HANDBOOKS

OF

ENGLISH LITERATURE

EDITED BY PROFESSOR HALES

THE AGE OF TENNYSON

THE
AGE OF TENNYSON

BY

HUGH WALKER, M.A.

FORMERLY PROFESSOR OF ENGLISH LITERATURE AT ST. DAVID'S COLLEGE
LAMPETER

LONDON
G. BELL AND SONS, LTD.
1947

First Published, September, 1897.

Reprinted, December, 1897 ; 1900, 1904, 1908,
1909, 1921, 1926, 1928, 1932, 1941, 1947.

PRINTED IN GREAT BRITAIN BY PURNELL AND SONS, LTD.
PAULTON (SOMERSET) AND LONDON

PREFACE.

THE age of Tennyson is defined, for the purpose of the present volume, as extending from 1830 to 1870. The date selected as the beginning of the period needs no explanation; but perhaps the question may be asked why the age of Tennyson should be supposed to end more than twenty years before Tennyson died. The answer is two-fold. First, I may plead the strong law of necessity. Sixty years, among the most fertile and varied in our literary history, could be compressed within the limits of a volume like the present only by completely changing the scale of treatment : and this again would have put it out of harmony with the other volumes of the series. But, secondly, about the year 1870 or before it there took place a change in the *personnel* of literature, less complete perhaps than that which marked the beginning of the epoch, but still sufficiently remarkable. Among the historians, Macaulay was dead and Carlyle had done his work. Among the novelists, Dickens died in 1870, Thackeray seven years before, and Charlotte Brontë still earlier; while, though George Eliot survived till 1880, the only great work of hers which lies beyond the limits of the period is *Middlemarch*. Mill, who had been so long the dominant power in philosophy, died in 1873. The poets, Tennyson, Browning, Matthew Arnold and Rossetti, survived. In poetry however Arnold's voice was by this time almost dumb. Browning continued to produce copiously; but after *The Ring and the Book* his style changed, and changed decidedly for the worse. Tennyson changed too, but in his case there was some gain to balance what was lost. The best of the younger poets, like William Morris and Swinburne, clearly show the influence of new ideals. The old order was changing, and new ambitions were beginning to sway men's minds. In short, if by the age of Tennyson we mean the period during which the influences which formed Tennyson and his contemporaries were dominant, we find that it came to an end long before Tennyson's life closed.

Tennyson and Browning, Arnold and Ruskin, therefore, have to be treated as survivors into a new period. But it is obviously undesirable to split a man's work in two; and consequently, though my period ends at 1870, I have included a sketch of the later work of these men as well. I have very rarely treated only a part of a man's work. I have preferred to leave wholly to my successor those writers who, though they had begun to write before 1870, seem on the whole to belong rather to the period still current.

In the plan of this book I have tried to follow out as faithfully as possible the general idea of the series to which it belongs; and thus I have been led rather to emphasise the thought of the greater men than to concern myself about including notices of a great number of minor writers. In a period so prolific it has therefore been necessary to enforce a somewhat rigid law of exclusion. The law has been made especially rigid in the case of fiction; because there is nothing that bears the test of time so ill as bad or mediocre fiction.

Variety is, after copiousness, the most striking feature of the period under review; and this variety somewhat

obscures the operation of ruling principles and ideas. I
have taken as my guide the conviction that the key to the
period is to be found in its search for truth and its resolve
to understand. We see this everywhere, in the development
of science, in the inquiry into the causes of the growth
and decay of nations, in the intellectual quality of the best
poetry, in the analytical psychology of so much prose
fiction.   It is the reaction against the extreme romanticism of the revolutionary period. The writers of the
Revolution sought to grasp truth by an act of faith. In
the Victorian period emotion plays a less and logic a
greater part. Or we may describe the change as a partial
reversion to the spirit of the eighteenth century. The
imaginative glamour of the romantic movement is not lost,
but there is conjoined with it a juster appreciation of the
clearness and precision and the logical coherency of the
age of Pope. Next to the eighteenth century the age of
Tennyson has been the most critical in our literature.

I owe thanks to Professor Hales for his uniform courtesy
and kindness in reading and considering my proofs, and
for many valuable and helpful suggestions.

H. W.

Lampeter,
   July, 1897.

CONTENTS.

THE AGE OF TENNYSON.

INTRODUCTION.

THE epoch of literature which opened about the year 1830 is perhaps best described, in the first place, by negatives. It is distinguished from the previous period, when the spirit which gave rise to the French Revolution was dominant, by the absence of certain characteristics then conspicuous. First and chiefly, it is distinguished by the failure of the hopes which at once produced and were produced by the Revolution. On the border-land between the two centuries literature was marked by buoyant and often extravagant expectation. Even pessimists like Byron were somewhat superficial in their pessimism. Byron looked upon the evils from which he and others suffered as due largely to the perversity of society. But this perversity might be cured, and if it were cured an earthly Elysium seemed a thing not wholly unreasonable to expect. To all who were animated by the spirit of Rousseau the problem, how to secure happiness, appeared almost identical with the comparatively simple one, how to remove obstructions. Nature unimpeded was perfect : it was the vain imaginings and evil contrivances of man that did the mischief. There were not wanting, even in the Revolutionary period, men who thought more deeply and who saw more clearly. The speculations of Malthus, destined afterwards, both directly and still more through the impulse they gave to Darwin, to prove among the most influential of the century, showed that some, at least, of the roots of evil reached far deeper than the orthodox Revolutionists and speculators of the type of Godwin had imagined. The exhaustion of Europe after the great struggle with Napoleon brought dimly home to multitudes who knew nothing about and cared nothing for abstruse speculation a sense of the difficulty and complexity of social problems. Exaggerated expectations bring their own Nemesis in the shape of proportionate depression and gloom; and the men of the new era set themselves somewhat wearily and with little elasticity of spirit to climb the toilsome steep of progress. The way seemed all the rougher because they had hoped to win the summit by a rush. Failure left them in the mood of Cleopatra on the death of Antony,—

'There is nothing left remarkable
Beneath the visiting moon.'

Hence in the beginning of the period there is on the part of all but the greatest a tendency to trifle. Sometimes even the greatest are not quite free from it; and in the early poetry of Tennyson we may detect evidence that the writer was as yet unmoved by any great interest.

But, though it was not clear at the moment, sixty years of subsequent history make it manifest that the generation then beginning had great work to do. In the first place, it had to work out, not the ideal of the Revolution as conceived by the Revolutionists, but that in it which was vital, and which had given it the power to move Europe. Modern democracy, though its roots stretch farther into the past, has been, as a realised political system, the work of the Age of Tennyson. The process whereby democracy has become dominant in the West of Europe has been marked by no great political convulsion comparable to the French Revolution. Even on the Continent the movement which in 1848 shook so many thrones was trifling in comparison with it ; and in England the agitations of the Reform Bill, of the Anti-Corn Law League, and even of the Chartists, either kept within the limits of the law or merely rippled the surface of social order. Nevertheless, the work done has been momentous. At the opening of the period we see political power placed by the first Reform Bill in the hands of the middle class ; at its close, this power is by the operation of the second Reform Bill, logically completed by the third, transferred to the working class. If we believe at all in the influence of social circumstances upon literature, we must believe that great changes such as these have left their stamp upon it ; and there is ample evidence that they have done so. Though Carlyle had little faith in popular government, his writings are everywhere influenced by the democratic movement. John Stuart Mill's works, and the whole literature of sociology, indicate how pressing the problem of the structure of society has been felt to be. Hood's *Song of the Shirt*, Mrs. Browning's *Cry of the Children*, Ebenezer Elliott's *Corn Law Rhymes* and Kingsley's *Alton Locke*, are a few examples of the way in which the social, political and economic condition of the poor pressed upon the imaginative writers of the time. Others in earlier days had been interested too. No reader of the *Canterbury Tales* can doubt that Chaucer was keenly alive to the state of all the grades of society. Shakespeare by a few vivid words in *King Lear* proves himself a humanitarian before humanitarianism became fashionable. Crabbe was the stern, and perhaps, after all, only half-truthful painter of humble life in the generation which had just closed. Burns gave to the peasant a citizenship in literature more sure than that conferred by Crabbe,

because he knew from personal experience that the life
hardest pressed by poverty need not be wholly sordid.
The interest is not new, but it has become more universal
and has grown in importance, and the proportion it bears
to other things is changed. The political revolution brought
this in its train. He who possesses power is sure of consideration and respect; and the classes which, to the Eliza-
bethans, were the 'rascal multitude,' have for sixty years
been struggling towards mastership, and have at last
attained it.

Among other results incident to this process, there has
been a great change in the character of the audience appealed to by literature. That audience is now far wider
than it ever before was. The spread of education through
all classes has vastly increased the number of those who
must and will read something. It was not till the year
1870 that the State took the great step which brought
primary education fully under its control; but for many
years before that date the elementary schools had been
partially supervised by the State, and from the year 1851
one of the greatest men of letters of the time, Matthew
Arnold, had laboured as an inspector in the cause of
popular education. The movement for the education of
women and for political equality between the sexes, if it
has not added a new class of readers, has certainly tended
to widen the range of interest among female readers.

It would be rash to assert that this increase in the
number of readers has been an unmixed benefit to literature. The proportion of those who have neither the
culture nor the time and inclination to study serious books
is probably greater now than at any former period. The
taste of such persons is gratified by the mass of fiction and
of periodicals which has grown and is still growing year by
year, not only in absolute, but in relative quantity; and it

cannot be considered satisfactory that growth is most vigorous just in those forms of literature which are least able to stand the test of time. It may be freely conceded that much of this growth would have taken place apart from any democratic movement or any extension of popular education; but nevertheless it has been stimulated by these causes.

In respect of periodicals the change, as compared with even the generation immediately preceding 1830, has been very great. The *Edinburgh Review* was for some years the only great critical periodical in Britain. The *Quarterly Review* was established to redress the political balance, shaken by the organ of the Whigs. A little later, *Blackwood's Magazine* gave scope to the fun and humour for which there was no place in the graver pages of its contemporaries. The *London Magazine* and the *Westminster Review* likewise did valuable service to literature and thought. But the great development of the magazines and critical journals has taken place during the last sixty years. In the course of it two tendencies have become manifest: first, a tendency to shorten the intervals of publication; and secondly, a tendency to multiply the organs of this periodical literature. The old quarterly has almost given place to the monthly magazine; the latter in its turn has had to abandon no small share of its province to the weekly journal; and recently the daily newspaper has been encroaching more and more upon the sphere of the weekly. Partly, no doubt, the change has been due to differentiation of function; partly too it has been brought about by impatience, and necessarily implies greater hurry and less mature consideration. The multiplication of organs has been equally remarkable. In early days a few magazines held the field alone; now their name is legion. One result is that there will probably never again be

concentrated on a single paper as much talent and
genius as we find in the early numbers of *Fraser's Magazine*.
Another is that in ever growing ratio the literary talent of
the age finds its outlet in the periodical. If Horace was
right in his celebrated maxim, the change is not one to
rejoice over.

The increase of the magazines has influenced all literature, but especially fiction. It has greatly stimulated the
demand, and it has changed the manner of publication.
In earlier days a book was as a matter of course finished
before the publication began. Chiefly by reason of the example of Dickens it became common to publish in parts;
and the magazines have made this the normal rather than
the exceptional form of publication, at least for authors of
sufficient reputation to command an audience first in the
periodical and afterwards when the parts are gathered into
a volume. Lately there have been indications that this
may come to be the mode of publication, not of fiction
only, but of serious historical and biographical works as
well.

We see then that a large popular audience, the majority
with little time, little money and little culture, is the
environment in which the man of letters in these days has
to live. For purposes of art it is neither the best nor the
worst possible. It is not so good as that of the Elizabethan
dramatists; for while many of the drawbacks are common
to the two, there is wanting in this later time that living
contact between author and public which invigorated
almost every page written then. Still less is it equal to
that of the golden age of Athens, when, as the commonest
remains of art still indicate, the mere journey-work of the
ordinary artisan proved the existence of culture in the man
himself, and of culture generally diffused among those to
whom his work appealed. In a less degree, but for similar

reasons, it is inferior to the environment of the Italian
Renaissance. On the other hand, it is better than patronage, whether individual or political, and better than the
terrible struggle out of patronage through which Johnson
passed. It is, in fact, the logical development of that
freedom which Johnson's struggle won. But the kind of
'natural selection' it implies is rough in its process and
crude in its results. The popular audience nourishes and
feeds fat a few classes who minister to its wants, but
there are many others, in a literary sense nobler and more
valuable, whom it barely enables to live. Darwin himself,
though he made earthworms far more fascinating than
many novelists can make the most romantic tale of love,
could not have lived if he had been really subject to this
competition. As late as the year 1870 Matthew Arnold
was assessed for £1,000 a year; but the evidence satisfied
the Commissioners that the assessment must be cut down
to £200; and the author said that he must write more
articles to prevent his being a loser even on the smaller
sum. Browning's *Paracelsus, Sordello* and *Bells and Pomegranates* were all published at his father's expense and
brought no return whatever. Edward FitzGerald, one of
the greatest poets of the age, lived and died almost unknown, and is even now known to comparatively few.
Tennyson alone among the greater poets of the time was
really successful in the financial sense. Even in fiction
there has been but little proportion between merit and re-
muneration. Dickens and George Eliot deserved and
won success; Thackeray's reward was comparatively inadequate; and it is hardly probable that Mr. George Meredith
ever received anything approaching the sums paid to not
a few of the favourites of a day. Evils such as these—
the accumulation of material rewards upon one class
of writers, want of discrimination even within that class,

and neglect, more or less complete, of others—must necessarily tend to cramp and fetter literature. They are not
new; perhaps they have been as bad in former times; but
at best we have done little or nothing towards finding a
remedy.

The development of physical science is another feature
of the time plainly visible in its literature. It is needless
to discuss its effect upon the material conditions of life;
for that has been not only fully recognised, but its importance, for the present purpose, has been greatly exaggerated.
Besides this however, the direct contributions of science to
literature have been considerable, and some of them possess literary qualities rarely equalled among the scientific
writings of past times. Moreover, science has so filled the
minds and possessed the imagination of men that its in-
direct has been far greater than its direct influence. Whatever its ultimate creed may prove to be, science has certainly been in part responsible for the growth of a spirit of
materialism, and has caused those who do not share that
spirit to examine themselves and to remould their arguments. Science has therefore tended to depress and to give
a tone of stoic resignation if not of pessimism to many
who, without accepting materialistic opinions, have been
affected by them.

But in another way science has been an elevating and
inspiring power. Its discoveries have stimulated men's
minds, and have done more than anything else to rouse
them from the lethargy consequent upon the apparent
failure of the Revolution. They have profoundly influenced
literature, both directly, and also through those philosophical and theological speculations which inevitably colour
all poetry and all imaginative prose. The new facts of
astronomy and geology have shaken many old theories and
suggested many new ones; and the results of biological

discovery have been still more striking. The transforming power upon thought of the theory of evolution may be measured by the fact that the majority even of those who dislike and deny Darwinian evolution still believe that there has been evolution of some kind. For thoughtful men, unless they are heavily fettered by preconceptions, the old view has become impossible; and no other except an evolutionary one has hitherto been even imagined. Here therefore there is a great unsettlement of popular ideas, and no little energy has been expended in fitting men's minds to the new conditions. Tractarianism, Pre-Raphaelitism, the satire, tempered with mysticism, of Carlyle, the idealistic optimism of Browning, and the creedless Christianity of Matthew Arnold, are all attempts to satisfy either the intellectual or the moral and artistic needs of modern times, and all show the influence of the scientific thought of the age.

Some of these forces however have been in the main reactionary. Side by side with the movement of science, which has on the whole tended to positivism, agnosticism, and in a word to negative views of things spiritual, there has gone on a remarkable revival of conceptions diametrically opposed to these. The old narrow Protestantism of England was powerful enough to struggle against Catholic Emancipation until the delay became a danger to the state. Yet hardly was this act of justice done when the great reaction known as the Oxford Movement began. It was, as its consummate literary expression, the *Apologia* of Newman, proves, the product of a double discontent,—a discontent, on the one hand, with that movement of science just spoken of; and a discontent, on the other hand, with what was felt to be the 'creed outworn' of English Protestantism. As against the latter it has achieved, among those who hungered for a more emotional religion, a

wonderful success. As against the former its utter failure
has been veiled only by that success.

Kindred in spirit and almost contemporaneous in origin
was the movement of the Pre-Raphaelite Brotherhood. On
the surface, this seems quite unrelated to Tractarianism;
for while the Tractarians were all for dogma, the Pre-
Raphaelites were indifferent to it. But both movements
were in essence protests on behalf of the imaginative and
æsthetic in human nature against the exclusive nourishment
of the intellectual element; and they proved their kinship
by each in its own way seeking to bring about a revival of
Mediævalism. In this fact moreover we see wherein their
value consisted. They fought a battle on behalf of aspects
of the truth temporarily threatened with neglect. In so
far as they asserted or implied the incompleteness of the
scientific view of life they were almost wholly right. In
so far as they asserted its positive falsity they were almost
wholly wrong. The latter was however the error principally
of the religious movement. The Pre-Raphaelites may have
been wrong in many respects in their conceptions of art;
but at least they generally confined themselves within their
own domain.

Both of these schools, though they differ in degree of
guilt, are chargeable with the sin of 'rending the seamless
garment of thought.' The Pre-Raphaelite, implicitly if not
in words, teaches that there is an intellectual world *and* an
æsthetic world. The Tractarians not merely implied but
insisted that there is a domain of reason *and* a domain of
authority.[1] Because of this fundamental error we must look
for the main current of modern thought elsewhere; for if
there is any one thing that modern philosophy unequivocally

[1] In later times this has been confused with the very different
doctrine that there is a domain of authority *within* the domain
of reason.

teaches, it is that all such divisions are unsound. And we find that all the greatest men of letters of the period are on this point in agreement with the philosophers. Carlyle, Browning, Matthew Arnold, Thackeray and George Eliot, all in various ways teach that art must not ignore the intellectual problem. Tennyson seemed for a time to hold aloof and to live in a lotos-land of artistic beauty, but he soon became restless, and all his greater works are charged with an intellectual as well as an artistic meaning. These men are not in all respects self-consistent. Browning in particular turned his back in his old age upon the principle which inspired his more youthful work. But in spite of inconsistencies he and the rest must all be classed as teaching, with the philosophers, the unity of intellectual and spiritual life, and the impossibility of ministering to the one without satisfying the other; and for this reason it is to them rather than to writers of more limited view that we must look for guidance in the labyrinth of contemporary life.

CHAPTER I.

THOMAS CARLYLE.

POETRY is so clearly the head and front of literature that in most periods the first and chief attention must be paid to the poets. The Victorian age is an exception, at least as regards the order in which prose and poetry claim notice, and perhaps partly as regards their relative prominence. The man who first gives us a key to the significance of the age of Tennyson is not Tennyson himself, nor Browning, nor any writer of verse, but one who believed that the day of poetry was past,—Thomas Carlyle (1795-1881). Considerably older than the poets, he had, notwithstanding his early difficulties, notwithstanding too the slow ripening of his own genius, made a name in literature and stamped his mark on his generation before either of them was widely known.

Carlyle was born at Ecclefechan (the Entepfuhl of *Sartor Resartus*) in Dumfriesshire. He was educated first at the local schools, and afterwards at the University of Edinburgh, to which he refers in *Sartor* as 'the worst of all hitherto discovered universities.' The purpose he had in view was to take the divinity course and enter the ministry of the Scottish Church. But this was rather the design of his parents than his own; as time went on 'grave prohibitive doubts' accumulated; and about the year 1817 Carlyle definitely abandoned his purpose. He was already supporting himself by school-mastering, an occupation which grew more and more irksome, and which in turn was thrown up in December, 1818. For some time he drifted, oppressed by doubts and dyspepsia, until in 1821 occurred the one fact recorded in *Sartor Resartus*, the incident in the Rue St. Thomas de l'Enfer (Leith Walk), wherein Carlyle, shaking off his doubts, stands up and confronts the Everlasting No and its claim, 'Behold, thou art fatherless, outcast, and the Universe is mine (the Devil's),' with the answer, '*I* am not thine, but Free, and forever hate thee.' This he ranks as his 'spiritual new birth;' and as such it ought to receive attention in any account, however brief, of a life which was mainly inward and spiritual.

But spiritual regeneration could not supply the need of daily bread. Carlyle supported himself partly by the tutorship of private pupils, a form of teaching less distasteful to him than his school work had been. He was at the same time studying hard and reading widely, in French, Italian, Spanish, and afterwards in German, as well as in English, and was slowly gravitating towards the profession of literature. He contributed articles to Brewster's *Encyclopædia*. Through Edward Irving, who had been for several years a generous friend, he was introduced to Taylor, the proprietor of the *London Magazine*, who published for him the *Life of Schiller*. About the same time the translation of *Wilhelm Meister* was issued through the agency of an Edinburgh publisher.

Carlyle's marriage occurred in 1826, and he was for a short time happy. But there still remained difficulties of finance as well as difficulties of temper. Literary occupation did not prove either as easy to get or as remunerative as Carlyle had hoped. His *German Romance* was financially a failure, and publishers were on that account the less

disposed to consider his books. He made unsuccessful attempts to find employment as a professor, first in the
London University, and again at St. Andrews. He had
lived since his marriage at Comely Bank, but had cherished
more or less all the time the purpose of retiring to his
wife's farm of Craigenputtock, a solitary moorland place in
Dumfriesshire. Moved probably by these disappointments,
he carried out his purpose in 1828. 'Hinaus ins freie
Feld,' to escape that necessity which ' makes blue-stockings
of women, magazine hacks of men,'—this had been the impulse which drove him thither. In less than four months
it was ' this Devil's den, Craigenputtock.' But ' this Devil's
den' was his home from 1828 to 1834, and, whatever doubts
may be entertained as to the wisdom and kindness of Carlyle in taking his wife there, if we judge by the result,
we must pronounce that he did what was best for his own
literary development. It was during those years that Carlyle grew to his full intellectual stature. There and then
were composed a great number of his essays; notably,
among the literary class, the essay on Burns, written at
the beginning of the Craigenputtock period, and, among
the historical class, *The Diamond Necklace*, written near
the end. There too was written that autobiography of
' symbolical myth' which, after being hawked in vain from
one publisher to another, at last appeared piecemeal in
Fraser's Magazine. There too the *French Revolution* was,
not indeed written, but planned and brooded over; and it
was with a mind already full of the subject that Carlyle in
1834 made his migration to London, his home for the rest
of his life. His character, moral and literary, was now
formed; all the influences subsequently brought to bear
upon it were of subordinate importance; and though in
length of years the future period exceeded the period past,
it may be briefly dismissed.

The *History of the French Revolution*, delayed though it was by the accidental burning of the manuscript of the first volume, was finished in January, 1837, and published shortly afterwards. It was the turning point in Carlyle's literary life. Hitherto it had been a long, hard, almost fierce struggle; but the *History* at once established him as one of the foremost men of letters of his day. Success came none too soon. His resources were all but exhausted, and, like his countryman Burns, so close to him in some of the circumstances of his early life, he contemplated emigration to America. From this he was saved by the project, devised by Harriet Martineau, which produced his lectures on German literature. The popularity of the *History* reacted on his earlier works; publishers sought him instead of waiting to be approached; a proposal was made for republishing even *Sartor;* and for the future Carlyle was sure, at any rate, of a competence. His next work of moment was *Chartism* (1839), written with a view to publication in the *Quarterly Review*. It was declined by Lockhart, but in such a way that the author and the editor retained for the future a strong mutual regard. In the year following Carlyle delivered the last of his courses of lectures, afterwards (1841) printed as *Heroes and Hero-Worship*. He was already deep in study for his *Cromwell*, and finding, as usual, great difficulty in beginning. Very different was his experience with *Past and Present*. This book, inspired by the same sense of social evils to which we owe *Chartism*, 'was written off with singular ease in the first seven weeks of 1843.' *Cromwell* was not finished till 1845. It was no sooner out than Carlyle began to think of *Frederick;* but of all the long 'valleys of the shadow' of his literary life, that was the longest. Before it took shape there appeared his *Latter-Day Pamphlets* (1850), of which the celebrated paper on *The Nigger*

Question was the precursor. The *Life of Sterling* (1851) is a strange contrast in tone and temper; for while the *Pamphlets* are among the most violent of Carlyle's writings, the *Life of Sterling* is one of the calmest. It was not until after the publication of *Sterling* that he seriously took to *Frederick the Great*, which had hitherto been only a project floating in his mind with many others. He visited Germany to see the scenes with which he had to deal and to gather materials. The first and second volumes were published in 1858, and the third followed in 1862. In the interval Carlyle had visited Germany a second time. *Frederick*, finished in January, 1865, set the seal on Carlyle's reputation as the head of the literature, at least the prose literature, of his time. It was also practically the end of his literary career. The world was ready to shower honours upon him. He was chosen Rector of the University of Edinburgh; but the triumph of his great inaugural speech was dashed almost immediately by the news of the sudden death of his wife. He wrote one or two minor articles, such as *Shooting Niagara*, and left the vivid and interesting, but frequently uncharitable, *Reminiscences*. With such exceptions, he lived henceforth, till his death on the 5th of February, 1881, the quiet retired life of a man whose work was done.

This man, so long neglected, was during a considerable part of his life, and especially in the years between the publication of the *Frederick the Great* and his death, the greatest literary force in England. The reasons which ultimately secured for him this power are in part just the reasons which so long stood in the way of his advancement. He was eminently original in his matter, and perhaps even more in his style. But there is always some difficulty in appraising the value of originality; and the difficulty is all the greater when the originality is

defiant and even borders on eccentricity. To a great extent
Carlyle's early struggles were necessary because no party,
creed or faction could attach him to itself or claim him as
its champion. Every party in turn found it possible to
assent to his negations, yet each in turn had to disapprove
of what he affirmed. In politics, how could such an
explosive force work in harmony with orthodox Toryism?
He was constantly ridiculing and denouncing a mere fox-
hunting and partridge-shooting aristocracy. 'Si monu-
mentum quaeris, fimetum adspice.' On the other hand,
if the Radicals thought they had his sympathy, they soon
found that the gulf between him and them was even wider,
if possible, than that which separated him from their
opponents. It was the disclosure of this gulf which led
to the breach with their best man, and one of his best
friends, Mill. They believed almost wholly in the machinery
of government, and he believed in it not at all. They
were economists, and he denounced economics as a mere
pretended science. They believed in government by
majorities, and he considered it 'the most absurd superstition which had ever bewitched the human imagination—
at least, outside Africa.' Again, he would admit no
accepted theological creed, and was consequently looked on
askance by the accredited leaders of religion. Anything
like superstition he abominated. Newman, he thought,
had 'not the intellect of a moderate-sized rabbit.' On
the other hand, he had no sympathy with the liberal party
of the Church of England. He condemned the writers of
Essays and Reviews. He respected Thirlwall, but wished
him anywhere but where he was. 'There goes Stanley,'
said he of a man whom he personally liked, 'boring holes
in the bottom of the Church of England.' He thought
Arnold of Rugby fortunate in being taken away before he
was forced to choose between an honest abandonment of an

untenable position and a trifling with his own conscience. He liked best the clergymen who could still honestly and literally and without misgiving accept the Prayer Book, but he did not respect their intellect. Again, if he did not like the ' liberals' within the Church, he liked still less the liberals outside it. However much he dissented from the champions of belief, he dissented still more from the apostles of unbelief. He had a faith, though not a creed. Separated thus from the orthodox by what he did not believe, and from the heterodox by what he believed, from one political party because he saw it would be fatal to remain inactive and leave *ill* alone, and from the other because he was convinced that movement in the direction they desired would be futile or worse, Carlyle stood alone. He had to create his own party, and the process was necessarily a slow one. But the very cause which made the work slow made it also great when it was accomplished.

One aspect of Carlyle's work not always duly recognised is its concentration of purpose. Superficially viewed, it has the appearance of a heterogeneous miscellany. Essays, literary, historical and mixed, biographies and mythical autobiography, histories drawn from different centuries and different peoples, idealised pictures of the past, and fierce pamphlets, not at all idealised, on questions emphatically of the present, succeed each other in his volumes. The very records of his literary life help to confirm this impression. No sooner has he finished one important work than he casts about to discover a subject for another. He makes no nation and no century specially his own, as it is the custom of the modern historian to do. In his longer works he jumps from the French Revolution to Cromwell, and from Cromwell to Frederick the Great. He seems to have been turned to the second subject almost by accident. He had been asked by Mill to write on Cromwell in the

London and Westminster Review. ' There is nothing,' says his biographer, ' in his journals or letters to show that Cromwell had been hitherto an interesting figure to him.' The projected magazine article was turned into a book through the impertinence of Mill's substitute, who in the absence of his superior wrote to Carlyle that he ' need not go on, for " he meant to do Cromwell himself." ' The choice of Frederick seems to have been hardly less fortuitous, and in itself it was more surprising than the choice of Cromwell.

Yet under this diversity it is always possible to detect a unity both of purpose and of effect. In the first place, there is the unity of Carlyle's own character. Everything he wrote was self-revealing; and it is scarcely too much to say that his whole works are an expansion and, as circumstances demanded, a modification, of the autobiographic *Sartor Resartus.* We see this in many ways. Carlyle is best when the conditions under which he works are such as to allow himself to appear freely, naturally, spontaneously, without fierce invectives and exaggeration. This, in his case, generally implies similarity without personal contact, or with contact from which the aspect of possible competition is removed. He is worst of all where there is a partial similarity without sympathy. Thus, the best perhaps of Carlyle's literary essays is that on Burns; and the reason why it is best is that Burns was in some ways so like himself. Both sprang from the Scottish peasantry, and the minds of both were deeply coloured by the experiences of their early youth. In writing of Burns and his father, Carlyle never forgets himself and his own father. On the other hand, the essay on Scott is certainly among the worst of his essays, just because Scott is at once too near to him and too far from him. Scott belonged to a different class in society, pursued different aims, and had a

widely different literary history from Carlyle. Yet both
were Scotch, and in the blood which they inherited as well
as in the mental and moral food on which they were
nourished there was much to bring them together. The
same contrast is illustrated by the *Reminiscences*. There,
every reference to his own family is distinguished by clear
comprehension and profound sympathy; while, unfortunately, nearly every reference to contemporaries not
related to him by blood is disfigured by acrimony and
depreciation. In the *Life of Sterling* friendship performs
the function which blood-relationship performs in the
Reminiscences. The essays on foreign writers, both French
and German, deal with men much farther removed from
Carlyle than Scott was; and if they have not that depth of
sympathy and that fineness of perception which are the
charm of the essay on Burns, they are free from the bitterness and ungenerous depreciation which mar the essay on
Scott. Take, for example, Carlyle's treatment of Goethe.
In many ways the great German was almost as far removed
as it was possible to be from his Scotch disciple. Yet
Carlyle's comprehension is clear, his appreciation ready,
his criticism wise. We see himself in it all, but just
because of their wide differences his own image never blurs
that of Goethe.

It will be found that the principle underlying Carlyle's
choice of historical themes was similar. He was bound to
reveal *himself*; but Carlyle's *self* was a particular view of
the universe. His subject therefore must illustrate this.
He was naturally attracted to the French Revolution. It
is the greatest movement of recent history; and Carlyle
invariably sought for lessons for the present. It dealt
the death-blow to many shams and hypocrisies; and
Carlyle waged a life-long war against these. While its
creed was the equality of men, no great movement has ever

more vividly illustrated their great and inevitable inequality; and Carlyle rejoiced to see the truth assert itself in spite of the prepossessions of a victorious mob, and rejoiced to point to the confirmation of his own favourite doctrine. Again, though Cromwell seems to have been brought to his mind almost by chance, the points of contact between the hero and his historian are sufficiently obvious. Cromwell's strength, his thoroughness, his roughness, his veracity, his piety, all contributed to endear him to Carlyle. The 'Calvinist without the theology' was fundamentally in sympathy with the great English Puritan. His boyhood and early training fitted him, better perhaps than any other training of the nineteenth century could possibly have done, to sympathise with the opinions of the Puritan of the seventeenth. It was the instinct which draws like to like that made him welcome the first suggestion of Cromwell as a subject; just as the same instinct made him afterwards ponder upon Knox as another possible subject.

The choice of Frederick is certainly that which requires most explanation, for in many ways his character seems strangely foreign to anything likely, *a priori*, to attract Carlyle. Complete explanation is perhaps not possible, but partial explanation certainly is. We must remember Carlyle's worship of force. He had been preaching all his life a form of the doctrine, might is right; and, as was usual with him, the doctrine had grown more extreme under contradiction and opposition. Thus we have the *Nigger Question* and the *Iliad in a Nutshell*. There is an element of truth in the doctrine, and under Carlyle's original application of it there had been a well-marked moral foundation, so that it could have been in many cases altered to read, 'right is might.' He meant not merely that 'Providence is on the side of the heaviest battalion,' but quite as much that the battalion is heaviest because Providence is on its side. In other words, he believed that the forces of the universe are moral forces and that true and permanent success mean being in harmony with them. As time went on however the qualifications were gradually stripped off, and latterly what Carlyle worshipped was little better than naked force. Now, in all the eighteenth century he could hardly have found a better example of successful force than Frederick. Destitute as he was of the piety of Carlyle's previous hero, he was at least an eminently successful governor, and Carlyle respected nothing so much as the faculty for the genuine government of men, not what he would have called sham government, the kind of government which follows while it seems to lead. If Frederick had not created a state, he had raised it from a position bordering on insignificance to one not far from the front in the European system. Moreover, this state was peculiarly interesting to Carlyle, for he saw in Prussia the future head of Germany, and in Germany a possible leader of Europe. These reasons induced him to turn to Frederick, and perhaps tempted him to clothe Frederick with attributes which were not all his. For the method of hero-worship has its dangers, and only prejudice would assert that the great hero-worshipper, keen as was his insight into character, has wholly escaped those dangers.

It was through these barriers, the barriers of an original and not infrequently eccentric genius, and of a personality strange and uncouth to the majority of his readers, that Carlyle had to fight his way to fame. It is true that at first the uncouthness and eccentricity were less prominent. The style of his earliest writings—the *Life of Schiller* for example—is simple and almost limpid; the arrangement is orderly, the development obeys the rules of a logic easily comprehended. But Carlyle speedily worked his way out of this style, and seldom used it afterwards. *Sartor Resartus*, the great product of the Craigenputtock period, presents all his peculiarities in their most aggressive form. Partly in fact, but still more in appearance, it is lawless and chaotic. Its style, difficult even now to a generation accustomed to and partly formed by Carlyle, was then unparalleled and, except after serious study, almost incomprehensible. It is full of evidences of German studies, German sympathies, and the influence of German thought. Carlyle has done more than anyone else to make these familiar in England; but before *Sartor* was published almost the only interpreters of Germany to England were men like Coleridge and De Quincey, who not only made the form English, but gave an English stamp to the matter as well. *Sartor*, moreover, was full of a humour deep and genuine but unfamiliar in kind, and, as regards the first impression produced, almost sardonic in character. Its subject was not calculated to arrest immediate attention. It was not the history of a nation or of a national hero. What it actually was could not be immediately perceived; but after bestowing some attention the reader discovered it to be the spiritual biography of a man then unknown, and his thoughts on human life and human society, presented humorously, whimsically, often enigmatically. It is not therefore altogether matter for wonder that this strange book with difficulty found a publisher, nor even that it threatened with ruin the magazine which at last received it. America, more tolerant of novelties, to her honour welcomed it; but in England the current opinion seems to have been expressed by the ' oldest subscriber,' who said to Fraser, ' If there is any more of that d——d stuff, I will, etc., etc.' We frequently boast of our progress. Is it certain that even now a phenomenon as strange as *Sartor* would meet with any better reception? John Stuart

Mill, a man as open-minded as he was intelligent, for a long time saw nothing in Carlyle's early essays but ' insane rhapsody;' and, though he was afterwards one of the warmest panegyrists of *Sartor*, which he thought Carlyle's greatest work, he read the manuscript unmoved. Not once nor twice, either in this island's story or in the history of the world, has the prophet been rejected by the generation he was sent to serve. Rather, rejection has been the general fate of prophets ever since the time when the children of Israel rebelled against Moses in the wilderness.

What redeemed *Sartor* in the eyes of those who had the patience to study it, was the discovery that the inner history of this unknown man had, in the first place, the interest which always belongs to human experiences told with absolute sincerity. For though *Sartor* contains little or no truth of fact, it is wholly true in idea. Carlyle, now as always, was intolerant of the very shadow of falsehood; and it was to his unswerving truth that he ultimately owed the greater part of his influence.

In the second place, the small band of careful readers discovered that *Sartor* was not only true and sincere, but that its truth was capable of an immediate and practical application. It was not something applicable only to a distant past or to another state of existence; its sphere was here and now. This is characteristic of Carlyle in all his works. He was always in intention, and generally in effect, the teacher first of his own generation, and secondly of the future. His interest in ancient history and literature was comparatively feeble, because he saw not how to bring them to bear so directly on the present. It was modern England, France and Germany, rather than ancient Greece and Rome, that nourished his mind. And for this reason, though his influence was of slow growth, it was deep rooted when it did spring.

Sartor Resartus is peculiarly important because of its chronological position. We have seen in the Introduction that the failure of the revolutionary ideal gives to the new period its most prominent characteristic. 'The gospel according to Jean Jacques' was accepted no longer. *Sartor* may be called a grim sort of gospel according to Thomas Carlyle. Carlyle himself had written before this; Macaulay had begun his brilliant career; among the poets, Tennyson, Browning and Elizabeth Barrett had published their earlier works; but *Sartor* is the first great book which faces the difficulties, and, in a way, embodies the aspirations of the new period. Its grimness no one will dispute. It is also a gospel, because the Everlasting No is routed, and under all the enigmas there is the promise of success and, if not Happiness, Blessedness, in work. It deals with quite a surprising range of modern problems. All the principal social, political and religious questions of the century are treated in greater or less detail. Carlyle's attitude towards economic and other science, his views on religion, the outline of his opinions as to the position and proper treatment of the poor, his conviction of the need of a better and stronger government, may all be seen in *Sartor*. He expanded greatly and illustrated in his later writings, but he did not add much. *Sartor* is his most original and probably his greatest work. It is peculiarly interesting to notice that in it the central point of his creed is the need of reconstruction. Religion must be reconstructed: the 'Hebrew old-clothes' have had their day and will serve for human garments no longer. But this is equally true of the tailoring of the French Revolution: society itself has to be reconstructed. And the reconstruction, in Carlyle's view, is a complex task. The salvation of mankind must be sought by the positive, not by the negative method. The way will be long and difficult, not short and simple as

the Revolutionists supposed. Neither will any amount of
political machinery suffice. Not by majorities, however
numerous, nor by ballot-boxes, however ingenious, can
sound government be carried on, but only by something
which goes to the root of character. Carlyle, writing in
the midst of a great agitation for improvement in political
machinery, merely looks on in contemptuous indifference,
convinced that at least the true solution lies not there. He
was too contemptuous, for the true solution lies not in any
one thing but in the union of many, and of these political
machinery is one.

Carlyle was not the only writer of this period who gave
thought to such problems, nor the only one who appreciated their complexity, but it was he who first adequately
expressed them; and it is *Sartor Resartus*, written in solitude on the Dumfriesshire moors, that summons the crowds
of modern cities to face and solve them. If the voice is the
voice of one crying in the wilderness, it is addressed to the
multitudes of human society wherever they are gathered
together.

The principle at the root of all Carlyle's other works is
the same. It has been already pointed out how his own
character forms, as it were, a background even to his
histories. As that character had been built up in the
struggle with, and continued to be absorbed in the con-
templation of, those problems, it follows that the histories
are just the presentation of the same problems under the
wider and more varied conditions of national existence.
There was artistic gain to Carlyle in the new conditions.
A longer dwelling in the regions of *Sartor* would have fed
the morbid blood in him. History, without smothering
his own personality, took him sufficiently out of it to
check this tendency. The *History of the French Revolution*
is much purer as an artistic conception than *Sartor*. It is

more orderly in development, it has more artistic unity. Indeed, with the exception of one or two of Carlyle's smaller works, like the *Life of Sterling*, it is in this respect the best he ever wrote. Among histories it is quite singular for its coherence. Few histories have the unity of works of imaginative art. Among early works we may find one or two, like the history of Herodotus, which simulate the character and rival the proportions of a national epic. Among later works we may find one or two, like Gibbon's, which derive an impressive unity from the stately march of events to a great far-off catastrophe. But probably nowhere is there a history which in every chapter, and almost in every sentence, breathes the artistic purpose as Carlyle's *History of the French Revolution* does. It has been frequently called the 'epic' of the Revolution. In point of fact, as Froude justly says, the conception is rather dramatic, and the best comparison is to Æschylus.

Carlyle had an infinite respect for facts, and as far as he could by industry and care, he assured himself that all he wrote as history was exactly true. It is of small moment that, like all the historians who have ever lived or ever will live, he has been proved to have made mistakes. But it is well to notice that, much as he revered facts, no one is farther removed than he from the school of Dryasdust. Few were so bold in making selection of their facts. The artistic principle always underlying his work saved him from the mistake into which so many recent historians seem prone to fall, the mistake of attempting to tell everything. To Carlyle, the fact must be illuminative, or he cast it aside. Moreover, while he denounced theorists, few bolder theorists than himself have ever written. Behind almost every sentence of his *French Revolution* there lies a theory, of character or motive, if not of cause and effect. The difference between him and the theorists he railed at was really that he presented poetically what they presented logically. He was aware of the limited truth attainable by their method; he was not perhaps fully aware of the dangers of his own. We see this imaginative element in the great part which character plays in the development of the French Revolution as Carlyle conceived it. It is in men, not in political machinery, that we must seek the clue to it. Hence the prominence, perhaps exaggerated, given to Mirabeau. Carlyle's facts are never left bare facts. He reverences them, not so much in themselves, as for the insight they give into the souls of men. This is the key-note of Carlyle's histories. They are essentially imaginative; and the writer spends his strength less in a narrative of events than in delineation of characters, and in the tracing of moral forces.

Carlyle's *Cromwell* is, more than either of the other histories, an illustration of his own doctrine of heroes, and less than either of the others is it a history of a nation as well as of a man. Cromwell to a great extent speaks for himself, and Carlyle expounds and comments on his uncouth and sometimes obsolete manner of expression. The commentary is free and even ample, yet there is less of Carlyle himself in this than in any other of his works. The great features of it are its delineation of the man Cromwell and the proof it presents of Carlyle's skill in the use of documents. Carlyle has not converted everybody to his own view of Cromwell, but he has at least coloured the opinion of everybody who has since studied the period.

If *Cromwell* is narrower in its scope than the *French Revolution*, *Frederick the Great* is even wider. The Revolution expanded into a European movement, but within the limits Carlyle set to himself it was essentially French. Frederick was the centre of a movement which Carlyle found could only be treated as a European one. He was

led by the relations, alliances and wars of his hero, to deal
at greater or less length with all the principal countries of
Europe, and his book, instead of being merely the history
of a man, became the history of one of the most momentous
series of events of the eighteenth century. In this respect
therefore the history of Frederick is his most ambitious
historical work ; and either to it or to the *French Revolution* must be adjudged the palm of excellence in its class.
Various arguments might be adduced on both sides, and
it would be rash to pronounce definitely. For the earlier
work it might be pleaded that it is clearly the more perfect in artistic conception. It is also true that, interesting
as is the Seven Years' War, and interesting as, in Carlyle's hands, the growth of the Prussian Monarchy becomes,
there is nothing in the subject-matter of *Frederick* quite as
enthralling as the volcanic scenes of the *French Revolution.*
It may also be pleaded that passages of eloquent writing are
more frequent, and individual passages probably greater
in the latter. The art in it moreover is purer, less inter-
mixed with the grotesque, and with what can only be set
down to Carlyle's individual eccentricities. On the other
hand, *Frederick* is even more forcible than the *French
Revolution.* Carlyle gathered power as years went on, and
he never expended it more lavishly than on this latest and
most ambitious of his works. Nowhere, except perhaps in
Sartor, are all his peculiarities more conspicuous; nowhere
is his gospel preached with more uncompromising energy ;
nowhere is his strange style more unrestrained and less
amenable to the ordinary laws of English composition.
For these reasons, combined with the wide range of the
work, which tasked his power of construction as it had
never been tasked before, *Frederick the Great* will probably
always win the suffrages of a large proportion of Carlylean
devotees. For the same reasons, those who, acknowledging

Carlyle's original genius and admiring his power, are only half reconciled to his sometimes wanton eccentricities, will doubtless continue to prefer the more regular *French Revolution*.

Regarding the purely historical essays as minor examples of the kind of works just discussed, Carlyle's remaining writings may be divided into two classes. These, in the order of their importance in his own eyes, and probably to the world, are, (1) works dealing with or bearing directly upon contemporary social and political problems ; and (2) literary essays, including under the latter head the translations and the two biographies of Schiller and Sterling.

Under the first class rank such works as *Chartism, Past and Present* and *Latter-day Pamphlets*. Under it too might be fairly brought some of the essays, such, for example, as the essay on the *Corn Law Rhymes*, which, though it deals primarily with a literary subject, was written because that subject opened immediately into a social one. But indeed all Carlyle's works are closely cognate to this section; for if he was not directly treating of such themes, his thoughts were never far away from them. Still, there is a difference between dealing directly with a subject and illustrating it by a borrowed light. In Carlyle's case the latter was the preferable method, and his wisest teaching on matters of immediate practical moment is not contained in the class of works here considered. The reason is that in discussing such questions he usually became violent and one-sided. Carlyle, as much as any man who ever lived, had ' the defects of his qualities.' We see in his own life how force and directness, his greatest qualities both literary and personal, become on occasion vices instead of virtues. He recognised the fact himself, and once humorously warned his own people, whom he had alarmed by his outcries, that they ought to know him

too well to believe that he was being killed merely because
he cried murder. But this habit of crying murder, trifling
perhaps in itself, had no little influence for evil on his own
life and on the life of her who was most closely associated
with him. Just the same fault may be observed in all his
works to some degree, but especially in the section of them
now under discussion. Carlyle habitually saw through a
magnifying glass. As he made an outcry if his own finger
ached, so he did in the case of the evils of his own time. The
'something in the state of Denmark' he could contemplate
with comparative equanimity, and the lesson he drew from
that state was apt to be more just because more temperate
than that which he drew directly from the present time
itself. Compare, for instance, the 'past' with the 'present'
in *Past and Present.* The former is calm, pure, beautiful,
and, we feel convinced, true. The latter is lurid, turbid,
exaggerated, repellent, only in part true. We cannot accept as true at all the contrast between the one age and
the other; only a most enthusiastic disciple can fail to
note that a select specimen of the past is pitted against
the average, or worse than the average, of the present.
But not thus is truth reached, and not thus is conviction
carried to the candid mind. Doubtless Carlyle wished to
reform, and the way to reform, it may be urged, is rather
to point out what needs amendment than to insist upon
the advantages of 'our incomparable civilisation.' This is
true, but justice is the prime requisite as a preliminary to
reform. The way to win men's acquiescence is not to paint
Hyperion on the one hand and a satyr on the other. The
better way is to point out how a society faulty, troubled,
but, it may be, not hopelessly corrupt, may be made in this
point and in that a little less faulty, less troubled, less
corrupt.

There is no such contrast in Carlyle's other works to

drive the sense of his error home; but the same error is
present in them. It is far from being the case that their
matter is essentially bad, or that Carlyle is essentially
wrong. There is much that is wholly sound and good in
Chartism; but it is unrelieved and unbalanced. The same
is true of the *Latter-day Pamphlets.* Even the much-
abused *Nigger Question* is fundamentally right. What it
means is that unless we organise free labour we had better
give up boasting that we have set it free. The liberation
of the West Indian slaves had brought to the verge of
bankruptcy what had previously been the richest of British
colonial possessions, robbed them of a prosperity which
they have never fully recovered, ruined the whites, and
deprived the blacks themselves of a government and
discipline which Carlyle believed to be morally necessary
to them, and therefore their right. There are several
points of contact between this and the theory of Aristotle;
there is also a general resemblance between it and the
bold doctrine of Carlyle's countryman, Andrew Fletcher
of Saltoun, who, impressed by the evil of unorganised free
labour degenerating into vagabondage, advocated the re-
introduction of slavery. It does not follow from the evils
pointed out by Carlyle that slavery ought to have been
maintained; but it does seem a fair inference that the
process of liberation actually adopted was ill considered, and was no subject for unqualified jubilation. If
Carlyle had advanced such ideas in a moderate and con-
ciliatory way he might have made converts. Instead of
that, he was aggressive. He sowed the wind of provoca-
tion, and he reaped the whirlwind of opposition, rejection,
sometimes of vituperation. It is vain to wish that he had
done otherwise; he could only do as his character allowed
him to do; but we shall do well to recognise that violence
proved to be not strength but weakness, and that with

more self-control he would probably have produced greater practical effect.

The class of writings dealing with literature and literary men is that to which Carlyle himself would have attached least importance. He was a man of letters by necessity rather than by choice. He would do nothing which did not promise him an opening into the sphere of the ideal, and literature was the only profession within his reach which seemed to do that. He would have preferred a life of action, provided the action had not for its end mere money-getting; and he declared there were few occupations for which he was not better fitted by nature than for that in which he spent his life. There may have been some exaggeration in this. If Carlyle had not by nature the faculty for writing, he made a marvellous faculty for himself. In favour of his own view, however, we may call to mind his well-known contempt for poetry, or rather verse, as it existed, and as he conceived it could alone exist, in his own day. Probably no born man of letters ever cherished such contempt, or ever submitted to be a writer of prose without some regret that he could not be a poet. Carlyle's half-dislike and more than half-disbelief in his own profession shows itself in the fact that he escapes as soon as possible from the region of pure literature ; and, while he remains himself a man of letters, he writes by preference about action and as little as may be about books and authors. His literary essays therefore belong principally to the first period of his authorship. Moreover, he betrays his tendency by his choice of subjects. He writes with most satisfaction on authors whom he can regard as teachers ; on others he writes only of necessity and with little sym-pathy.

Carlyle's creed was that a critic must first stand where his subject stood before criticism could be other than misleading. The way to write either fruitful criticism or true history was to read and reflect until it was possible to think the thoughts of men of the time or of the country to be commented on. He carried out these precepts by way of biography as well as of critical essays. Of his two biographies, the *Life of Schiller*, though good, is much the less interesting and valuable. The *Life of Sterling* by common consent ranks among the best in English literature. Carlyle's work is, as a rule, remarkable rather for the presence of merits than for the absence of faults, but the *Life of Sterling* has few faults. It is exceedingly well proportioned, both in its several parts and with reference to its subject. Carlyle has moreover, while showing sincere friendship everywhere, preserved a wonderful sanity of judgment. It is impossible to rank Sterling's performances high, and his biographer, while respecting the man and steadily believing him greater than his works, steadily refuses to eulogise mediocre writings. An air of moderation, of charity and of kindliness breathes over the whole, as if Carlyle still felt the influence of his dead friend. He has written greater things, but none perhaps equally delightful.

It is necessary to add a word about Carlyle's much-debated style. But, in the first place, we ought in propriety to speak of Carlyle's *styles*. He had two, practised mainly, though not exclusively, in different periods of his life. His early style was a clear, strong, simple English, almost wholly free from the ellipses, inversions and mannerisms associated with his name. These gradually grew, and appeared fully developed for the first time in *Sartor Resartus*. Carlyle retained but seldom exercised the power of writing in his earlier style. The *Life of Sterling* has more affinity to it than to his later mode. But when Carlyle's style is spoken of, what is meant is invariably the style of his later books. It is over this that the battle has raged. There is no style more strange and unexampled in English, or more at war with ordinary rules. It is in the highest degree mannered, it seems to be affected, it is anything but simple. Certainly it is the last and worst of all styles to select for imitation. No man would ever advise another to give his days and nights to the study of Carlyle in order to learn how to write English. In the abstract, if it were possible to take it in the abstract, it would be described as an exceedingly bad style; but whether it was bad for Carlyle is less clear. Though it is not natural in the sense of being born with him, it is natural in the sense that it seems peculiarly adapted to his turn of thought. Could Carlyle have expressed his humour and irony otherwise? It is difficult to say; but at least he never did it with perfect success until he developed this style. If the style was really necessary to the complete expression of what was in Carlyle, then that is its sufficient justification. Among the various ' supreme virtues ' which have been assigned to style, the only genuine one is just this, that it and it alone, whether simple or ornate, curt or periodic, best expresses the thought of the writer. Yet we are apt to exclaim after all, ' the pity of it! ' If only the humour and irony, the intensity and passion, could have found a voice more nearly in the key of other voices! This style will almost certainly tell against the permanence of Carlyle's fame. The world is a busy world, and the simple, clear, direct writer, the man whom he who runs may read, has a double chance of the busy world's attention. Swift, whom Carlyle resembled in not a few ways, wrote a style unsurpassed for clearness and simplicity, yet he is not much read. How much less would he be read were *Gulliver's Travels* written in the style of *Sartor Resartus!*

CHAPTER II.

POETRY FROM 1830 TO 1850.   THE GREATER POETS:
TENNYSON AND BROWNING.

WHILE it is in the prose of Thomas Carlyle that we first find
a key to the ultimate and deeper tendencies of literature,
it is in verse that we see most clearly its characteristics for
the moment. In the interesting preface to *Philip van
Artevelde*, published in 1834, Henry (afterwards Sir Henry)
Taylor remarked that the poetry which had been recently
popular, of which he took Byron's as typical, was marked
by great sensibility and fervour, profusion of imagery and
easy and adroit versification ; while it showed inadequate
appreciation of what he called the intellectual and immortal
part, and a want of subject-matter. ' No man,' he adds,
' can be a very great poet who is not also a great philosopher.' About the poetry of his own days, he says that
' whilst it is greatly inferior in quality, it continues to be
like his [Byron's] in kind.'

The criticism is just, and the aspiration is not only towards a desirable reform, but towards that which in point
of fact has redeemed literature in the later decades of the
century, and has given the Victorian age a position among
the great poetic epochs of English literature. At the
moment when Taylor wrote, the sinking so frequently
noticeable between two great periods of literature was
plainly to be seen, and it was far deeper in poetry than in

prose. The great poets were somewhat later in coming than their brethren in prose, Macaulay and Carlyle; and, still more, it was longer before they proved to the satisfaction of criticism their title to be considered great. The field was for the time in possession of a band of minor poets, some of them not merely minor but insignificant. It is not enough to say that they are inferior to Byron, they belong to a different order altogether; for Byron, with all his faults, was great. It was however in his footsteps that they trod. As Keats and Shelley and Wordsworth have been the ruling powers since 1840, so during his brilliant life, and from his death down to about that year, was Byron. The poetry of the opening years of this period is therefore rightly affiliated to him. Even Tennyson, a man of wholly alien genius, felt the influence, as the *Poems by Two Brothers* shows; while the verse of Letitia Elizabeth Landon proves that sex was no barrier to it.

Want of subject-matter and of capacity for the intellectual and immortal part is precisely the defect of the poetry of those years. It is essentially trivial. It leaves the impression that the poet is writing not because he must, but because he has determined to do so. For the present purpose it is safer to draw conclusions from the work of a single great man than from that of many mediocre writers; and when we find Tennyson, already great in technical skill and graceful in style, sinking to triviality in subject and to commonplace sentiment, we look for an explanation not wholly confined to himself. We find it in the fact that those years were an interregnum between the philosophy of Rousseau and that gospel of work of which even Carlyle was as yet only half master, and which no one else had then grasped at all. Men were oppressed by a sense that the Revolution had shattered the old foundations of society; and they had scarcely gathered courage to attempt the task of reconstruction. To call therefore for a philosophy in poetry was right; but to supply it was impossible until the hour had come, and the man. Meanwhile the ordinary writer of verse groped in darkness or walked by a borrowed light. But in a sense, the man, or the men, had come, and the hour was rapidly approaching. Just three years before the beginning of the period Alfred Tennyson began to write, and just three years after it Robert Browning published his first poem.

Alfred, Lord Tennyson, was born at Somersby in Lincolnshire, of which place his father was rector. He was educated at Trinity College, Cambridge, where he was contemporary with and made the acquaintance of an unusual number of men afterwards highly distinguished. Tennyson's most intimate friend was Arthur Henry Hallam (1811-1833), son of the historian, and himself a writer of high promise, both in verse and prose. The literary remains published after Hallam's death can only be regarded as the promise of something that might have been. There is nothing great in them, but there is evidence of power which would probably have led the writer to greatness. Dying so young however, Hallam is memorable not so much for anything he did himself, as for his influence on his friend, and especially for the fact that he inspired *In Memoriam.*

During his course at Cambridge Tennyson won the Chancellor's prize with the poem of *Timbuctoo,* a piece above the ordinary prize-poem level, but not in itself remarkable. Still earlier, in 1827, he had joined with his brother Charles in a small volume entitled *Poems by Two Brothers.* But these compositions were merely boyish, and Tennyson's first noteworthy contribution to literature was the *Poems, chiefly Lyrical,* of 1830. This was followed by another volume bearing the date 1833, and entitled simply *Poems*. Then came nine years of almost complete silence, broken, in 1842, by two volumes entitled once more, *Poems*. These mark the end of Tennyson's first period of authorship. In the volumes of 1830 and 1833 we may look upon him as in many respects an apprentice in poetry; in those of 1842 he has passed far beyond mere apprenticeship. *The Princess* (1847) indicates a change in his method and in the nature of his ambitions; while *In Memoriam* (1850), though it has its roots in the early life of Tennyson, and was in part at least written when the grief it commemorates was fresh, is connected by its subject-matter rather with Tennyson's later work and with the interests of the second half of the century. In the year when *In Memoriam* was published Tennyson succeeded Wordsworth in the laureateship, an office which he held for a longer period than any of his predecessors. His appointment was the public recognition of him as the chief poet of his time.

The most interesting feature of Tennyson's writings during those years is the evidence of development they present; and this is especially important in any attempt to gauge the tendencies of the time. This evidence has been much obscured by changes and omissions. Part of the contents of the volumes of 1830 and 1833 has been incorporated in the collected editions of Tennyson's poems. About half of the collection of 1842 consisted of select poems from the earlier volumes; but many pieces were omitted, and of those retained almost all were freely changed, and some nearly re-written. For this reason it is difficult for the reader of the present day to appreciate fairly the early criticisms of Tennyson. It is well known that he was severely handled, especially by Lockhart in the *Quarterly Review;* and it is supposed, on the ground of the poet's great achievements, that this is only another example of perverse and utterly mistaken criticism. But such a judgment is hardly fair to the critic. Carlyle long afterwards condensed the criticism in his expressive way into a word,—'lollipops.' A great many of Tennyson's early poems were 'lollipops,' dainty, exquisite, delicious to taste, but not food. They are elegant, not strong. They are deficient in two things essential to great poetry, depth of thought, and fervour of passion. The need of passion to poetry will be universally admitted; and to the need of thought, especially in the present century, one of the greatest of English critics has borne emphatic testimony. 'I do not think,' says Matthew Arnold in his *Letters*, 'that any poet of our day can make much of his business unless he is intellectual.'

Now, among the early poems of Tennyson there are many pieces in which the want of these qualities is felt. He was certainly not in those days a poet of passion. His pulse temperately keeps time all the while he is drawing his Lilian, his Margaret and his Adeline. Though these pieces deserve, within certain limits, warm praise, they cannot be ranked as great poetry. They are masterpieces of grace, but they want depth. The writer is himself unmoved, and in consequence he leaves his readers equally calm. The same holds true of the thought in these volumes. It is usually cold and somewhat superficial. The critics, alive to these defects, were, it is true, both incautious and unfair. The early volumes contained a few poems showing no small force of mind, as well as a technical skill remarkable in so young a man. They contained, in particular, *The Palace of Art* and *A Dream of Fair Women*, both, even in their original shape, indubitably the productions of a strong intellect. In them also we find the exquisite *Lotos-Eaters*, with its wonderful melody, one of the most poetic poems Tennyson ever wrote, and one which, for suggestive beauty of thought as well as for rhythm, ranks among the masterpieces of the English language.

Tennyson then, judged by those early volumes, was a man who might prove to be less gifted intellectually than artistically. He certainly had grace, but it might be reasonably questioned whether he had much strength. On the other hand, it might prove that the surface show of weakness was the fault rather of the time than the man. For the production of truly great poetry two things must co-operate,—great gifts in the individual, and a great life in the community in which his lot is cast. Without the latter the former will lie dormant, like the strength of Samson till the Philistines are upon him. Now, this is exactly what has been described as the position of matters when Tennyson began to write. The old impulse which had stirred the giants of the Revolution was failing or was undergoing transformation; the new impulse was only beginning to be felt.

As the poet was, so to speak, in the balance, his next publication is an object of special interest. He had taken plenty of time; and an interval of nine years, considerable at any time of life, is great in the space between twenty and thirty. He had moreover undergone a great personal sorrow in the death of his friend Hallam. If any change was ever to take place in his work it might be expected now. And we do find a great change, partly in the tone of the new poems, and hardly less in the omissions and revisions of the old. The purely trivial pieces are not reprinted. It is hardly less instructive to note that in the lighter pieces which are retained the changes made are comparatively slight; for they were already nearly perfect of their kind. Very different is the treatment of the more weighty poems. Tennyson evidently felt that he had been less successful with these; and accordingly he freely revised all, and nearly rewrote some of them. The new pieces present similar evidence of development. The poet is still an artist first of all, but in a large proportion of the pieces he is a thinker as well. The whole tone of these volumes is therefore more thoughtful and more profoundly serious than that of their predecessors. *Ulysses*, *Locksley Hall*, *Morte d'Arthur* and the *Vision of Sin* may be mentioned as typical of the new work. Edward FitzGerald thought that Tennyson never rose above, nor even equalled, the poems of 1842; and, if we judge by the perfect balance of thought and expression, much might be said in defence of this view. At any rate, he had proved himself a poet who must be taken seriously, and it is from this date that we may regard his position among the greater English poets as assured. We have glimpses of artistic ideals to be realised and of intellectual problems to be solved. On the artistic side, the ideals are fundamentally a development from Keats, but they are a development by an original genius. On the intellectual side, *Locksley Hall* presents social problems, and the *Vision of Sin* raises moral and religious difficulties similar, it is true, in essence to those which men had discussed in former days, but seen in the light of the poet's own time.

Hitherto Tennyson's pieces had all been short. In 1847 he published his first long poem, the medley of *The Princess*. This serio-comic production on what is called ‘ the woman question ’ will probably not hold for long a high place among Tennyson's works. The main body of it contains no great illuminating thought. The reflexions upon the position of women and the relations of the sexes are not beyond the range of an intelligence considerably short of genius, and the jest and earnest are not very happily mingled. The poem is remarkable rather for fine passages than for greatness as a whole. In point of length it was the most important experiment Tennyson had yet made in the most difficult but most flexible form of English metre, blank verse. There is however no part of *The Princess* of similar length which can be ranked as equal to *Morte d'Arthur*; and its best feature, the lyrics between the parts, were a subsequent addition. But whatever may be the intrinsic merit of *The Princess*, it is valuable as a symptom. The poet who had at first held so far aloof from the interests of everyday life is now found devoting his longest work to a social question of the day. He is at least endeavouring to be what Sir Henry Taylor says the great poet must be, a philosopher as well as an artist. If 'art for art's sake' be the proper creed of the poet, then Tennyson is wrong, and he remains wrong all the rest of his life. We must rank him among those poets who seek to base their work on an intellectual foundation, not among those who hold that feeling alone is sufficient. He seeks to see Truth as well as Beauty, instead of resting satisfied, like Keats, with their ultimate identity.

Robert Browning is the only poet of that time who can be placed beside Tennyson, and it is only in respect of greatness that the two can be conjoined; for in the great features of his poetry Browning stands apart, not only from Tennyson, but from all contemporary writers. The Browning family were dissenters in religion, and in those days dissenters were to a large extent cut off from society and from the usual course of education. The young poet went to no public school, and his higher education was given not at Oxford or Cambridge, but in the University of London, afterwards University College. There he remained only one year, and the travels on the continent which followed were unquestionably more important for his intellectual

Robert Browning (1812-1889).

development. On his return he settled down to a literary life, and, notwithstanding narrow means and want of appreciation, became a poet by profession. His works consequently are the landmarks of his life. The most important event, outside the record of his publications, is his marriage in 1846 to Elizabeth Moulton Barrett, who was already known as a poetess. This union is unique in the records of English literature, and indeed, it would be hardly too much to say, of all literature. It has been said that men of genius usually marry commonplace wives. The two Brownings were, the one certainly among the greatest of nineteenth century poets, the other generally regarded as the greatest of English poetesses. The health of Mrs. Browning necessitated their living abroad ; and the works of both bear deep marks of the influence of their long residence of fifteen years at Florence.

Browning, like Tennyson, lived and worked all through the present period, and far beyond its lower limit ; but, unlike Tennyson, he neither illustrates in his own writings the characteristic influence of the time, nor did he in the early years make any deep mark upon it. One reason for his escape from the influence was that his interests were during those years more purely intellectual than those of any other poet. He had moreover a native buoyancy which saved him from the paralysing effect of disappointment and of fading hopes. He was an idealistic optimist born into a world where pessimism, or faith only in material prosperity and material progress, prevailed. Hence we find that from the start his works, unlike those of Tennyson or his contemporaries in general, were characterised by an even extravagant largeness of design. His first work, *Pauline* (1833), though it contains more than one thousand lines, is a mere fragment of a most ambitious scheme, which the poet afterwards admitted to have been far beyond his strength. *Paracelsus,*

Sordello, Strafford, and the other dramas, all exhibit a similar boldness. While the other poets of the time had to be slowly made conscious of their strength and encouraged to undertake great things, Browning had by degrees to become aware of the limits of his powers, and to learn that he must reach through small things up to great. It was after what we may call an apprenticeship in the shorter dramatic monologue, such as we find in *Dramatic Romances, Dramatic Lyrics* and *Men and Women,* that he achieved his greatest triumph, *The Ring and the Book.*

Pauline is interesting chiefly for the evidence it presents of the poet's early tastes. Shelley was the poet to whom in this piece he owed most; but Shelley's genius was not in harmony with Browning's, and afterwards his influence vanished almost as completely as did that of Byron from the works of Tennyson. *Pauline* was followed by *Paracelsus* (1835), a poem in which the writer seemed to spring all at once to the full maturity of his powers. He failed however to maintain his ground. *Strafford* (1837) was the first of a series of dramas published between that year and 1846, when the last number of *Bells and Pomegranates,* containing *Luria* and *A Soul's Tragedy,* appeared. Browning never afterwards attempted the drama proper, for *In a Balcony,* first published among *Men and Women,* is rather a dramatic episode than a drama. Besides the dramas, there had appeared during those years *Sordello* (1840), the most enigmatical poem Browning ever wrote. Despite the beauty of the descriptive passages in the poem, it may be questioned whether the enigma is worth the trouble of solution; at any rate, all the ingenuity bestowed upon it has not yet suggested a satisfactory explanation. There had appeared also, as parts of the series of *Bells and Pomegranates, Dramatic Lyrics* (1842) and *Dramatic*

Romances and Lyrics (1845). *Pippa Passes* (1841) is sometimes misleadingly classed as a drama. It is far more closely akin to the dramatic romances and dramatic lyrics.

The decade between *Strafford* and *A Soul's Tragedy* may be described then as, for Browning, a period of dramatic experiment. The result was to demonstrate that, though his genius was in some respects intensely dramatic, he was not fitted to write for the stage. His failure is all the more remarkable because of his keen interest in character and his great success, under certain conditions, in understanding and interpreting it. The question naturally arises whether there is any connexion between Browning's failure and the often-noted incapacity of the present century to nourish a dramatic literature. This incapacity is conspicuous in the preceding period as well as in that now under discussion. Scott failed completely as a dramatist. The once great reputation of Joanna Baillie has withered away. The dramas of Byron are striking, but their centre is always George Gordon. Shelley succeeded once, in *The Cenci;* for, great as is *Prometheus Unbound*, its greatness is not dramatic. With respect to the present period, the most convincing proof of the scarcity of dramatic talent is the fact that there is no need to devote a separate section to the criticism of this form of literature. To most writers the drama has been a mere interlude among other literary work, and this in spite of the fact that fiction alone can compare with it in respect of the material rewards it offers. Almost the sole exception, among those who can be regarded as rising into the ranks of literature, is James Sheridan Knowles who belongs more to the preceding period than to this. As literature, his plays are far from remarkable. His tragedies are of little interest, and his comedies, while ingenious, are pieces of skilful mechanism rather than works inspired by the poetic spirit. Men like Tom Taylor and James Robinson Planché and Douglas Jerrold, gifted with fluency, and capable of writing as many dramas as the theatres might demand, have a place only in ephemeral literature. Even better men, such as Thomas Noon Talfourd (1795-1854) and John Westland Marston (1819-1890), hold but a low position in its annals. The cold dignity of Talfourd's style hardly atones for the commonplace character of his thought; and Marston betrays an incapacity, fatal in a dramatist, to draw clear and consistent characters. Henry Taylor, who ranks much higher, will be considered elsewhere. As a rule, such drama as there is in the period comes under names more conspicuous in other departments. Great as are his literary defects, Bulwer Lytton is pretty nearly the best in the dramatic list; and, like Charles Reade, he is a novelist first and a dramatist only in the second place.

In some of these cases it might be fairly urged that the cause of failure is want of dramatic talent in the man himself; but this does not explain the strange fact that in one age, the Elizabethan, nearly all writers should prove themselves capable of producing dramas, always respectable and often great; while in another, our own, no one, except Tennyson in his old age, has written a drama that is likely to rank permanently among the treasures of literature. We can only account for this by the operation of the law of development in literature. We observe, in point of fact, that particular literary forms flourish at particular times. We observe, further, that in ancient Greece and in modern France and Spain, as well as in England, the golden age of the drama is neither at the beginning nor at the end, and that in each case it coincides with a period of great national activity and exaltation. The fact is susceptible of a psychological explanation. The drama requires an even balance between the spirit of action and the spirit of reflexion. On the one hand, we can hardly conceive of the drama being as naïve as the poems of Homer; on the other hand, the growth of self-consciousness is apt to interfere, as it did in Byron's case, with true dramatic portraiture.

Herein we find the secret of Browning's failure. Though he rightly proclaimed that all his poetry was 'dramatic in principle,' yet he never wrote a successful drama. The reason is that in him the spirit of reflexion predominates unduly over the spirit of action. In his plays the action stagnates, because he has no interest in it. All his wealth of intellect is devoted to the unfolding of motive and inner feeling, because, little as he cares for what a man does, he cares very much for what he *is* and *why* he does it. The characters therefore, in Browning's mode of conception, are seen individually, each in himself; they are not developed, in accordance with the true dramatic method, by mutual interaction. Hence too it comes that Browning's stage is never more than half filled, and that even of the sparse *dramatis personæ* only one as a rule, or at most two or three, are brought out with tolerable fulness of detail.

In the dramas then we may say that Browning was merely learning what he could not do. Side by side with them he was doing work which taught him what he could do eminently well. His name is associated, more than that of any other poet, with the dramatic monologue. Excluding the regular dramas, nearly all his work of the period under consideration is either dramatic monologue or closely akin to it. *Pippa Passes* is only slightly different, a series of dramatic scenes, bound together by a lyric thread and by the character and doings of the girl Pippa. Most of the *Dramatic Lyrics* and *Dramatic Romances* are pure monologues. *Paracelsus* may be described as modified monologue. And not only during these years, but throughout his life, Browning's success depended principally upon two things; first, on the fidelity with which he kept to monologue; and secondly, on his remembrance of the fact that the poet must be not only intellectual, but artistic. With few exceptions Browning's greatest things—in *Men and Women*, in *Dramatis Personæ* and in *The Ring and the Book*, as well as in the works above named—are monologues in which he bears this fact in mind. With few exceptions his failures in later days are due to the fact that he forgets the poet in the philosopher.

Reasons may easily be found to account for the fact that dramatic monologue proved so much more suitable to the genius of Browning than either the regular drama or any other form of verse. It gave scope to his interest in character, without demanding of him that interest in action which he only showed spasmodically. Moreover, it suited his analytic method. For Browning is not, like Shakespeare, an intuitive but a reflective artist. His delineations are the result of a conscious mental process; and hence he can hardly call up more than one character at a time. Further, he does not care to trace character through a train of events. His pictures are usually limited to moments of time, to single moods. They reveal the inner depth seen through some crisis in life; and therefore, though they are highly impressive, they do not exhibit growth. Now, for purposes such as these the monologue is admirably adapted. It leaves the poet free to choose his own moment, to begin when he likes and end when he likes; and this is essential to the effect of many of Browning's poems, as for instance *In a Gondola* and *The Lost Mistress*. It explains likewise the extraordinary suddenness of his style, which is one among the many causes of the difficulty so often felt in understanding him. There is no preparation, no working up to the crisis. The scene opens

abruptly on some tempest of the soul, and the reader has
to penetrate the mystery amidst thunder-claps and light-
ning-flashes. Yet the method does not always give rise to
difficulty. There is no better example of it in Browning
than the magnificent sketch of *Ottima and Sebald* in *Pippa
Passes*. It is not a monologue, for there are two inter-
locutors; but they stand isolated from all the world, bound
together by crime, and are seen only in their moment of
supreme tension. Yet everything is so clear that dulness
itself could hardly mistake the meaning.

Paracelsus is so much the most important of the works
of this period that it demands separate notice. Although
several characters appear in the course of it the method is
fundamentally that of monologue. The whole interest is
concentrated on the fortunes and spiritual development of
Paracelsus; but in this instance they are followed through
a life. The poem may be described as a poetical treatise
on the necessity of a union of love with knowledge and of
feeling with thought. But though loaded with reflexion it
never, like Browning's later works, ceases to be poetical,
and it must be ranked very nearly at the head of its author's
writings. The intellectual theory of the universe which
underlies all Browning's poetry is never afterwards as
fairly stated, nor are the difficulties as fully faced, as in
Paracelsus. It has the advantage therefore, not only as
poetry but also as philosophy, over the works written after
The Ring and the Book.

Boldness of design then, and an even excessive opulence
of intellect, were from the first the characteristics of
Browning. He did not acquire them, they were his
birthright. Carlyle stood out from among his contemporaries by virtue of conquests won through toil and pain,
Browning entered into his inheritance at once and without
effort. The one might have said, like the chief captain,

"With a great sum obtained I this freedom;" and the other might have answered, with St. Paul, "But I was free born." Yet the advantage was not all on one side. Carlyle had the deeper sympathy with the difficulties of the time, and laborious as was his way upwards he had far more power over his own generation than Browning. The latter was for many years one of the least popular of poets, and what influence he possessed operated slowly and unseen. It was men of less vigorous intellect who stamped their character upon this early part of the period.

CHAPTER III.

THE MINOR POETS, 1830 TO 1850.

THE view presented in the last chapter is that even Tennyson in his early works displays the qualities to be expected in a time of lowered energy, and gradually, by native force, rises superior to its limits. If this view be sound we should expect the characteristics in question to be much more prominent in lesser men. And this we find to be the case. Besides Tennyson himself and his brothers, the principal poets who had begun to write before 1830, and who may be taken as representative of the early years of the period, were: Letitia Elizabeth Landon, Mrs. Hemans, Elizabeth Moulton Barrett, Thomas Hood, Henry Taylor, and William Motherwell. We may include also Winthrop Mackworth Praed, for, though his poems were not collected and published till long afterwards, a number of them were written before this date. The *Poems* of Hartley Coleridge came a little later ; and in the last year of the decade then beginning Philip James Bailey won by the long and ambitious poem of *Festus*, a great reputation which has for many years been fading away.

These writers are unusually hard to classify, because of the absence of any dominant note or of any absorbing interest. The two women first named, Mrs. Hemans and ' L. E. L.,' belong rather to the preceding period, though they overlap this. Both are sentimentalists, and time has taken from their work the charm it once possessed. Mrs. Hemans is now unduly depreciated, but the difference between the most favourable and the least favourable critic can only be with regard to the degree of weakness charged against her. L. E. Landon (1802-1838), who became by marriage Mrs. Maclean, was in her own day even more popular than Mrs. Hemans, but she has since been much more completely forgotten. Even the mystery of her death, which was believed by many to be due to foul play, but which in all probability occurred through misadventure, has failed to keep alive the interest in her. Yet, though her verse is of little value, she is one of the best examples of the tendencies of the time. She followed Byron as far as her talents and the restraints of her sex would allow. Her longer poems are on the whole poor; some of her shorter pieces are very readable, but they are chargeable with the fault of an excess of rhetoric. Such as she was in poetry, her work was mostly done before 1830. After that date she wrote some mediocre prose stories, but was comparatively inactive in verse.

Both of Tennyson's brothers, Charles and Frederick, were, like himself, poets. It has but recently become known that Frederick as well as Charles had a share in the *Poems by Two Brothers*. Except for this the eldest brother's publications were of much later date; but Charles Tenny-

Charles Tennyson
Turner
(1808-1879).

son, afterwards Charles Tennyson Turner, followed up the joint venture with another of his own, a slim volume of *Sonnets and Fugitive Pieces*, published in 1830. This attracted the attention of Coleridge, who bestowed warm but discriminating praise upon the sonnets. Both as to fame, and probably as to his own productiveness, Charles Tennyson Turner was crushed, as it were, under his greater brother. He wrote little more, though he carefully revised and in some respects decidedly improved his sonnets. It is by virtue of them that he takes his place among English poets. They are graceful and sweet, but the substance is not always worthy of the form. They reveal everywhere the interests and the pursuits of the Vicar of Grasby, and they are honourable to his peaceful piety. It is evident that both Charles and Frederick Tennyson, and especially the latter, might have been disposed to adapt to themselves the humorous complaint of the second Duke of Wellington, and exclaim, ' What can a man do with such a brother ? ' Though the eldest of the three, Mr. Frederick Tennyson belongs by the date of his publications rather to the period after than to the period before 1870.

Of the other writers, Praed, accomplished and exceedingly clever, but never impelled to do anything really great, may be regarded as a victim of the prevalent want of purpose. So may Hood, in respect of that section of his works which naturally goes along with those of Praed. Hood, it is true, was too great a man to be dismissed as merely a writer of the transition ; yet, just because of his greatness, his history shows better than that of any other man how earnestness was discouraged and triviality fostered. Seldom have so great poetic gifts been so squandered—with no dishonour to Hood—on mere puns. The poet, as an early critic pointed out, was a man of essentially serious mind ; but he had to earn bread for himself and his children, and as jesting paid, while serious poetry did not, he was compelled to jest.

Thomas Hood inherited from a consumptive family a feeble constitution, and the latter part of his life was a gallant but painful struggle against disease. His literary life began in 1821, when he was made 'a sort of sub-editor' of the

Thomas Hood
(1799-1845).

London Magazine. Lycus the Centaur, a boldly imaginative piece for so young a man, appeared in 1822. *The Plea
of the Midsummer Fairies,* a fine specimen of graceful
fancy deservedly ranked high by himself, and the powerful
and terrible *Eugene Aram's Dream,* were likewise early
pieces. The latter may be contrasted for its treatment of
crime with Bulwer Lytton's well-known novel on the
story of the same murderer. The advantage in imaginative force and insight, as well as in moral wholesomeness, is
all on the side of Hood.

These pieces prove that the vein of serious poetry was
present from the first in Hood. The vein of jest and pun
was equally natural to him. Jokes of all kinds, practical
and other, enlivened and sometimes distracted his own
household. This liking for fun inspired the *Odes and
Addresses to Great People,* written in conjunction with John
Hamilton Reynolds, the *Whims and Oddities,* and the succession of *Comic Annuals,* the first of which appeared in
1830. The presence of such a light and playful element in
a great man's work is by no means to be regretted; but in
Hood's case, unfortunately, there was for many years little
else. Hood was blameless, for he had to live. With
characteristic modesty he seems for a time to have been
persuaded that the public were right, and that nature
meant him for a professional jester. It was fortunate that
he lived to change this opinion, for much of his finest
poetry belongs to his closing years.

Perhaps the most original fruit of Hood's genius is
Miss Kilmansegg, which conceals under a grotesque exterior
deep feeling and effective satire. It has been sometimes
ranked as Hood's greatest work; and if comparison be
made with his longer pieces only, or if we look principally
to the uniqueness of the poem, the judgment will hardly be
disputed; but probably the popular instinct which has

seized upon *The Song of the Shirt* and *The Bridge of Sighs*, and the criticism which exalts *The Haunted House*, are in this instance sounder. The grotesque element cannot be employed freely without damage to the pure poetic beauty of the piece in which it occurs; and *Miss Kilmansegg* certainly does suffer such damage.

The Song of the Shirt and *The Bridge of Sighs* are by far the most popular of Hood's poems. They have the great merit of perfect truth of feeling. Handling subjects which tempt to sentiment, and even to that excess of sentiment known in the language of slang as ' gush,' they are wholly free from anything false or weak or merely lachrymose. Pity makes the verse, but it is the pity of a manly man. *The Haunted House*, first published in the opening number of *Hood's Magazine*, stands at the head of the writer's poetry of pure imagination. Few pieces can rival it for eeriness of impression, and few exhibit such delicate skill in the choice of details in description. The centipede, the spider, the maggots, the emmets, the bats, the rusty armour and the tattered flags, all help to deepen the sense of desolation and decay. This piece, with the more serious ones already mentioned, and a few others, such as *Ruth* and *The Death-Bed*, are Hood's best title to fame. The growth in their relative number as time went on, the increasing wealth of imagination and the greater flexibility of verse, all show that Hood was to the end a progressive poet. If he had lived longer and enjoyed better health his fame might have been very great. He was the victim of the transition, and through tardiness of recognition and the want of any influence to draw him out, he failed to leave a sufficient body of pure and great poetry to sustain permanently a high reputation. As the author of a few pieces with the unmistakable note of poetry he can never be quite forgotten

Passing mention may be accorded along with Hood to

Laman Blanchard
(1804-1845).

Laman Blanchard, a very minor poet, who showed the same combination of seriousness with fun. He was an agreeable writer, but not, even at his best, a distinguished one.

The man of closest affinity to Hood was Winthrop

Winthrop
Mackworth Praed
(1802-1839).

Mackworth Praed, who began by contributing at school to *The Etonian*, and continued at Cambridge to write for Knight's *Quarterly Magazine*. He entered Parliament, and if he had lived he would probably nave risen to eminence there. Praed belongs to the class of writers of *vers de société* of which Prior is the earlier and Locker-Lampson the later master; and it is not too much to say that he surpasses both. It is a species of verse well adapted to such a period as that in which Praed lived. Great earnestness is not required, and is even fatal to it. The qualities essential to success are culture, good-breeding, wit and lightness of touch. Praed had them all. The cleverness and wit and delicacy which nature had given him were all increased by the influence of his school and university, where he acquired all the grace of scholarship without any of the ponderosity of learning. But Praed had one more gift, without which his verses must have taken a lower place—the gift of a refined poetic fancy. It is this that gives his wit its special charm, and it is this too that saves his verse from being that merely of a very clever and refined jester. The well-known character of *The Vicar* is one of the best examples of this combination of feeling with lightness. Herein we detect the difference between Praed's wit and the wit of Hood. The latter commonly separated jest from earnest, and gave himself wholly over to one or the other. He is far the more pronounced punster. The pleasant surprises

of Praed's verse usually arise from some delicate turn of
thought rather than from a twisting of words. Hood's
fun is sometimes almost boisterous, Praed's is never so.
As regards the lighter verse, the advantage on comparison
is all on the side of the younger man. But there is no
other aspect to Praed. Notwithstanding the undertone of
seriousness, notwithstanding too the strange power of that
masterpiece of the grotesque, *The Red Fisherman*, it remains doubtful whether he had the capacity to be more
than what he is, the prince of elegant and refined writers
of light verse. Hood is indubitably a poet.

It is likewise as a writer of *vers de société* that Richard
Monckton Milnes, Lord Houghton, is
best known, and is happiest. But
though he shines as a writer of what
may be called, without disparagement,
poetical trifles, there is also a serious
strain by no means contemptible in his verse. *Strangers
Yet* is a fine specimen of pathos. In *Poems, Legendary
and Historical*, however, Houghton is less successful, and
the best of them do not bear comparison with Aytoun's
Lays of the Scottish Cavaliers, which belong to the same
class. Houghton's critical work in prose is on the whole
more valuable than his verse, for there his culture told, and
the lack of high imagination is less felt.

Richard Monckton
Milnes,
Lord Houghton
(1809-1885).

Richard Harris Barham represents a type of humour
much broader than that of Praed. His
Ingoldsby Legends have enjoyed a popularity
wider, probably, than that of any other
humorous verse of the century. They are
clever, rapid in narrative, and resourceful in phrase and in
rhyme. Yet a certain want of delicacy in the wit and of
melody in the verse is evident when we compare them with
the work of Hood and Praed, or that of such later

Richard Harris
Barham
(1788-1845).

humorists as Calverley, or J. K. Stephen, or Lewis Carroll. Barham's last composition, 'As I laye a-thynkynge,' contains the promise of success if he had written serious poetry.

Hartley Coleridge was a poet of a totally different type;
Hartley Coleridge (1796-1849). and we must ascribe the fact that he never redeemed his early promise to hereditary weakness of will rather than to any adverse influence of the time. Against the latter he had a defence that did not in the same measure shield any other contemporary. He was the special inheritor of the great traditions of the so-called Lake school; and he was cradled in poetry. His infancy and childhood are celebrated both by his father and by Wordsworth. Derwent Coleridge tells a story of his brother, which shows that Wordsworth accurately described Hartley as one 'whose fancies from afar are brought,' and who made 'a mock apparel' of his words. 'Hartley, when about five years old, was asked a question about himself being called Hartley. "Which Hartley?" asked the boy. "Why! is there more than one Hartley?" "Yes," he replied, there's a deal of Hartleys." "How so?" "There's Picture-Hartley (Hazlitt had painted a portrait of him) and Shadow-Hartley, and there's Echo-Hartley, and there's Catch-me-fast Hartley"; at the same time seizing his own arm very eagerly.' Evidently this boy lived in a world of day-dreams, in a 'perpetual perspective.' The problem of the education of such a young idealist is a difficult one; but it seems clear that its principle ought to have been a judicious, not a harsh or pedantic, regularity. His father's aspiration of 'wandering like a breeze' was not for him. But instead, Hartley's actual education was irregular and desultory. Nothing was done to improve his natural defect and to discipline his will; and weakness

of will wrecked his life. The fellowship he had won at Oriel College was forfeited for intemperance, and he never conquered the habit, but sank from depth to depth, a pitiable example of genius gone to waste.

Though Hartley Coleridge wrote prose as well, his name is now associated only with his poems. A volume of these was published in 1833. It was marked Vol. I., but no second ever appeared. The poems however were re-edited, with additions, by Derwent Coleridge, in 1851. Hartley Coleridge nowhere shows the supreme poetic gift his father possessed; but as in sheer genius the elder Coleridge was probably superior to any contemporary, so Hartley seems to have been the superior by endowment of any poet then writing, Tennyson and Browning alone excepted. Weakness of will, unfortunately, doomed him to excel only in short pieces, and to be far from uniform in these. It would have been wiser to omit the section of ' playful and humorous' pieces. But the sonnets are very good, and some of them are excellent. A few of the songs take an equally high rank, especially the well-known *She is not fair to outward view*, and *'Tis sweet to hear the merry lark*. There are many suggestions of Wordsworth, but Hartley Coleridge is not an imitative poet. Without any striking originality he is fresh and independent. His verse betrays a gentle and kindly as well as a sensitive character. He evidently felt affection for all living things, and especially for all that was weak, whether from nature, age, or circumstance. Some of this feeling turns back, as it were, upon himself, in the numerous and often pathetic poems in which he appears to be contemplating his own history. He is of the school of Wordsworth in his love for and his familiar communion with nature; and here at least he gathered some fruit from the ' unchartered freedom ' of his existence.

Hartley Coleridge belonged to a family unique in its

power of transmitting genius. His sister Sara likewise inherited intellectual and imaginative gifts probably little if

Sara Coleridge
(1802-1852).

at all inferior to his; but circumstances
prevented her from making a great name.
She married another Coleridge of genius,
her cousin, Henry Nelson, whose untimely death threw a
burden upon her, as editor of her father's literary remains,
that absorbed her time and energies. Her only book is
Phantasmion, a fairy tale, whose lyric snatches prove her
worthy of remembrance among English poetesses.

Of the other poets who have been named, William

William
Motherwell
(1797-1835).

Motherwell was the least considerable both in
achievement and in gifts. He had a taste for
research in old popular poetry, but he took
such liberties that his versions are not to be
trusted. He also allowed the pseudo-antique to mar some
of his own work, especially the fine *Cavalier Song*. He is
happiest in the vein of pathetic Scotch verse, of which the
best specimen he left is his *Jeanie Morison*. He had the
feeling and sensibility of a minor Burns, but not the force.
Contemporary with Motherwell and, on the Scotch side of
his work, not dissimilar, was William Thom (1798-1848),
'the weaver poet,' best known for *The Blind Boy's Pranks*.
Dialect alone unites with these two George Outram (1805-
1856), a man little known out of Scotland, but, in his best
pieces, one of the most irresistibly humorous of comic
poets. Nothing but unfamiliarity with the legal processes
and phrases on which the wit frequently turns, prevents
him from being widely popular. For rich fun *The Annuity*,
his masterpiece, has seldom been surpassed.

Henry Taylor
(1800-1886).

Henry Taylor lifts us once more into a
higher sphere of art. He lived an even
and unruffled life, the spirit of which
seems to have passed into his works. The son of a

country gentleman, he procured an appointment in the Colonial office, gradually rose in it, was knighted, and after nearly half a century of service, retired in 1872. The comfortable and easy life of office permitted Taylor to develop his powers to the uttermost. For a greater man its very smoothness might have been damaging. Great poetry requires passion : either the passion of the emotional nature, or that passion of thought which, as Mr. William Watson has lately reminded the world, is no less valuable for the purposes of art. Official life fosters neither ; but it would seem that Sir Henry Taylor's nature contained the germ of neither. Hence perhaps, in part, his disapproval of the school of Byron. His practice would have been as excellent as his theory had he been one of those who know

> 'A deeper transport and a mightier thrill
> Than comes of commerce with mortality.'

But he was wanting in the second kind of passion, as well as in the first. His work is like his life, smooth, calm, unchargeable with faults ; but it is not the kind that animates mankind.

Sir Henry Taylor wrote prose as well as verse, in particular a very readable autobiography. It is however chiefly as a dramatist that he is memorable. His plays are the closet studies of a cultured man of letters, who knew little and cared little about the conditions of the stage. *Isaac Comnenus* (1827) was followed by his masterpiece, *Philip Van Artevelde* (1834). *Edwin the Fair* appeared in 1842, and his last play, *St. Clement's Eve*, in 1862. He also wrote one other piece, *A Sicilian Summer*, a kind of comedy, not very successful.

Philip Van Artevelde is so clearly Taylor's best work that his literary faculty may be judged, certainly without danger of depreciation, from it alone. It is a historical drama, and the title sufficiently indicates the age and country in which the scene is laid. The whole drama is long, and the slow movement adapts it rather for reading than for representation. It is composed of two parts, separated by *The Lay of Elena*, a lyrical piece in which may be detected echoes both of Wordsworth and Coleridge, with an occasional suggestion of Scott. The weakest element of the drama is the treatment of passion. Taylor's incapacity to comprehend it is strikingly illustrated in the passage where Philip, immediately after his declaration of love to Elena, reflects upon the caprice of a woman's fancy which

> ' Takes no distinction but of sex,
> And ridicules the very name of choice.'

The thought is a little trite, and the words are extraordinary in the mouth of a newly-accepted lover. We may confidently look to Taylor for careful and workmanlike delineation of character, but we shall find in him no profound insight. Philip proses about the burden he takes up and the cares he endures. But notwithstanding defects, the interest is fairly well sustained, some of the situations are impressive, and the verse is frequently lit with flashes of imaginative power. A man of talent with a touch of genius, Taylor saw clearly what the poetry of his time needed, but for want of the ' passion of thought ' he failed to supply it.

One contemporary at least showed by his practice that he agreed with Taylor as to the necessity of setting poetry on a philosophical basis. Philip James Bailey published *Festus* in 1839. It has been the work of his life, for though he wrote other pieces afterwards, most of them have been

Philip James
Bailey
(1816-1902).

incorporated, wholly or in part, with *Festus*. The consequence is that the poem, long originally, has grown to
enormous dimensions.   It is an ambitious attempt to settle
all the fundamental problems of the universe, and it was
once hailed with a chorus of praise that would almost have
sufficed for Homer or Milton.   This praise remains one of
the curiosities of criticism for later days to marvel at.
Festus is not profound philosophy, and still less is it true
poetry.   The thought when probed is commonplace.   A
vigorous expression here and there is hardly enough to
redeem the weak echoes of Goethe and Byron.   Frequently
the verse is distinguishable from prose only by the manner
of printing.   'Swearers and swaggerers jeer at my name' is
supposed to be an iambic line.   We are told that a thing is
in our 'soul-blood' and our 'soul-bones;' and we hear of
'marmoreal floods' that 'spread their couch of perdurable
snow.'   Yet this passes for poetry, and *Festus* has gone
through many editions in this country, and still more
in America.   The aberration of taste is not quite as great
as that which raised Martin Farquhar Tupper and his
Proverbial Philosophy to the highest popularity, but it is
similar in kind.

A more interesting and far superior example of the class
of thoughtful poets was Richard Henry,
Richard Hengist   or, as he called himself in later life,
Horne   Richard Hengist Horne.   Horne was a
(1803-1884).   man of versatile talent who, after an adventurous youth in which he saw something of warfare
and passed through many adventures on the coasts of
America and, at a later date, in the Australian bush,
settled down to a literary life.   His first memorable works
were two tragedies, *Cosmo de' Medici* and *The Death of
Marlowe*, both published in the year 1837.   A third tragedy,
Gregory VII., appeared in 1840.   Horne's dramas are

thoughtful, and they have the vigour which marked his own character. Yet Horne seems to have felt that there was something not wholly satisfactory in his dramatic work, and, except *Judas Iscariot* (1848), his more noteworthy writings in later days are either prose, or lyrical verse, or epic blank verse. He is best known by *Orion, an Epic Poem* (1843). It is an epic with a philosophic groundwork, 'intended,' as the author himself explains, ' to work out a special design, applicable to all time, by means of antique or classical imagery and associations. . . . Orion, the hero of my fable, is meant to present a type of the struggle of man with himself, *i.e.*, the contest between the intellect and the senses.' Horne sarcastically hinted his sense of the improbability that such a poem would find a sale by publishing the first three editions at a farthing, with the explanation that he did so ' to avoid the trouble and greatly additional expense of forwarding presentation copies.'

Orion is Horne's masterpiece. The philosophic thought clogs the epic movement, but the thought is weighty enough, and expressed with sufficient terseness and force, to be worthy of attention for its own sake. The verse is almost always good and sometimes excellent. Horne is indebted more to Keats than to anyone else. Sometimes he appears to echo him consciously ; at other times the reminiscence is probably unconscious. But as Horne was always a bold and original thinker his discipleship was altogether good for him. The sonorous quality of his verse is partly due to his model ; the meaning remains his own.

Another true poet whose work belongs largely to this early period was William Barnes, author of *Poems of Rural Life in the Dorset Dialect*. This collection, published in 1879, and embracing the work of more than forty years,

William Barnes (1801-1886).

may be said to sum up his literary life; for, though he wrote prose as well as poetry, it is only by his verses in dialect that he has any chance to be remembered. Barnes began writing his Dorset poems in 1833, and continued to do so at intervals all through his life. The great charm of his poetry is its perfect freshness. The Dorset poems are eclogues, wholly free from the artificiality which commonly mars compositions of that class; they are clear, simple, rapid and natural. There is no affectation of profound thought, and no straining after passion, but a wholly unaffected love for the country and all that lives and grows there. The vital importance of language to poetry is nowhere more clearly seen than in Barnes, for all the spirit of the Dorset poems evaporates, and all the colour fades from the specimens the poet was induced to publish in literary English.

There were numerous inferior writers, a few of whom claim a passing notice. James Clarence Mangan (1803-1849) is one of those Irishmen with regard to whose work a wide difference of opinion exists between his countrymen and English critics. He had certainly an ear for verse and a gift for making it, and if his equipment of ideas had been proportionate he would have been a great poet. His weakness is that, while he can say things pleasantly, he has but little to say. Charles Whitehead (1804-1862) was one of those who attempted dramatic composition, but his best work was *The Solitary* (1831), a reflective poem in the Spenserian stanza, thoughtful but slow in movement, and as a whole somewhat tiring. Thomas Wade (1805-1875) was likewise a mediocre dramatist, whose name is now associated only with *Mundi et Cordis Carmina*, a book which bears many traces of the influence of Shelley.

Ebenezer Jones (1820-1860) also, though much younger

than these men, falls, by reason of his principal work, *Studies of Sensation and Event* (1843), within the same period. Jones was crushed by circumstances and the want of appreciation, otherwise his sensitive nature might have produced good, though hardly great poetry.

... these principles, the principal works
... Chaucer, and Percy ... when the failure
... Jones was rewarded by ... and the want
... objection others ... nearly might have
... good, though hardly great poetry.

CHAPTER IV.

THE EARLIER FICTION.

THE characteristic literary form of the last two generations has been the novel. After a certain interval Scott was
followed zealously, and by constantly increasing numbers ;
so that for every novelist who was writing in the first
decade of the century, there were probably ten in the
fourth ; and, as the great increase of readers has been
principally in the readers of fiction, the growth has
naturally continued down to the present day. No one can
believe that this immense preponderance of fiction has
been altogether wholesome. It is questionable whether
the novel is capable of producing the highest results in art ;
certainly we do not find in prose fiction the equivalent of
Hamlet or of *Faust,* of the *Iliad* or the *Divine Comedy.* It
may be that the Shakespeare of novelists has not yet come ;
but it may also be that the form is inherently inferior to the
drama and the epic. The latter is the conclusion suggested
by the fact that of all kinds of imaginative art the novel is
the one which has least permanence. Novels are like light
wine in respect that, while pleasant to the taste, they do
not keep long ; they resemble it too in the fact that a man
may read much, as the disappointed toper found he could
drink much, without making great progress. Notwithstanding the hostility, avouched by Horace, of gods and
men and booksellers to the mediocre poet, the versifier

who has just a little of the poetic spirit is, after two or three generations, far more readable than the merely competent novelist. There are few literary experiences more melancholy than to turn to an old novel, once famous, but not quite the work of genius. Moreover, the novel has yielded more than any other form of literature to certain influences of the time inimical to high art. It is in fiction above all that the periodical system of publication has been adopted; and we can trace its evil effects in the work even of men like Thackeray and Dickens. The novel tends at the best to looseness of structure, and periodical publication fosters the tendency.

In at least one other way the influence of the novel must have been partly evil. The gains of literature have been to an altogether disproportionate extent showered upon novelists; and the ordinary laws of human action force us to believe that some talent must have been thus diverted to fiction which would have been better employed otherwise. Theologians like Newman and historians like Froude are tempted from their own domain into the field of fiction. Yet on the other hand it must be said that the greater writers have been on the whole remarkably faithful to their true vocation. The leading novelists are those whose talents find freest scope in fiction. Historians, philosophers, novelists, poets, the great men everywhere remain what nature intended them to be. Still, the evil, though not as great as it might have been expected to be, is real. Matthew Arnold, it is said, ceased to write verse because he could not afford it. But for the absorption of the mass of readers in fiction he probably could have afforded it.

In the year 1830 literature in general, but especially fiction and the more fugitive forms both of verse and prose, received a notable stimulus from the establishment of *Fraser's Magazine*. The idea of the magazine originated with William Maginn and a Bohemian acquaintance of his, Hugh Fraser, from whom, and not from the publisher James Fraser, it received its name. Maginn had been a contributor to *Blackwood*, and partly through his connexions with its staff he soon drew around him a band as brilliant as that of *Blackwood* itself. Coleridge, Carlyle, Lockhart, Thackeray and Southey were among the early contributors. Theodore Hook, famous for his somewhat coarse but copious and ready wit, also wrote for it. He was at that time one of the most popular of the novelists; but though he could tell a story well he could not draw a character, and it is for impromptu jests and for the clever fun of his articles that he is now remembered. Maginn himself was no mean contributor. He was never the editor of the magazine, but he was one of the most energetic and effective of its staff. Thackeray has immortalised him in Captain Shandon; but if he had the weaknesses of that well-known character he had certainly all his cleverness and more than all his accomplishments. For Maginn's more serious articles show no inconsiderable learning; while his best humorous articles are simply excellent. *Bob Burke's Duel with Ensign Brady* is a model of what the Irish story ought to be. Maginn was helped by others in giving an Irish flavour to the early *Fraser*. Crofton Croker, author of the *Fairy Legends and Traditions of the South of Ireland*, was one of his colleagues; and the witty Francis Mahony was another. The famous *Reliques of Father Prout* first appeared in *Fraser*.

William Maginn (1793-1842).

Men like Theodore Hook and Mahony were however merely the free lances of fiction, and it was Scott who moulded the legitimate novel. It is strange that his great success did not more speedily produce a crop of imitations. A few appeared during the twenties, but Scott's life was near its close before any writers came forward of calibre sufficient to be called his successors. Of those who had begun to write before 1830, the chief were Bulwer Lytton, Disraeli and Marryat. Two others, worthy of mention though inferior to these, were the prolific but commonplace G. P. R. James and Harrison Ainsworth. All of these men were stimulated by Scott, but the greater ones were more than mere imitators.

The first Lord Lytton was by baptism Edward George Earle Lytton Bulwer. On succeeding to his
Lord Lytton mother's estate of Knebworth he became
(1803-1873). Bulwer Lytton; and in 1866 he was raised to the peerage as Viscount Lytton. The union of politics with fiction is one of the points of contact between him and Disraeli; but while in the case of Disraeli the politician is first and the man of letters second, the order of importance is reversed in the case of Lytton. In politics, Lytton was at the start a Whig, but afterwards attached himself to the Conservative party, and became, under Lord Derby, Colonial Secretary.

Lytton's literary career began in boyhood with *Ismail and other Poems* (1820), and it ended only with his death. Perhaps fluency and versatility were his most remarkable characteristics. He distinguished himself as a novelist and as a dramatist, achieved a certain success as a lyric poet, believed that his greatest work was an epic, and attempted criticism and history. He had however the good sense and good taste to leave his historical work, *Athens, its Rise and Fall*, unfinished on the appearance of the histories of Thirlwall and Grote. It is only as a novelist and dramatist that he demands serious consideration; and in these departments he is the more worthy of attention because he is perhaps the best literary weather-gauge of his time.

Lytton's first novel was *Falkland* (1827), which he after-

wards called his Sorrows of Werther. It proves his literary
affiliation to Byron, and the proof is strengthened by
subsequent works. Lytton, who was not proud of the
relationship, both thought and said that he had done much
to put Byron out of fashion. Possibly he was right, but
the kinship is none the less real. The posing and foppery
of *Pelham* are both like and unlike the attitudinising of
Byron; and the similarity of the sentimental and romantic
criminals, Eugene Aram and Paul Clifford, to the heroes of
Byron's tales is obvious. Moreover, as Lytton once at
least, in *Pelham*, sat for his own portrait, and Byron did so
many times, the likeness was recognised as a personal one,
so that one of Lytton's early lady correspondents nicknamed
him Childe Harold. Lytton was too sensitive to influences
to escape the Byronic fever. But his Byronism is Byronism
a little damaged. 'The Hero as Criminal,' as presented by
him, is a being more sentimental and sickly, less violent and
less forcible, but not a whit less dangerous to society, than
his Byronic prototype.

Lytton's excursions into the domains of dandyism and
criminality drew down upon him the satire of Carlyle and
Thackeray, both sworn foes of affectation, from which
Lytton was never free. But in spite of hostile criticism
the new novelist had caught the popular taste; and he
retained it, perhaps because his own never remained long
constant. Shortly after the publication of *Eugene Aram*
(1832) he underwent a marked change, due immediately to
a journey to Italy, the influence of which is seen both in
the subject and the treatment of *The Last Days of Pompeii*
(1834), and of *Rienzi* (1835). These, with *The Last of the
Barons* (1843), form a group of historical romances, glittering and clever, but destitute of charm. The strength and
the weakness of Lytton is nowhere more easily detected
than in these novels. They show abundance of talent,

supported by a quality not usually associated with such powers as those of Lord Lytton—indefatigable industry. Yet they fall short of excellence. To say that Lytton's treatment of history will not bear comparison with Shakespeare's, or with Scott's, or with Thackeray's, is only to say that he is not equal to the greatest masters. But there are other men, markedly inferior to these, who yet overtop Lytton. Such, for instance, is Charles Reade, in his *Cloister and the Hearth*. What Reade has in common with his greater brethren, and Lytton has not, is the light and shade of life. In Lytton all is polished glittering brilliance. The light is neither the sunlight of common day nor 'the moonlight of romance,' but the glare of innumerable gas lamps,—the rays from the footlights to which he was about to betake himself. All the softer shades disappear, and quiet effects are impossible. There is nowhere in these novels, and there is rarely in Lytton's later works, that atmosphere of a home which we always breathe in the novels of the greater writers.

After the Italian novels Lytton for a time turned his energies to dramatic writing. The fantastic romance of *Zanoni* (1842) and *The Last of the Barons*, which followed it, are exceptions. With *The Caxtons* (1849) we find him entering upon a new period of prose fiction. *My Novel* (1853) was a sequel to it; and these two are generally ranked with *What will He do with It?* (1859) as a group devoted to contemporary life. Perhaps *Kenelm Chillingly* (1873) ought to be added. These novels are altogether mellower than the historical romances, and wholesomer than what may be called the criminal group. To a great extent the theatrical glare has disappeared. It is clear that in writing these novels Lytton was catering for the taste which had been partly indicated and partly created by Dickens and Thackeray. The difference is that, whereas

Dickens and Thackeray are habitually in touch with nature, Lytton is so only in moments of inspiration. His true field was not the natural, but rather the fanciful and fantastic. Two of his most successful works are *Zanoni*, which flings probability to the winds, and *The Coming Race* (1871), in which the faculty exercised is that of prophecy. In the latter Lytton showed again his extraordinary sensitiveness. Forecasts like *The Coming Race* have been characteristic of recent literature, and he seems to have divined their approach.

Lytton's dramas are remarkably like in tone to his novels, and the popularity they have enjoyed has been due to much the same causes. But whereas the novels are overshadowed, in critical opinion at least, and largely even in popularity, the dramas remain what they were when they were written, among the best plays of a non-dramatic age. Not that they can compare in literary merit with even such semi-failures as Browning's plays, still less with Tennyson's one great success, *Becket*. They are melodramatic, and the striving for stage effect is evident; but yet they are interesting and well adapted for representation, and the melodrama is good of its kind. Lytton's first play, *The Duchess de la Vallière*, was a failure; but *The Lady of Lyons* (1838) speedily became, and still remains, a favourite on the stage. It is the best specimen of Lytton's dramatic work. Attempts have been made to put the prose comedy, *Money* (1840) above it; but, though effective, *Money* is very flimsy in construction and characterisation. Lytton's third drama, *Cardinal Richelieu* (1838), is like one of the historical novels adapted to the stage; though, curiously enough, it is less meretricious than they are.

The epic of *King Arthur* is scarcely worthy of mention; but Lytton's lyrics deserve a few words, if only because they are in danger of being forgotten. They are not original; perhaps indeed it is as echoes that they are most interesting. We have already seen how Lytton appears to veer with every breath of popular taste; and it is curious to detect in a man so different by nature the occasional echo of the pensive reflexion of Arnold, and sometimes even a suggestion of the philosophy of Browning. It will appear hereafter that this faculty proved hereditary and descended to Owen Meredith. Two stanzas from *Is it all Vanity?* deserve to be quoted, because the modern note sounds so clear in them:

'Rise, then, my soul, take comfort from thy sorrow;
   Thou feel'st thy treasure when thou feel'st thy load;
Life without thought, the day without the morrow,
      God on the brute bestow'd;

'Longings obscure as for a native clime,
   Flight from what is to live in what may be,
God gave the Soul;—thy discontent with time
      Proves thine eternity.'

Benjamin Disraeli, Earl of Beaconsfield, was the man of letters most closely related in spirit and methods to Lytton; but even from the beginning his ambition was for eminence in the state. Political interests and a political purpose are features in his earlier works, and they are the essence of the intermediate novels, *Coningsby* and *Sybil*. Disraeli began his career with *Vivian Grey*, the first part of which was published in 1826, and the second in the following year. He next spent three years in the south of Europe; after which, in the interval between his return and his entrance into Parliament in 1837, came the period of his greatest literary activity. Between 1831 and 1837 there appeared, besides some minor works, five novels,—*The Young Duke, Contarini*

Benjamin Disraeli,
Earl of Beaconsfield
(1804-1881).

Fleming, The Wondrous Tale of Alroy, Venetia and *Henrietta
Temple.* Parliamentary work checked his pen and profoundly influenced what he did write, as we see in *Coningsby* (1844), *Sybil* (1845), and *Tancred* (1847). After
Tancred Disraeli wrote no fiction till *Lothair* appeared in
1870, followed by the disappointing *Endymion* (1880).

As literature, Disraeli's novels are not great, because,
using the word in an artistic and not in a moral sense, they
are not pure. They are pretentious and unreal, and the
rhetoric rings false. The impression of insincerity, conveyed
to so many by his statesmanship, is conveyed also by his
novels. But notwithstanding all defects, Disraeli's novels
have that interest which must belong to the works of a man
who has played a great part in history. They throw light
upon his character, they mark the development of his
ambition, it may even be said that they have helped to
make English history. It is worth remembering that
Tancred foretells the occupation of Cyprus; and it is quite
consistent with the character of Disraeli to believe that,
when the opportunity came, the desire to make his own
prophecy come to pass influenced him to add to the
British crown one of its most worthless possessions, and
to burden it with one of its most intolerable responsi-
bilities, the care of Armenia. Indeed, the most remarkable feature in Disraeli's novels is the way in which
they reflect his life and interpret his statesmanship. The
magniloquence, the flash and the glitter of the early novels
seem of a piece with the tales current regarding the
author's manners and character, his dress designed to
attract attention, and his opinions cut after the pattern
of his dress. So in the *Coningsby* group we are struck
with the forecast of the writer's future political action.
His later policy seems to be just the realisation of his
earlier dreams.

Impartially considered, these novels, notwithstanding their air of unreality, tell in favour of Disraeli's sincerity. Many even of his own party believed him to be cynically indifferent to the real effect of his measures, and to aim only at party, and, above all, at personal success. But it ought to be remembered that the originator of Tory democracy was also the leader of Young England. *Coningsby*, and still more *Sybil*, advocate the claims of the people to a more careful consideration than they had hitherto received at the hands of government; and their advocacy was no mere passing thought. In the case of *Sybil*, at least, Disraeli's views were the outcome of personal observation during a tour in the north of England. When he afterwards declared that sanitation and the social improvement of the working classes were the real task of government, he was only repeating what he had written many years before. Men who knew Disraeli well have said that his most wonderful quality was an almost portentous power of forecast. This is certainly confirmed by his literary works. There are no writings of the century which so distinctly foreshadow the actual course of politics and legislation as this group of Disraeli's novels.

Of the other men selected as representative of this early period, Ainsworth and James, though younger than Marryat, claim treatment first, because their work is more closely connected with the novels of the preceding period. They were direct imitators of Scott, as Scott himself perceived in the case of Ainsworth at least; [1] and criticism of one side of their work could not be better expressed than in his words. The great novelist compares himself to Captain Bobadil, who trained up a hundred gentlemen to fight very nearly, if not quite, as well as

---

[1] *I.e.*, if Ainsworth was the author of *Sir John Chiverton*.

himself. He goes on: 'One advantage, I think, I still have over all of them. They may do their fooling with a better grace; but I, like Sir Andrew Aguecheek, do it more natural. They have to read old books and consult antiquarian collections to get their knowledge; I write because I have long since read such works, and possess, thanks to a strong memory, the information they have to seek for. This leads to a dragging-in of historical details by head and shoulders, so that the interest of the main piece is lost in minute descriptions of events which do not affect its progress.'

Little or nothing need be added about the historical novels of William Harrison Ainsworth. What Scott says is strictly true of *The Tower of London* (1840), reputed to be Ainsworth's masterpiece, of *Old St. Paul's* (1841), and of *St. James's, or the Court of Queen Anne* (1844). The censure is indeed too mildly expressed.

William Harrison Ainsworth (1805-1882).

Ainsworth had another side. Like Lytton, he showed a kind of perverse regard for interesting criminals. *Rookwood* (1834), with its famous description of Turpin's ride to York, and *Jack Sheppard* (1839), are studies of the highwayman. The latter was severely criticised as demoralising in tendency, and the censure induced Ainsworth to abandon this species of story.

George Paine Rainsford James was even more prolific than Ainsworth. He is said to have written more than one hundred novels, besides historical books and poetry. No wonder therefore that the name of James became a by-word for conventionality of opening and for diffuse weakness of style. More perhaps than Ainsworth he has suffered from time, because he remains more constantly on a dead level of mediocrity. James trusted,

George Paine Rainsford James (1801-1860).

and in his own day trusted not in vain, to adventure; but unless there is some saving virtue of style, or of thought, or of character, each generation insists on making its own adventures. James has sunk under the operation of this law, and he is not likely to be revived.

Frederick Marryat was a man of altogether higher merit than these two. Indeed there

Frederick Marryat (1792-1848).

are several points, of vital moment for permanence of fame, wherein he surpasses Disraeli and Lytton as well. He was by far the most natural and genuine of the whole group. He was also, *qua* novelist, the most original. There is no affectation, no pretentiousness, in Marryat. Through his breezy style there blows the freshness of an Atlantic gale, rude and boisterous, but invigorating. He is moreover the best painter of the naval life of that day, and the fact that it has passed away for ever, by closing the subject to future writers, or condemning them to write at second-hand, gives to his works a special promise of permanence.

Marryat's literary career reaches from *Frank Mildmay* (1829) to the posthumous *Valerie* (1849). His stories embody many incidents of his own life, and his characters are often reproductions of actual men. Thus, the Captain Savage of Peter Simple is partly a picture of Marryat's first commander, the great Cochrane, to whose adventurous spirit he owed an experience richer, though crowded within a few years, than a lifetime of the 'weak piping time of peace.' This was his literary stock-in-trade. His rattling adventure, his energetic description, his fun and liveliness, are the charm of his best books—*Peter Simple, Jacob Faithful, Midshipman Easy, Japhet in Search of a Father*. His plots are rough but sufficient; his characters show little penetration; but the habit of drawing from the life prevented him from going far wrong.

From the nature of his subjects and from his mode
of treatment Marryat invites comparison with his predecessors, Smollett and Fenimore Cooper, as well as with
his contemporary, Michael Scott, who, next to Marryat
himself, is the best of the naval story-tellers of that time.
Marryat is by no means the equal of Smollett in richness of
humour. His is rather the humour of boisterous spirits
than that intellectual quality which gives so fine a flavour
to books. On the other hand, Marryat is much more
humane than Smollett. The life depicted by both is rough
to the last degree. In Smollett, the roughness frequently
passes over into brutality; while Marryat, though he
depicts brutality, never seems to share it. As against the
American, Cooper, Marryat has the advantage, in his sea
stories, of greater familiarity with the life he paints;
Cooper's strength is elsewhere, and there he reaches higher
than Marryat's highest point.

Michael Scott, one of the *Blackwood* group of writers,
would be not unworthy to be bracketed
with Marryat if a man could be judged by
parts of his books without regard to the
whole; but unfortunately *Tom Cringle's Log* (1829-30)
and *The Cruise of the Midge* (1836) are little more than
scenes and incidents loosely strung together. Perhaps
Scott was influenced by the *genius loci;* at any rate his books
resemble the *Noctes Ambrosianæ* in so far as they are the
outlet to every riotous fancy and every lawless freak of the
writer's humour.

Marryat had several imitators, the best of whom were
Glascock and Chamier, the latter still fairly well known by
name as the author of *Ben Brace* and *The Arethusa*. But
though they had practical experience of sea life, like
Marryat, Glascock and Chamier had not his literary
faculty. At a later date, James Hannay, the essayist and

Michael Scott
(1789-1835).

critic, essayed the naval tale with more literary skill, but
without the practical knowledge possessed by these men.

To a wholly different class belonged the once famous

Samuel Warren. He was a barrister and

Samuel Warren
(1807-1877).

the author of several legal works, but
his literary career was determined rather
by a short period of medical study in Edinburgh, before he
resolved to be a barrister. His acquaintance with Christopher North opened the pages of *Blackwood* to him, and
he utilised his medical training in the *Diary of a Late
Physician*, an unpleasantly realistic book which first appeared in that magazine. *Ten Thousand a Year* (1841),
though commonplace in substance, was interesting. Warren
lived upon the reputation of this book. His subsequent
attempts were failures, and he was known through life as
the author of *Ten Thousand a Year*.

CHAPTER V.

FICTION: THE INTERMEDIATE PERIOD.

WHERE dates so overlap it is impossible to find, and therefore misleading to seek for, absolute divisions. Some of the writers to be treated in this chapter began to publish only a few years after those dealt with in the last, and great part of their career was strictly contemporaneous. The division only means that, on the whole, we can recognise in the earlier writers a closer relationship with the preceding period, a more direct debt to Scott and Byron. In the fourth decade of the century we begin to see the romance of the Middle Ages and of the East giving place to the humours of low life in Dickens, to satire on society in Thackeray, and to the novel of passion in the Brontës. These writers may be said to form ideals of their own, and though they do not constitute a school they are each distinguished by characteristics which we recognise as the growth of the present period.

The difference between good work and excellent work is

Charles Dickens
(1812-1870).

seen when we turn from even the best of the earlier writers to Charles Dickens. The novelist's father, John Dickens, was a clerk in the navy pay-office; and the circumstances of the lad's early life are universally known from *David Copperfield*, a novel largely autobiographical. Forster's biography proves that the picture of the miserable little drudge, David, is even painfully accurate. The sordid life, both of his home, with its mysterious 'deeds' leading up to his father's imprisonment in the Marshalsea, and of the London streets and the blacking warehouse, was the best possible for the development of his talents; but the bitterness of it never faded from his memory. Neither can it be denied that certain of the faults of Dickens may with probability be explained by his early life. His many fine qualities were marred by a slight strain of vulgarity, visible both in his works and in his life, from which the surroundings of a happier home would almost certainly have preserved a nature so sensitive.

The family circumstances improved, and in 1824 Dickens was sent to a school at once poor and pretentious, where he remained for two years. He afterwards spent some time in a lawyer's office, but left it to become a reporter. After much toil he became, in his own words, which are confirmed by the estimate of others, 'the best and most rapid reporter ever known.' Journalism is akin to literature, and Dickens gradually drifted into authorship. His first article, *A Dinner at Poplar Walk*, now entitled *Mr. Minns and his Cousin*, appeared in the old *Monthly Magazine* for December, 1833; and the collected papers were published in 1836, under the title of *Sketches by Boz*. They were in some respects crude, but they contained the promise of genius. The first drafts of some of Dickens's best characters are to be found in them, and the sketches are eminently fresh and independent. Few books owe less to other books than the early works of Dickens. His book was the streets of London; and even what he read was best assimilated if it had some connexion with them. George Colman's description of Covent Garden captivated him. 'He remembered,' says Forster, 'snuffing up the flavour of the faded cabbage-leaves as if it were the very breath of comic fiction;' and

Forster adds, with justice, ' it was reserved for himself to give a sweeter and fresher breath to it.' For to the honour of Dickens it may be said that, despite certain lapses of taste, he seldom forgot that ' there is as much reality in the scent of a rose as in the smell of a sewer.'

The extraordinary rapidity with which Dickens rose to popularity is indicated by the advance in the value of his copyrights. He sold the copyright of *Sketches by Boz* for £150, and before *Pickwick* was finished in the following year, he found reason to buy it back for no less than £2,000. *Pickwick*, scarcely equalled for broad humour in the English language, was published in monthly parts, and finished in November, 1837. It was *Pickwick* that led to the first meeting between Dickens and Thackeray; for on the suicide of Seymour, the original illustrator, Thackeray was one of those who offered to execute the sketches. *Oliver Twist* was begun before *Pickwick* was finished; and in the same way *Nicholas Nickleby* overlapped *Oliver*. Thus the stream flowed on for many years; and though towards the close of his life the rate of production was slower, Dickens, like Thackeray, was writing to the last.

The life of Dickens was purely literary, and was diversified by few incidents. But he was liable to overstrain, as men of great nervous energy are apt to be, and was consequently forced to allow himself occasional holidays. During one of these, in 1842, he visited America, and wrote, in consequence, the not very wise or generous *American Notes*. This journey bore fruit in *Martin Chuzzlewit*. Two years later he made a journey to Italy, and subsequently he was several times on the continent and once again in America. The influence of the continental journeys can be traced in *A Tale of Two Cities*, though the story is rather due to Carlyle's *French Revolution* than to the personal observation of Dickens. A more serious inter-

ruption than any holiday he ever allowed himself was
his indulgence, for so it may be described, in public readings.   They increased his wealth, and they gratified the
vanity which, in spite of his biographer, was one of the
weaknesses of Dickens; but they impaired his literary
work, and in all probability they hastened nis death.   Besides these readings, the nervous strain of which was very
great, Dickens encumbered himself with editorial work.
He conducted *Household Words* from its start in 1850; and
when it stopped in 1859 he started *All the Year Round*,
with which he was connected till his death.   Through these
various distractions both the quantity and the quality of
his original work declined.   Probably after *David Copperfield* he never wrote anything altogether first-rate.   His
health too gave way under the strain, and he died at the
age of 58, on June 9th, 1870.

Dickens has enjoyed a popularity probably unparalleled
among English writers.   Forster has calculated that during
the twelve years succeeding his death no fewer than
4,239,000 volumes of his works were sold in Britain.   The
secret was in the first place originality.   Dickens had
lived the life he depicted.   With a strong memory and
keen powers of observation he had been storing up from
early boyhood information which in his maturer years
served him well.   'Sam's knowledge of London was extensive and peculiar,' he writes of Weller, when Mr. Pickwick
addresses him with a sudden query about the nearest public
house; and he illustrates Sam's knowledge by making him
answer without a moment's hesitation.   Dickens himself,
if put down suddenly in any quarter of London, could
probably have answered the question with equal readiness.
He was emphatically a man of cities, was restless when he
was long away from streets, and loved above all things the
streets of London.

But he was still more an observer of persons than an observer of places. Even in boyhood he judged men with great accuracy; and after he had won fame he asserted that he had never seen cause to change the secret impression of his boyhood with regard to anyone whom he had known then. Moreover, he never forgot. In his troubled and wretched boyhood, therefore, he was 'making himself,' though involuntarily and in an unpleasant fashion, as much as Scott was by his Liddesdale raids.

It is however the something added to observation that gives literary value; and had Dickens added nothing he would have been far on the way to oblivion now. Shakespeare may have based Falstaff on observation; but probably no man, except Shakespeare himself, was ever quite as humorous as the fat knight. Similarly, it is safe to assert that Dickens never met a Londoner with all the wit and resource of Sam Weller. 'The little more, and how much it is.' What the artist adds creates the character. Incidents he has seen, phrases he has heard, are only the raw material for his imagination. Humour is practically non-existent unless it is understood; and, as a more recent humourist has whimsically insisted, there may be here a kind of division of labour, the humour being lodged in one mind and the comprehension of it in another. It is so with Dickens. He sympathises, appreciates, interprets, and thus in part creates. He frequently makes the fun by his own keen sense of it.

But while Dickens was excellent within his own sphere, that sphere was comparatively small. He was good only as a painter of his own generation and of what had come under his own experience. Living in the days of the historical novel, Dickens nevertheless felt that his talent lay in the delineation of contemporary manners. Neither his education nor the bent of his mind fitted him to excel

in the historical romance. Twice he tried the experiment—
in *Barnaby Rudge*, and in *A Tale of Two Cities*; but on
both occasions he wisely kept pretty close to his own time.
Barnaby Rudge is, by general consent, second-rate, and
whatever may be the true value of *A Tale of Two Cities*, its
merit is not essentially of the historical kind. It is Scott
who has written the history of the Porteous riot and of the
rebellion of '45; and our most vivid impression of society
in Queen Anne's time comes from *Esmond*. But there is
no danger of Carlyle's *French Revolution* being superseded
by *A Tale of Two Cities*.

Neither has Dickens command over a wide range of
character. He is completely at home only in one grade of
society, and, as a rule, the farther he moves from the lower
ranks of Londoners the more he falls short of excellence.
Coachmen, showmen, servants of all kinds, beadles, self-
made men of imperfect education, he could depict with
wonderful force and vivacity; but his triumphs in the
higher ranks are few. The reason lies partly in the
character of the experience he had acquired, partly in
his manner of conception. Dickens was theatrical and
had a tendency to farce; above all, he was by nature a
caricaturist. If anyone, man or woman, presented some
conspicuous peculiarity, whether of disposition, or of
physical appearance, or of dress, Dickens was happy and
made the most of it. But education and social convention
tend to smooth away angularities and prominences, and
hence among the classes influenced by them he rarely
found the material he needed.

The characters of Dickens, then, are personified humours,
his method is the method not of Shakespeare, but of Ben
Jonson. Pecksniff is just another name for hypocrisy,
Jonas Chuzzlewit for avarice, Quilp for cruelty. The
result is excellent of its kind. The repetitions and catch-

words are, within limits, highly effective. Sometimes they
are genuinely illuminative; but sometimes, on the other
hand, they reveal nothing and are used to weariness. The
'waiting for something to turn up' of the Micawber
family goes to the root of their character. But 'ain't
I volatile?' 'Donkeys, Janet,' the sleepiness of the Fat
Boy, Pecksniff and Salisbury Cathedral, even the jollity of
Mark Tapley, are worn threadbare. Mrs. Harris herself
is heard of rather too often. Exaggeration has no law, it
is rather the abrogation of law; and the writer who adopts
the method of exaggeration pays the price in losing all
check upon himself.

In exaggeration too we find the defect of Dickens's
highest quality. His humour, like the humour of the
country he at first satirised so bitterly, rests too much on
exaggeration. It is ready, copious, irresistible; but, while
it wins and deserves admiration, it rarely provokes the ex-
clamation, 'how natural,' or 'how true.' Micawber is one
of the most comical characters in fiction, but we are not
struck by his fidelity to nature. Though he is drawn from
the life he is not representative, but rather belongs to
the class of curiosities whose natural resting-place is a
museum.

The mannerism of which this is one form runs through
the whole of the work of Dickens, affecting style as well as
substance, the description of nature as well as the delineation of character. The English is nervous and vivid, but
little regard is paid to proportion. The minutest detail, if
it happens to strike the writer's fancy, is elaborated as if it
were vital to the story. The moaning of the sea, the
freaks of the wind, the fluttering of a leaf, are dilated upon
in paragraph after paragraph. It is the romantic method
liberated from all restraint. There is no poetry more
heavily charged with the 'pathetic fallacy' than the prose

of Dickens; and in prose it is more dangerous because
of the absence of the trammels of verse.

The dangers of this style and this manner of conception
become more conspicuous when we turn to other mani-
festations of them.   Dickens was in his own time thought
to be a master of the pathetic equally with the mirthful
strain.   It was correct taste to weep over little Nell; and
Jeffrey, no very indulgent critic of contemporaries, declared
that there had been nothing so good since Cordelia.   Dickens
has been dead only a quarter of a century, but few critics
would pronounce such a judgment now.   His humour
so far retains its power; but the veneer has already worn
off his pathos.   Little Nell and little Emily may still draw
tears, more tears perhaps than were ever shed for the fate
of Cordelia.   But this is not the best test of the quality of
pathos.   That which, from Homer to Shakespeare, has conquered the suffrages of the world, is solemnising and sad-
dening, rather than tear-compelling.   Tears are within the
range of a very ordinary writer, but to produce a tragic
Cordelia or Antigone is only possible to a Shakespeare or a
Sophocles.   The truth is that the faults of Dickens, apparent in his humour but pardonable there, become offensive
in his pathos.   His touch is not sufficiently delicate, he does
not know when to leave off, he unduly prolongs the agony.
The death-scene of Cordelia and Lear, perhaps the most
tragically pathetic in all literature, occupies some sixty or
seventy lines.   How different from this are the scenes relating to the death of Little Nell!   Their very diffuseness
has contributed to their popularity, but it damages them
as literature.

Many of the other faults of Dickens are cognate to this.
He sacrifices everything for effect, and hence his proneness
to horrors.   The pictures are often wonderfully done, but
they are unwholesome.   The murder by Jonas Chuzzlewit,

and still more the murder of Nancy, are examples. Sometimes Dickens goes wholly beyond the reach of pardon, as in the purely horrible and sickening description of spontaneous combustion in *Bleak House*. More frequently the sin is rather against proportion. We hear too much of the dragging of the river for dead bodies in *Our Mutual Friend*. Dickens never could learn where to stop. His highly pictorial imagination presented to him every detail of the scene; and, like a Pre-Raphaelite, he forgot that to the reader a general impression conveyed more truth than minute accuracy in every detail.

The faults of Dickens grew with time, his merits tended to decline; but even to the end the characteristic merits are to be found. It was not unjustly said that his death had once more eclipsed the gaiety of nations.

While Dickens, as has been seen, leaped into fame, his only contemporary rival, William Makepeace Thackeray, slowly and with difficulty forced his way to it. He was the senior of Dickens by rather more than half a year, having been born at Calcutta on July 18th, 1811. He was educated at the Charterhouse; and if his feelings may be inferred from his works they must have changed considerably. In his earlier writings it is Slaughter House; in *The Newcomes* it is the celebrated Grey Friars. After leaving school Thackeray went in 1829 to Cambridge, but he left the University in 1830 without taking his degree. While he was there he contributed to *The Snob*, the name of which suggested to him a title in after years. One of his papers was an amusing burlesque on *Timbuctoo*, the subject for the prize poem, won by Tennyson, for 1829. In 1830 Thackeray went to Weimar, and he spent a considerable time there and in Paris training himself as an artist. The inaccuracy of his draw-

William Makepeace
Thackeray
(1811-1863).

ing was a fatal bar to his success in art; but he turned
his studies to account afterwards in illustrating his own
books; and there are probably no works in English in
which the illustrations throw more light upon the text.
In 1832 he became master of his little fortune of about
£500 per annum, all of which was lost within a year or two.
Most of it was sunk in an unprofitable newspaper adventure, reference to which is made in *Lovel the Widower*,
and, with less accuracy of circumstance, in *Pendennis*. But
if he lost his money by a newspaper, it was by journalism
that he first gained his livelihood. He wrote for *The
Times*, for *Fraser's Magazine*, and for the *New Monthly
Magazine*, contributing to the second some of the most
important of his early works; and for about eight years
(1842-1850) he was one of the principal literary contributors
to *Punch*. In these periodicals there appeared during the
ten years, 1837-1847, *The Yellowplush Papers*, *The Great
Hoggarty Diamond*, *Barry Lyndon*, *The Book of Snobs* and
The Ballads of Policeman X. Thackeray had also published independently *The Paris Sketch-Book* and *The Irish
Sketch-Book*.

Vanity Fair (1847-1848) was Thackeray's first novel on
the great scale. *Barry Lyndon* was indeed an exhibition
of the highest intellectual power; but it was not of the
orthodox length, and it failed to bring the writer wide fame.
Vanity Fair did bring him fame among the more thoughtful readers, though not a popularity rivalling that of
Dickens. It was followed by *Pendennis* (1849-1850),
Esmond (1852) and *The Newcomes* (1854-1855). *Esmond*
was the only one that was published as a whole, and it is
significant that it is by far the best constructed of the four
usually accepted as Thackeray's greatest novels. The
periodical method of publication had peculiar dangers for
him. He was constitutionally indolent, almost always left

his work to the last moment, and sometimes had to patch up his part anyhow.

In 1851 Thackeray delivered the lectures on the *Humourists of the Eighteenth Century*, and repeated the course in America in 1852-1853. The lectures on *The Four Georges* were delivered first in America (1855-1856). Of all Thackeray's writings these two courses have probably had the most scanty justice meted out to them. Critics are frequently apologetic, sometimes condescending. Nobody need apologise, and few can afford to condescend with respect to what are really among the richest and best criticisms of this century. Thackeray knew not only the literature but the life of the eighteenth century as few have known it. In minute acquaintance with facts he has doubtless been surpassed by many professional historians ; but there is no book to be compared to *Esmond* as a picture of life in the age of Queen Anne ; and the lectures on the humourists are saturated, as *Esmond* is, with the eighteenth century spirit. The figures of the humourists live and move before our eyes. We may not always agree with the critic's opinion, but we can hardly fail to understand the subject better through his mode of treatment. Strong objection has been taken, perhaps in some respects with justice, to his handling of Swift. Yet, much as has been written about Swift, where does there exist a picture of him so vivid, so suggestive and so memorable ? Who else has done such justice to Steele ? Who has written better about Hogarth ? Thackeray succeeded because he not only knew the work of these men but felt with them. He was at bottom of the eighteenth century type. Much of Swift himself, softened and humanised, something of Fielding, whom he justly regarded as a model, and a great deal of Hogarth may be detected in Thackeray. The best criticism is always sympathetic ; and it is because sympathy is so easy to him here that Thackeray is so excellent. The treatment even of Swift is far from being unsympathetic.

With the four Georges Thackeray was certainly not in sympathy. But they afforded him an ample field for the exercise of his satiric gifts, and he found occasion in his treatment of them for some passages of his most eloquent writing. The objection taken to this course of lectures has been as much political as literary. Thackeray is supposed to have treated the throne with scanty reverence ; but it is the throne itself that is lacking in reverence when such lives are led ; and the day for the concealment of disagreeable truths has long gone by.

The Virginians, a continuation of *Esmond*, ran its periodical course from 1857 to 1859. In the latter year Thackeray became editor of the *Cornhill*, for which he wrote *Lovel the Widower* (1860), *The Adventures of Philip* (1861-1862), and the delicious *Roundabout Papers*, which he contributed occasionally from the beginning of his editorship to his death. *Denis Duval* had not even begun to appear in the magazine, and only a small part had been written when the author was suddenly cut off at the age of fifty-two.

It would not be easy to name two great contemporary writers, working in the same field of letters, more radically unlike than Dickens and Thackeray. Even the qualities they possess in common diverge as far as qualities bearing the same name can do. Both are humourists; but the humour of Thackeray is permeated through and through with satire ; that of Dickens has not infrequently a touch of satire, but its essential principle is pure fun, and it is largely burlesque. We look for it in the absurdities of the Micawber family, in the Jarley wax-works, in the ridiculous adventures of the Pickwick Club, and in the solemn

fatuity of Silas Wegg. Thackeray was a master of burlesque too, as his imitations of contemporary novels—*Phil
Fogarty, Codlingsby, Rebecca and Rowena*—and his *Ballads
of Policeman* X prove. But it is a totally different burlesque. That of Dickens moves to laughter, and the
laughter is frequently uproarious; Thackeray only excites
a smile and a chuckle of intellectual enjoyment.

The two writers differ equally in their pathos. Dickens,
as we have seen, draws it out, paragraph after paragraph,
chapter piled on chapter. Thackeray concentrates, partly
from the artist's knowledge that concentration is necessary
to permanent effect, in greater degree because of a personal
dignity, accompanied by reticence, in which Dickens was
certainly deficient. Just as there are substances which will
not bear light, so there are feelings which seem to be pro-
faned if they are too long exposed to view. All art involves
exposure; but the difference between perfect taste and defective taste lies in knowing just in what manner and how
long to make the exposure. In *The Four Georges* two
paragraphs contain all we are told about the last tragic
years of George III.; and just a few lines of eloquence and
pathos rarely equalled close the story.

When we search back from symptom to cause we find the
secret of these and many other differences in the fact that
the work of Dickens is primarily sentimental, while
Thackeray's is primarily intellectual. This is by no means
equivalent to saying that Dickens is deficient in intellect,
or Thackeray in sentiment. It means rather that the
strong intellect of Dickens is the servant of sentiment, the
strong sentiment of Thackeray the servant of intellect. It
is another way of saying that Thackeray is essentially of
the eighteenth century, the century of predominant understanding. It follows from his satirical way of viewing
life; for the satirist must not wholly lose himself even

in his *sæva indignatio*. The effect of his satire depends upon his keeping aloof, critical, superior. The Romans were great satirists because they did so; the English are great satirists in so far as they do so likewise. Something is lost in emotion, as art, something is gained in comprehension, for practical application.

No one can doubt that Thackeray is thus reflective and satirical. Critic after critic has called attention to his habit of staying the course of his story for comment and exposition. Not only so, but there is subdued and disguised comment all through. The artist makes each character criticise itself; and the effect is as if we were walking constantly in the light of those rays which pierce through the opaque and reveal what lies beneath. Thackeray's satire plays continually over the characters he creates for warning and example. Blanche Amory, Becky Sharp, Major Pendennis, all have their inner motives exposed by this searching and pitiless light. So much is this the case that Thackeray has been described as not properly a novelist at all, but first of all a satirist. The difference is that the novelist primarily exhibits life as it is, while the satirist comments upon it. That Thackeray does the latter is obvious; but it seems an exaggeration to say that he is not properly a novelist. Though most of his stories are loosely constructed, though plot and incident are of subordinate importance, yet without the story his books would be vitally different. Moreover, the pure satirist commonly deals with types rather than individuals. Juvenal does so, Horace does so, Swift does so. So does Thackeray himself in *The Book of Snobs*. But Becky Sharp and Major Pendennis and Beatrix Esmond all have individuality.

Further, in what may fairly be regarded as Thackeray's highest effort, satire sinks to a secondary place. *Esmond,* though not the best known of Thackeray's works, is his purest piece of art. It is so, partly at least, because the conditions presupposed by the story put a curb upon the satirical tendency, in which undeniably Thackeray was too prone to indulge. In *Esmond* the writer is restrained in two ways. First, as the hero is himself the narrator, the sentiments have to be fitted to his character. And Henry Esmond was not the familiar compound of weakness and selfishness, crossed with some good nature and with occasional higher impulses, but, on the contrary, Thackeray's ideal man. He is endowed with a power of satire, but it is rarely exercised. The second restraint arose from the need of unceasing watchfulness to use language consistent with the time in which the story is laid. If Thackeray was tempted to be careless, this necessity must have kept him constantly in check. And so well did he satisfy the requirements that *Esmond* is admitted on all hands to be, of all books in English, that which most accurately reproduces the style of a past age.

It is remarkable that the same book which contains the noblest figure Thackeray ever drew contains also the most lovable of his good women, and the most brilliant and fascinating of the class that cannot be called good. All critics have been struck with Thackeray's tendency to make his good women weak and colourless, or else sermons incarnate. Amelia and Helen Pendennis are examples of the former class, Laura of the latter. Lady Castlewood escapes the censure. She has greater strength of character than Amelia or Helen; and her human weaknesses win a sympathy Laura does not command. Moreover, there is no other woman of her type shown in the light of passion as she is in that perfect chapter, *The 29th December*. Beatrix, on the contrary, ranks among the reprobate. She is not so wonderfully clever as Becky Sharp, but she has what Becky has not, fascination. Becky has only her intellect. Beatrix, clever too, has, besides her social position, splendid beauty, and above all the indescribable magnetic power of attraction. She can win men against themselves, and though they are alive to all the evil of her character. Becky can only win those whom she has blinded.

The other novels, less perfect as pictures of life, are not inferior in sheer intellect. *Vanity Fair* and *Barry Lyndon* are superlative examples of force of mind. The latter is so faithfully written from the scoundrel's point of view that only the excess of scoundrelism prevents Barry from commanding sympathy. The former contains in Becky Sharp the cleverest and most resourceful of all Thackeray's characters. It also contains, especially in the chapters on the Waterloo campaign, some of the finest English he ever wrote. *Pendennis* has its special interest in the thread of autobiography interwoven with it ; while *The Newcomes* has its crowning glory in the old colonel, and in the famous scene in Grey Friars. After *The Newcomes* the quality of Thackeray's work, or at least of his novels (for the lectures and the *Roundabout Papers* stand apart) declined. He did not live long enough to demonstrate whether the decline was permanent or not ; but certainly there is no lack of power in the *Roundabout Papers ;* and in spite of his own dictum that no man ought to write a novel after fifty, Thackeray should have been just at his best when he died.

Thackeray was a poet and an artist as well as a novelist ; and sometimes in a copy of verses or in a sketch the inner spirit of the man may be seen more compendiously, if not more truly and surely, than in longer and more ambitious works. It is so here. The spirit that pervades *Vanity Fair* is the same that inspired the *Ballad of Bouillabaisse,* the concluding stanzas of *The Chronicle of the Drum,* The

End of the Play, Vanitas Vanitatum, and others of his more serious verses. There is a touch of satire in these verses, but there is far more of pity than scorn. Still more vividly this spirit shines through a triplet of sketches labelled respectively Ludovicus, Rex and Ludovicus Rex, the shivering little atom of humanity, the imposing trappings of royalty, and then the poor little mortal clothed in this magnificence. Here we have the quintessence of Thackeray's sermon through all his books, the difference between the humble reality and the vast pretensions, moral, intellectual and social, too often based on it. There is frequently scorn in the sermon, the more in proportion to the greatness of the pretensions. But there is almost always pity behind the scorn. Ludovicus Rex is, after all, the sport of fate. It is fate that decrees

> ' How very weak the very wise,
> How very small the very great are !'

It is the neglect of this fact that has led to the common judgment that Thackeray is a cynic. The gulf that divides him from cynicism is seen when we compare him with Swift. There is always in Thackeray a sensitive kindliness not to be found in the older writer. Thackeray's bitterest satire is on individuals who are worse than their neighbours. There is something amiss with society when Barry Lyndon and Becky Sharp are possible ; but we are not led to think that all men are Barry Lyndons, or all women Becky Sharps. *Gulliver,* on the contrary, is a satire on the human race.

A group of Irish novelists, rather older than Thackeray and Dickens, may be noticed together for the sake of certain features they have in common. If fineness of literary quality alone were in question, the first place must be assigned

William Carleton
(1794-1869).

to William Carleton, whose *Traits and Stories of the Irish Peasantry* are the most carefully executed of their class. Carleton however had neither the verve nor the copiousness of Lever, who has been fixed upon by popular judgment as the leading Irish novelist of his time.

Samuel Lover
(1797-1868).

Still less can the versatile Samuel Lover, song-writer, dramatist and painter as well as novelist, compete with Lever; for although the former did many things with a certain dexterity he did nothing really well. His *Handy Andy* is a formless book, and the fun of it grows tedious.

Charles James Lever came in direct literary descent from

Charles James
Lever
(1806-1872).

neither of these, but from William Hamilton Maxwell (1792-1850), whose *Stories from Waterloo* turned Lever's attention to the literary possibilities of the great war. This book begot *Harry Lorrequer*, begun in the *Dublin University Magazine* in 1837; and *Lorrequer* was followed by *Charles O'Malley* (1840). The former derived its name from the ' rollicking' quality generally recognised as characteristic of Lever. Both books have whatever attraction high spirits and plenty of fun and fighting and adventure can give; but in the literary sense they are rough and unpolished to the last degree. *Tom Burke of Ours* (1844) shows the same qualities slightly chastened and reduced to a more literary shape. The change went on, and Lever paid more and more attention to construction and to literary law and rule. He himself considered *Sir Brook Fossbrooke* (1866) his best book; but it may be questioned whether the gain in smoothness and regularity is sufficient to compensate for the partial loss of that rush of adventure and copiousness of anecdote which won for Lever his reputation, and still preserves it.

It is singular that this typically Irish novelist was by blood more English than Irish. But the debt which

Ireland owed to England in Lever was repaid with interest in that family of genius, the Brontës. Their father, himself a minor poet, left behind him, when he left Ireland, the name by which he was known, Brunty, from O'Prunty, and was afterwards known as Brontë. He married a Cornish girl, and settled as a clergyman at Haworth, on the wild moors of the West Riding of Yorkshire. All his children who grew to maturity possessed talent, if not genius. His son, Patrick Branwell Brontë, who was in boyhood considered the most promising of all, squandered his own life and clouded the lives of his sisters by his debauchery. The three sisters, Charlotte, Emily Jane and Anne, all won a place in literature, and two of them a conspicuous one. Their lives were uneventful, but gloomy and sometimes tragic. They were poor, they had a dissipated brother, they were constitutionally liable to consumption, and their story is a record of dauntless efforts frustrated by failing health. Their works bear deep marks of the people and the place amidst which they were conceived, but even more of their own family history. This was in fact inevitable. The sisters had no wide culture; still less were they accustomed to mingle in society and meet many types of men and women. Besides their few books, greedily read until the favourites were so tattered and worn that they had to be hidden away on private shelves, the men dwelling near them, the scenes around them and the tales current in their family were the only food for their imagination.

Charlotte
Brontë
(1816-1855),

Emily Jane
Brontë
(1818-1848),

Anne Brontë
(1820-1849).

An outline of Charlotte's life can be easily traced in her writings. Her first place of education, Cowan Bridge School, for the daughters of clergymen, appears in *Jane Eyre;* and Helen Burns represents her hapless eldest sister Maria, who died at eleven. A residence in Brussels to improve their French and qualify them for higher teaching, furnished much matter for *The Professor* and *Villette*. They meant to receive pupils at the parsonage; but their brother's intemperance made that impossible, even if pupils had offered themselves, and, until his death in 1848, he was a heavy burden and a bitter grief.

The sisters had long loved to write as well as to read; and Charlotte has told how, in the autumn of 1845, the thought of publication was suggested by a MS. volume of Emily's poetry. Her criticism of the verses is generous, but by no means extravagant. 'I thought them,' she says, 'condensed and terse, vigorous and genuine. To my ear they had also a peculiar music, wild, melancholy, and elevating.' The other sisters had written poems also, and after various difficulties a small volume of *Poems* by Currer, Ellis and Acton Bell was published in 1846. It attracted little attention, and Charlotte says with truth that only the poems of Emily deserved much. Hers display a genuine poetic gift. Had she lived to write much more verse she would certainly have been one of the greatest of English poetesses, and might have been the first of all. Strength, sincerity and directness are the characteristics of her verse; and the individuality of the writer gives it distinction:

'I'll walk where my own nature would be leading:
  It vexes me to choose another guide:
Where the grey flocks in ferny glens are feeding;
  Where the wild wind blows on the mountain side.

'What have these lonely mountains worth revealing?
  More glory and more grief than I can tell:
The earth that wakes *one* human heart to feeling
  Can centre both the worlds of heaven and hell.'

The volume of verse was followed by several volumes of prose. Each sister had a story ready, and the three were offered simultaneously for publication. Emily's novel, *Wuthering Heights*, and Anne's, *Agnes Grey*, were accepted, though 'on terms somewhat impoverishing to the two authors.' Charlotte's, *The Professor*, was rejected by one publisher after another, and ten years passed before it appeared. Meanwhile the dauntless author set to work and wrote *Jane Eyre*. This was accepted, and was published, like the stories by the other sisters, in 1847. Unlike theirs, it won a rapid and remarkable success and finally fixed the career of Charlotte Brontë.

It will be convenient to take the work of the three sisters in the reverse order. That of Anne Brontë may be speedily dismissed. She was a gentle, delicate creature both in mind and body; and but for her greater sisters her writings would now be forgotten. Her pleasing but commonplace tale of *Agnes Grey* was followed by *The Tenant of Wildfell Hall*, in which she attempted, without success, to depict a profligate.

In sheer genius Emily Brontë probably surpassed Charlotte, though in art she was certainly the inferior of her elder sister. All that she wrote bears the stamp of her sombre imagination and of the gloomy strength of her character. Despite the Celtic strain in her blood, she, like the rest of her family, had more in common with the austere Yorkshire character than with that of the typical Irishman. She had a perfect comprehension of it. She was, as the northern character is by so many felt to be, personally unattractive. She was almost savagely reserved. Even her sisters, in her last illness, dared not notice 'the failing step, the laboured breathing, the frequent pauses' with which she climbed the staircase. But she had also the better qualities of the northern nature. She never shrank from duty or evaded a burden; and her courage was boundless. With her own hand she applied cautery to the bite of a dog she believed to be mad; and she conquered a savage bull-dog by beating it with the bare hands, though she had been warned that if struck it would fly at her throat.

Such a character explains all that Emily Brontë is in literature. *Wuthering Heights* is her only novel, for she died the year after its publication. It remains therefore uncertain whether she would have mastered her errors, or whether, as in her sister's case, her first work was to be her greatest. The probability is that she would have improved. She was only thirty; and the defects of *Wuthering Heights* are artistic,—faulty construction, want of proportion, absence of restraint. These are defects which experience might be expected to overcome; especially as Emily Brontë's verse showed that she was by no means without taste. There are flaws in the substance too; and it is less likely that these would have disappeared. Even Mrs. Gaskell could not deny that there is some foundation for the charge of coarseness brought against Charlotte; and there is more in the case of Emily. It is not merely that her characters are harsh and repulsive: there are not a few such characters in life, and there were many of them within the experience of the Brontë family. But besides, Emily Brontë appears to sympathise with, and sometimes to admire, the harsher and less lovable features of the characters she draws. Heathcliff is spoilt for most readers by the seemingly loving minuteness with which the author elaborates the worst characteristics of his nature, characteristics familiar to her from family legend.

For several reasons Charlotte Brontë holds a higher place in literature than her sister. She has not to be judged by one work only. *Jane Eyre* was followed by *Shirley* (1849), by *Villette* (1853), by *The Professor* (1857), published posthumously, and by the fragment, *Emma*

H

(1860). In none of these did she equal her first novel, but she exhibited different sides and aspects of her genius, she multiplied her creations, and she proved, as long as life was given her, that she had what in the language of sport is called 'staying power.' Moreover, Charlotte was decidedly more of the artist than Emily. She understood better the importance of relief. Her imagination too was prevailingly sombre; yet though *Jane Eyre* is sufficiently gloomy, it is less uniformly so than *Wuthering Heights*. The shadow is flecked here and there with light. Again, Charlotte is more versatile in her imagination and much more pictorial than Emily. All the members of the Brontë family had a love and apparently some talent for art; but it is in the works of Charlotte that this talent leaves the clearest traces. There are few things in *Jane Eyre* more impressive than her description in words of the picture her imagination, if not her brush, drew. More ample scope, greater variety, a more humane tone,—these then are the points in which Charlotte surpasses Emily.

Notwithstanding the wonderful force and vividness of their imagination, the Brontës were in several respects singularly limited, largely because their experience was so limited. It was only genius that saved them from the narrowest provinciality. Even genius did not enable them to reach beyond a few well-marked types of character, nor did it save them from errors in the drawing of these. Both Rochester and Heathcliff would have been more endurable, as members of society, if their creators had themselves known more of society. They are brutal because the Brontës had seen and heard about much brutality, and had not learned that polish is by no means synonymous with weakness, and that gentleness is quite consistent with manliness and strength of will.

Partly however the narrowness was in the Brontës

themselves. They show little power of invention. Not only are their types few, but the individual characters are nearly all reproductions from life. Probably no English writer of equal rank has transcribed so much from experience as Charlotte Brontë. Many of her characters were so like the originals as to be immediately recognised by themselves or by their neighbours. Shirley Keeldar was her sister Emily, Mr. Helstone was her father, the three curates were real men, and some of Charlotte's school friends were depicted, it is said, with the accuracy of daguerreotypes. This minute fidelity to fact occasionally brought Miss Brontë into trouble; for she was not particularly sagacious in estimating the effect of what she wrote. We may argue from it, moreover, that if she had lived she would soon have exhausted her material.

Charlotte Brontë was likewise deficient in humour. This might be safely inferred from her works, where there are hardly any humorous characters or situations; and the inference would be confirmed by her life. Her letters, often excellent for their common sense and their high standard of duty, and sometimes for their dignity, are almost destitute of playfulness. Neither does she seem to have readily recognised humour in others. She admired Thackeray above almost all men of her time, but she was completely puzzled by him when they met. She lectured him on his faults, and quaintly adds that his excuses made them worse. The humourist was playing with the too serious mind. Had Miss Brontë been as Irish in nature as she was by blood she would not have made this mistake.

In the case of the Brontës it would be peculiarly ungenerous to insist on defects. All life long they fought against odds. With inadequate means and imperfect training, without friends and without advice, they won by their own force and genius alone a position in literature which is higher now than it was forty years ago. Charlotte is one of the half-dozen or so of great English novelists of the present century; and in all probability it is only her early death that has made Emily's place somewhat lower.

Senior in years to the Brontës was the biographer of

Elizabeth Cleghorn
Gaskell
(1810-1865).

Charlotte, Elizabeth Cleghorn Gaskell. Mrs. Gaskell's fame was won chiefly as a novelist, but, both for its intrinsic merits and as a memorial of a most interesting literary friendship, her *Life of Charlotte Brontë* deserves mention. If not equal to the best biographies in the language, it is worthy of a place in the class nearest to that small group. It gives a delightful impression both of the subject of the memoir and of her biographer. There was sufficient difference between the two to make Mrs. Gaskell's generous appreciation peculiarly creditable to her. Two contemporaries of the same sex, reared amidst men closely akin in character, and confronted, as *Mary Barton* and *Shirley* prove, by similar social problems, could hardly present a greater contrast than there is between Charlotte Brontë and Mrs. Gaskell; the former austere, intense, prone to exaggeration and deficient in humour; the latter genial, balanced, and among the most successful of female humourists. The contrast extended to the personal appearance of the two women. Charlotte Brontë was plain and diminutive, while in her youth Mrs. Gaskell was strikingly beautiful.

The events of Mrs. Gaskell's life were almost wholly literary. Her first novel, *Mary Barton*, published in 1848, remains to this day probably her best known, though not her most perfect book. It deals with the industrial state of Lancashire during the crisis of 1842, and it won, by its vivid and touching picture of the life of the poor, the admiration of some of the most distinguished literary men of the time.

The subject was gradually drawing more attention. The evils which begot the socialism of Robert Owen and drew the protests of Carlyle and of Ebenezer Elliott had been brought into prominence by the Luddite riots and by Chartism. Most of the novelists were awakening to a sense of them. Disraeli had anticipated Mrs. Gaskell; and Kingsley as well as Charlotte Brontë followed her. The treatment varies greatly. Mrs. Gaskell, like Kingsley, has much more sympathy with socialism than Charlotte Brontë has. The social aspects of *Mary Barton* caused it to be admired and praised on the one hand, and to be censured on the other, for reasons outside the domain of art; but on the whole they certainly increased its popularity.

The success of *Mary Barton* won for Mrs. Gaskell an invitation from Dickens to contribute to *Household Words*, and some of her best work, including *Cranford* (1851-1853) and *North and South* (1854-1855), first appeared there. She was also a contributor to the *Cornhill*, where her last story, *Wives and Daughters*, was running when she died, with startling suddenness, in 1865.

' George Sand, only a few months before Mrs. Gaskell's death, observed to Lord Houghton: " Mrs. Gaskell has done what neither I nor other female writers in France can accomplish; she has written novels which excite the deepest interest in men of the world, and yet which every girl will be the better for reading." ' This is high praise ; and it is deserved. It must not indeed be pressed to mean that Mrs. Gaskell is the equal in genius, far less the superior, of writers like George Sand or George Eliot. Neither is she the equal of her friend, Charlotte Brontë. There is a sweep of imagination and a touch of poetry in *Jane Eyre* quite beyond the reach of Mrs. Gaskell. But her work is at once free from weakness and wholly inno-cent. She is of all the more remarkable female novelists of this period the most feminine. The traits of sex are numerous in her books, but they never appear unpleasantly. Her women are generally better than her men; yet her men are not such monsters as the Brontës loved to depict. On the contrary, she is fond of painting men of quiet worth, such as the country doctor whose 'virtues walk their narrow round,' who lives unknown, but who is sadly missed when he dies. Her best stories are quiet tales of the life of villages and small towns, and they show the shrewd, kindly, genial observation with which all her life she regarded those around her. She was happy in her own domestic life, and she believed that life in general, though chequered, was happy too. In her picture of human nature the virtues on the whole prevail over the vices.

Mrs. Gaskell saw everything in the light of a sympathetic humour. It is this quality that has served hitherto as salt to her books and has preserved their flavour while that of a great deal of more ambitious literature has been lost. If her humour is not equal to the best specimens of that of George Eliot, it is more diffused; if less powerful, it is gentler and quite as subtle. In style she is easy and flowing; and her later books show more freedom than her first attempt. At the same time, her writing rarely rises to eloquence. She had more talent than genius. She has created many good, but no great characters; and she stands midway between Thackeray and Dickens, who are emphatically men of genius, and writers like Trollope who, with abundant talent and exhaustless industry, have no genius whatever.

CHAPTER VI.

THE HISTORIANS AND BIOGRAPHERS.

CARLYLE was so much besides being a historian, and seems, when we look back from a distance of sixty years, so clearly the leader of thought in the early part of this period, that it has been deemed advisable to treat him by himself.   But even without him the volume and the quality of historical work accomplished during those forty years is very great.   Besides Macaulay, who surpassed Carlyle in popular estimation, Thomas Arnold, Grote, Thirlwall and Froude were all men who, in most periods, might well have filled the first place in historical literature.

Several reasons may be assigned for the concentration of talent upon history.   In the first place, the circumstances of the time made an examination of the foundations of society imperative.   This necessity reveals itself everywhere, in poetry, in philosophy, and in theology, as well as in history.   The cry is on all sides for reconstruction ; and there is a growing sense that the reconstruction must take place upon a groundwork of fact, discoverable only by a study of the past.   The pre-Revolutionary writers had relied upon *a priori* theory, but the immediate results were so different from their anticipations that their successors were little disposed to repeat the mistake.   Modern history teaches above all things the lesson of continuity. institutions change and grow, but they never spring up suddenly like a Jonah's gourd; and even revolutions only modify, they do not annul the past.

Science too has had a powerful influence, and the success of the scientific method has encouraged the application of a method similar in principle, though necessarily different in minor points, to the facts of history. The last two generations have witnessed a great extension of the principle of induction in the sphere of history; and as the first step in a complex process of induction is the accumulation of masses of facts, we have here perhaps an explanation of some of the weaknesses of the modern school of history. It is apt to lose itself in detail. The reach of Tacitus or of Gibbon seems no longer attainable, because their successors must know everything, and can with difficulty restrain themselves from stating everything. Some one, doubtless, whether he be called a philosopher or a historian, will ultimately assimilate the masses of information thus laboriously compiled, and the world will once more have the principal results compactly stated and in orderly sequence. Buckle's experiment proves that it is possible to attempt this too soon; but at the same time the welcome that experiment received is an indication that we shall not be permanently satisfied with the fragments and aspects of history which alone the new method as yet yields. Unity of treatment is ultimately as essential in history as codification is in law; and it is essential for much the same reason. The old proverb tells us that the wood may be invisible by reason of the trees.

We may trace the influence of science also in the greatly deepened sense of the importance of origins. In science the chief triumphs have been won by tracing things to their beginnings; in physical structure to atoms and molecules, in animal life to nerve cells, protoplasm, or whatever is simplest and most primitive. Exactly the same effort is made in modern history ; and nothing is more distinctive of it, in contrast with the comparatively superficial historical school of the eighteenth century, than the determination to trace the starting-point and original meaning of institutions. Ages which had been previously left to legend and myth have been patiently investigated, and it is to them that we are now referred for the explanation of our own times.

But not only has the ideal of history changed; the material from which it is written, old in one sense, is to a large extent new in the sense that it is now for the first time accessible. The men of earlier times, even when they had the industry and the will for minute investigation, had seldom the means. The vast increase of accessible documents has caused history to be written afresh, to an extent best measured by the fact that, except those who rank as original authorities, Gibbon alone among historians prior to the present century still holds his ground.

Thomas Babington Macaulay felt these modern influences, though not quite in their full force. He was the son of Zachary Macaulay, celebrated for his exertions in the Anti-Slavery crusade. At Cambridge, whither he went in 1818, young Macaulay had for contemporaries a very brilliant set of young men, including Derwent and Henry Nelson Coleridge, Moultrie, Praed and Charles Austin, 'the only man,' says Sir George Trevelyan, 'who ever succeeded in dominating Macaulay,' the man who weaned him from the Toryism in which he had been brought up, and ' brought him nearer to Radicalism than he ever was before or since.' A constitutional incapacity for and hatred of mathematics was punished by the omission of his name from the Tripos list of 1822. He had been 'gulfed.' Nevertheless, in 1824, he was elected to a Fellowship of Trinity College. He was

Thomas Babington
Macaulay
(1800-1859).

called to the bar in 1826, but never took seriously to the
law as a profession. He had received an earlier call to
another profession, and during his stay at Cambridge he
had been a frequent contributor to *Knight's Quarterly
Magazine.* But we may date from 1825, when his essay on
Milton appeared in the *Edinburgh Review,* the opening
of his career in literature. For many years afterwards he
was a frequent and certainly the most effective contributor
to the review.

Macaulay's connexion with Jeffrey's review was profit-
able in several ways to himself as well as to it. He gained
money, and fame, and political connexions which determined the course of his life for many years, and which by
doing so unquestionably influenced his historical work.
Through the influence of Lord Lansdowne, who had been
struck by his articles on Mill, Macaulay became, in 1830,
member for Calne. He soon made his mark, rather as a
speaker of set speeches than as a debater. His speeches
have much the character of his essays, the rhetorical style
of which is not ill adapted to verbal utterance. The clearness which Macaulay never failed to give made the rhetoric
effective. His great knowledge, and especially his wonderful command of historical illustration, enabled him often to
clinch his argument where abstract discussion would have
failed. The most telling passage in one of his best known
speeches, the speech on copyright, is a long list of concrete
instances of the effect of the proposal he was advocating as
contrasted with that of the proposal he was combating. At
the close, with well-founded confidence, he challenges his
opponent to match it. While therefore Macaulay had but
a small share of the highest faculty of the orator, the
power to sway the passions of his audience, he had in
a high degree the power to interest their intellect. For
neat, crisp statement, apt and copious illustration, and

effective rhetoric occasionally rising into eloquence, his speeches have few equals.

As a reward for his services in the cause of reform Macaulay was appointed a member of the Supreme Council of India. In 1834 he sailed from England, and he resided in India till the beginning of 1838. Soon after his return to England he was elected M.P. for Edinburgh, and in 1839 was raised to the Cabinet as Secretary at War. But he gradually became absorbed in his history and devoted less and less time to politics. His defeat in 1847 in the parliamentary election for Edinburgh contributed to wean him still more from public life. He was hurt, and the smart of wounded pride is apparent in the most beautiful verses he ever wrote. They were composed on the night of his defeat, and they declare that the writer's true allegiance belongs to that Spirit of Literature who, when all the 'wayward sprites' of Gain, Fashion, Power and Pleasure have passed away, draws near to bless his first infant sleep. The verses are transparently sincere. Macaulay's love for letters was the passion of his life; and, acting on such a character as his, the unmerited rebuff dealt by Edinburgh proved a turning point in his career. He retired into private life, and though after the repentance of Edinburgh in 1852 he sat again for his old constituency, it was with the fixed intention not to immerse himself in parliamentary work, and above all not to accept office. He was now completely absorbed in his history; and as he gradually became conscious of the greatness of his task, and felt that life was slipping away with only a fragment of it accomplished, he grudged more and more any deduction from the time which, he foresaw, must be too short at best. For his previously excellent health had broken down soon after his election, and he never fully recovered it. He resigned his seat in 1856. In the following year he was raised to the peerage as Baron Macaulay of Rothley, and he died on December 28th, 1859, leaving his history a fragment.

The works of Macaulay are remarkably easy to classify and not very difficult to appraise. They fall under four heads,—speeches, essays, including the biographical articles contributed to the *Encyclopædia Britannica*, the *History of England*, and poetry.

The speeches have been already noticed. The essays, which are described as 'critical and historical,' are only to a very minor degree critical. The well-known paper on Robert Montgomery, irresistibly amusing in its severity, is exceptional in the fact that, starting with a literary subject, it treats that subject throughout from a literary point of view. In most of his essays, as he himself confessed, Macaulay escapes as soon as possible from criticism and glides into history. This is the case even in the essay on Milton, who would have enchained him to criticism if anyone could. Where he is really critical, Macaulay always shows the qualities of good sense, sound judgment and extensive knowledge; but few will think that he shows any remarkable fineness of critical faculty. On occasion he could characterise a style exceedingly well. His contrast between the simple, nervous and picturesque expression of Johnson's familiar letters and his Latinised pomposity when his sentences are done out of English into Johnsonese, cannot be forgotten; and his treatment of Bacon's style is as sound and excellent as his treatment of Bacon's philosophy is mistaken and false. But his mind was of too positive a type to admit of the finest kind of criticism. He saw nothing in half-light, and he was deficient in sympathy. His criticism of the Queen Anne writers, whom he knew best, will not bear comparison, in respect of insight and sensitive appreciation, with Thackeray's criticism of them in the *English Humourists.*

Macaulay's strength lay elsewhere; and though he carried into all he did the deficiencies revealed by his criticism, as well as deficiencies due to political prejudice and personal bias, yet all faults are forgotten, for the time at least, in admiration of wide knowledge, boundless energy and brilliant style. Macaulay's extensive reading, backed by his wonderful memory, served him well. His knowledge was always at hand. If he wanted a reference or an allusion he could in a moment supply it. Yet his quotations, references and allusions are never pedantic, nor are they allowed to clog and weight his style. They serve their proper purpose of illustrating and enforcing his point. He defends his position by parallel after parallel, contrast after contrast. It was this wealth of illustration that forced acquiescence from men of less knowledge among his contemporaries; it is the suspicion that the parallels are not always accurate, and the contrasts not always sound, that has since caused so many of his conclusions to be regarded with suspicion. But frequently the historical illustrations are poured out, not to defend any thesis, but simply because they crowd spontaneously into the writer's mind; and some of the most effective passages in Macaulay's writings are of this character. Take, for example, the well-known passage from *Warren Hastings* beginning, 'The place was worthy of such a trial,' or the description in the *History* of the spot where the dust of Monmouth was laid. Less crowded with historical names and details, but still deriving most of its charm from the same cause, is the almost equally well-known paragraph in the essay on *Ranke's History of the Popes*, beginning, 'There is not, and there never was on this earth, a work of human policy so well deserving of examination as the Roman Catholic Church.' There is a rapidity, fire and vividness in such passages by which we may in great measure account for

Macaulay's popularity. He had no more marked literary gift. It shows itself even more spontaneously in his letters than in his formal writings; and the letters have sometimes moreover a touch of humour rare in the works he intended for publication. Few things of his are more purely delightful than the letter to his friend Ellis, describing the division in the House of Commons in 1831, when the Reform Bill was carried by a majority of one: 'You might have heard a pin drop as Duncannon read the numbers. Then, again, the shouts broke out, and many of us shed tears. And the jaw of Peel fell; and the face of Twiss was as the face of a damned soul; and Herries looked like Judas taking his necktie off for the last operation.'

It is true that the vivid colouring of the essays sometimes becomes too glaring, that the characters, especially when they have relation to politics, are apt to be too dark or too bright for human nature, and that the writing is throughout that of a partisan. But if this detracts from it is far from destroying their value; and Macaulay's biographer is pardonably proud of their popularity, and insists, with justice, that it is an element in their greatness as well as an evidence of it.

The first two volumes of the *History of England* were published in 1848, and the third and fourth in 1855, while the fifth was left unfinished at Macaulay's death. The history repeats in great measure both the merits and the defects of the essays. Written with a steady eye to permanence, it is far purer and more perfect, better proportioned, more restrained and more harmonious than they; but it is marked still by the same limitations. We find the writer's strength in a great command of facts and in clearness and force of style. His weaknesses are partisar bias, exaggeration and a certain want of depth.

The story of Macaulay's ambition to write a history which every young lady should read in preference to the latest novel has been often repeated and often ridiculed. The ridicule is ill judged.   To aim at popularity is in itself innocent and even laudable; in truth it is universal.   Carlyle himself with reason felt aggrieved that he remained so long unrecognised.   The desire for popularity becomes vicious only when it leads the man who cherishes it to pander to a taste which he knows to be depraved, or to write something worse than his best, because he knows that his best would not be as popular.   There is no trace of such conduct in Macaulay.   His faults were inherent in his nature, and could have been eradicated only by making him anew.

Of late years Macaulay's history has been often challenged on the score of inaccuracy and untruth.   The charge is brought against every historian in turn; and we must remember, on the other hand, that Freeman, one of the most competent of judges, warmly praised Macaulay for his command of facts.   It is necessary to distinguish three things: falsity of statement, incompleteness of statement, and the drawing of disputable conclusions.   In the first respect Macaulay was rarely, in the second and third he was frequently, at fault.   His omissions are often indefensible. The whole evidence of his character is against the supposition that they were due to conscious dishonesty.   It is far more probable that, approaching his subject with a strong prepossession, he was positively blind to anything that told against his own view.   Partly for the same reason, and partly because his philosophic endowment was not equal to his literary talent, his inferences too are often questionable.   And this perhaps will prove in the end a more serious objection to his history than his partisanship; for, after all, there are worse things, even in historical writing, than partisanship. The man who is free from all temptation to take a side, if not from political affinity then from moral sympathy, must run some risk of being dull and colourless.

Macaulay did much to enlarge and liberalise the conception of history. More than any of his predecessors, he attempted to base his views on a wide consideration of the literature and life of the people, as well as on their constitution and campaigns and treaties. He cast all pseudo-dignity to the winds. His method was sound; and herein Carlyle, though he applied the principle differently, was quite at one with Macaulay. Another honourable characteristic, wherein the two historians likewise agreed, was their care in visiting the scenes about which they had to write; and both have gained in vividness and in topographical accuracy from this habit. Macaulay's notes on the scenes of the Irish war were 'equal in bulk to a first-class article in the *Edinburgh* or *Quarterly Review.*'

The style of Macaulay is at its best in the *History*, where it is more chastened, more varied and sonorous than in the *Essays*. The same tricks and mannerisms reappear, but they are softened and restrained. The trick of a rapid succession of curt sentences, at times so effective, but also at times monotonous and jarring, is kept within bounds. Short and simple are mingled with comparatively long and complex sentences; for Macaulay, scornful of 'the dignity of history' when it is merely cramping and obstructive, is scrupulously mindful of it when the phrase has a legitimate application. He rejects as meretricious ornament and illustration which, as he himself declared, he would have considered not only admissible but desirable in a review. The just censure that his style is hard and metallic applies with far more force against the *Essays* than against the *History*. Greater care and higher finish deepen and enrich the tone.

Macaulay's verse must be dismissed with few words. He is best known by his *Lays of Ancient Rome*, compositions which, like his prose writings, are historical in principle. They neither are nor pretend to be great, but they rank high among the modern imitations of popular poetry. At the same time, they display no such sympathetic genius as, for example, Scott's ballad of Harlaw, no such loftiness of mind as his *Cadyow Castle*. They are clear, rapid and vigorous, like their author's prose. The generous judgment of Elizabeth Barrett, quoted in Ward's *English Poets*, is essentially just : 'He has a noble, clear, metallic note in his soul, and makes us ready by it for battle.' That he makes us ready by it for battle is eminently true of the splendidly martial *Battle of Naseby*, the most stirring piece of verse Macaulay ever wrote. It is interesting to note that the historian of England thus, at the age of twenty-four, reached his highest point in ballad verse in a subject taken from the country and the century which all his life long attracted his most serious study.

In several respects Macaulay is the natural antithesis to Carlyle : to some extent they may even be regarded as complementary. We may correct the excess of the one by the opposite excess of the other. Macaulay was an optimist, Carlyle a pessimist ; Macaulay was the panegyrist of his own time, Carlyle was its merciless critic ; Macaulay devoutly believed all the formulas of the Whig creed, and had great faith in Reform Bills and improvements in parliamentary machinery, Carlyle accepted no formulas whatsoever, and set small store by any reforms that were merely parliamentary ; Macaulay was orthodox in his literary tastes and methods, Carlyle was revolutionary and scornful of rule. The contrast applies equally to their personal history and character. Macaulay was sunny, genial and healthy, Carlyle dyspeptic, irascible, 'gey ill to deal wi';' Macaulay suddenly sprang into fame, Carlyle slowly and with difficulty fought his way to it. They are contrasted in their very biographies. Macaulay's is one of the pleasantest in the language; Carlyle's awoke an acrimonious discussion, due in part certainly to the sins of the subject, but in part also to his injudicious treatment by the biographer.

The truth lay between them. If Macaulay was too easily optimistic, Carlyle was too gloomy. To paint a picture all shadow is as untrue to art, and generally to fact, as it is to paint one all light. It is true that the great problem of society, wise government, cannot be solved by franchises and ballot-boxes; but proper regulations as to these may help to solve it. Carlyle sometimes forgot that the practical problem usually is, not to secure that complex and difficult thing, wise government, but to effect some little improvement which will conduce to the comparative, wiser government, if it does not lead us to the unattainable positive.

The example of German thoroughness had no small influence in fostering the new movement in history. It acted most directly on the students of ancient history, and Niebuhr was the channel through which it was transmitted to England. Before the middle of the century his authority was hardly questioned, though a little later we can trace the reaction in the works of Sir George Cornewall Lewis and others; and now it is no longer possible to conjure with the Pelasgians. But whatever doubts may cloud some of the conclusions of Niebuhr, it was he who enabled the English historians to breathe life into the dry bones of ancient history. Thomas Arnold, Thirlwall and Grote were all inspired by him. Taking these writers as a group, we may remark one important difference between them and the writers of modern history. The historians of the ancient world are wider in their range, and in their works it is still possible to trace the whole life of a people. Thirlwall and Grote embrace all the history of Greece down to the period of decay, and only Arnold's early death prevented him from being equally comprehensive. The reason is that there is a certain finality about ancient history. The materials are manageable in quantity, and there neither have been nor can be such additions to them as to those on which modern history is based.

Thomas Arnold was a man of untiring energy, and he found for his energies three channels, two of them practical and one literary. It is as a schoolmaster that he has won his widest, and what will probably prove his most enduring fame. Some unfavourable critics have insisted that Arnold's Rugby boy could only be described by the slang term, prig. But such criticism is merely the revolt against excessive praise. There may have been some intellectual and moral coxcombry developed in early years by many of Arnold's pupils; but that is not the mature characteristic of men like Clough and Stanley and Dean Vaughan. Moreover, Thomas Arnold was emphatically one of those men from whom virtue goes out; and a result due to affectation can hardly have come from a character so simple and so sincere.

Thomas Arnold (1795-1842).

But Arnold was ambitious likewise to have a hand in determining the doctrines and shaping the thought of England. He, a clergyman, naturally took an ecclesiastical view of what would do that; but it was at the same time a broad view. His position was singularly interesting. The two great evils of the age, in his eyes, were that materialism which he believed to be centred in the University of Lon-

don, and the Catholic revival associated with the University
of Oxford. He stood upon a ground of rationalism, but it
was a rationalism which he firmly believed to be consistent
with faith. He hated materialism because it left no room
for a religious creed; he hated Tractarianism because
it was irreconcilable with reason, and he was convinced
that whatever was irrational must and ought to go to ruin.
He would have accepted the aphorism of a living writer,
'Nothing that is intellectually unsound can be morally
sound.' 'It is,' says he, 'because I so earnestly desire the
revival of the Church that I abhor the doctrine of the
priesthood.' It was this, the combination of faith with
fearless loyalty to reason, that gave him his peculiar interest
in the eyes of observers. The keenest of these however
thought the permanent maintenance of that position impossible; and Dr. Arnold's son, Matthew, in his *Letters* expresses in another way an opinion substantially identical
with that which Carlyle had expressed before.

Arnold's *History of Rome*, published between the years
1838 and 1843, has in great part lost its importance through
the researches of Mommsen and other German scholars; but
there are portions which can never lose their importance.
The point of view is essentially Arnold's own. The impulse
to write came to him because he found in Rome the ancient
analogue to the 'kingly commonwealth of England.' He
found in the great republic lessons both of encouragement
and of warning to his own country; but he sinned less than
some others, notably Grote, in the way of drawing these
lessons direct from the ancient state to the modern. In
another respect, dignity of style, he had an immense advantage over his more widely-read contemporary. Arnold's
English is always forcible, and in the best passages it is eloquent. He is strongest in his account of military operations,
and his description of the campaigns of the Second Punic War

remains still the most vivid and readable in our language, and probably in modern literature. Certainly Mommsen, powerful as his work is, cannot rival Arnold as a military historian. It is rather in depth of scholarship, in mastery of facts, in comprehension of the early history, and consequently of the subsequent working, of the constitution, that Arnold has been surpassed.

The other two historians of the ancient world both chose Greece for their subject. The more interesting and abler man of the two, and the profounder scholar, had the singular ill fortune to see his work superseded, almost as soon as he had written it, by that of his rival. Connop Thirlwall was celebrated in his day as one of the best of English scholars; but no man was ever less of the mere grammarian. Trenchant intellect and sound judgment were his characteristics. He impressed all who encountered him with his capacity to be a leader of men; and his early enterprises seemed a guarantee that he would redeem his promise. As one of the translators of Niebuhr he moulded English historical thought; and his translation of Schleiermacher's essay on St. Luke made an equally deep impression on English theology. It almost stopped his professional advancement. When, in 1840, Thirlwall was suggested to Lord Melbourne for the bishopric of St. David's, Melbourne, with the characteristic oath, objected: 'He is not orthodox in that preface to Schleiermacher.' After some investigation the pious minister convinced himself that the writer of the preface was sufficiently orthodox for the purpose. Thirlwall, perhaps to the cost of his permanent fame, became Bishop of St. David's, and held the office till the year before his death. As Bishop he was bold and independent in judgment. On two memorable occasions he stood alone among his order. He was the solitary bishop who refused to sign

Connop Thirlwall
(1797-1875).

the address calling upon Colenso to resign, and he alone voted for the disestablishment of the Irish Church. Nevertheless he was in a position unfortunate for himself. His nature demanded unfettered freedom of thought; and the controversy with Rowland Williams over the question of *Essays and Reviews* proved that such freedom was not to be found on a bishop's throne.

Thirlwall's principal contribution to literature is his *History of Greece* (1835-1847). The completed work is unfortunately marred by traces of the original design. It had been meant for *Lardner's Cyclopædia*, but overflowed the limits set. Thirlwall thereupon revised the scheme; but he never attained the freedom he would have had if he had begun to write on his own plan and his own scale. His profound scholarship, penetrating judgment, nervous though severe style, and critical acumen, all show to advantage in the *History*. He is far more concentrated than Grote; and though the latter caught the meaning of certain movements and certain institutions which Thirlwall neglected or misinterpreted, he presents a more luminous and a less prejudiced view of Greek history than his successful rival.

But if the *History of Greece* is Thirlwall's most solid contribution to literature, that which gives the best impression of the man, regarded by contemporaries as a rival of the greatest, is his *Letters to a Young Friend*.[1] Few collections of letters give a more charming view of a relation of pure friendship between two people of widely different age. They are weighty too because they touch at many points on questions of universal interest. It has been said that the letters a man writes ought to be

[1] The 'Young Friend' to whom these remarkable letters are addressed is now Lady Hills-Johnes, of Dolancothy, Carmarthenshire.

ascribed to his correspondent in equal measure with himself; and it is certain that from the sympathy he found in this friendship Thirlwall drew an inspiration nothing else in his life ever gave him.

George Grote, the schoolfellow, friend and rival of Thirlwall, was a man in most respects widely different from the great Bishop. Thirlwall's thought was German in origin, though it was coloured by English ecclesiastical opinion. Grote was a Benthamite, and had all the hardness without quite all the force of that school. It was the rising school, and part of Grote's success was due to the fact that he was moving along the line of least resistance. He was a persevering, clear-sighted, determined man. As a historian of Greece he was patient and thorough. He had marked out the subject as his own more than twenty years before the publication, in 1846, of his first two volumes; and ten years more passed before the work was finished. Indeed, we may say that his whole life was devoted to it; for, according to his conception of history, *Plato and the other Companions of Sokrates* (1865), and the incomplete Aristotelian studies issued posthumously in 1872, were parts and appendages of the history.

George Grote
(1794-1871).

Grote was spurred on to this work by political feelings more nearly related to the present time. He was irritated by the Toryism of Mitford's *History of Greece*, which he exposed in an article in the *Westminster Review*. Yet one of his own most conspicuous defects is that he too evidently holds a brief on the opposite side. He does not slur facts, still less does he falsify, but his arguments have sometimes the character of special pleading. Democracy becomes a kind of fetish to him. Its success in the Athens of the fifth century B.C. is made an argument for extending the English franchise in the nineteenth century A.D.; and

Grote is wholly blind to the fact that the wide difference of circumstances makes futile all reasoning from the one case to the other.

Grote's style is heavy and ungainly. He plods along, correct as a rule, but uninspiring and unattractive. He is similarly clumsy in the use of materials. Skilful selection might have appreciably shortened his history; but Grote rarely prunes with sufficient severity, and often he does not prune at all. His habit of pouring out the whole mass of his material in the shape of notes lightens the labour of his successors, but injures his own work as an artistic history. Nevertheless, though Grote had no genius, and nothing that deserves to be called a style, his *History of Greece* holds the field. It does so because of its solidity and conscientious thoroughness, because of its patient investigation of the origin and meaning of institutions, and because its very faults were, after all, faults which sprang from sympathy. Grote was the first who did full justice to the Athenian people; and he may be pardoned if he sometimes did them more than justice.

As these three, Arnold, Thirlwall and Grote, dealt with the ancient world in its glory and greatness, so there were two, Milman and Finlay, who traced its decay, or the process of transition from the ancient to the modern world.

Henry Hart Milman in his earlier days wrote poetry. The turning-point in his literary career was the publication of the *History of the Jews* (1830), the first English work which adequately treats the Jews in their actual historical setting, not in the traditional way as a 'peculiar people' with practically no historical setting at all. Milman afterwards edited Gibbon and wrote a life of the historian; and in 1840 the result of his studies appeared in the *History*

Henry Hart
Milman
(1791-1868).

of Christianity under the Empire.   In 1855 the *History of Latin Christianity down to the Death of Pope Nicholas V.* set the crown upon his labours.   This work is Milman's best title to remembrance, and though errors have been detected in it, the tone and spirit are good, the method sound and the scholarship admirable.

George Finlay has suffered from an unattractive theme,

George Finlay
(1799-1875).

for few care about the obscure fortunes of Greece after its conquest by the Romans. But Finlay was an enthusiast who not only wrote about Greece but lived in it; and this residence (continuous after 1854) imparts to his history its most valuable qualities.   Finlay published a series of works on Greece between 1844 and 1861, all of which were summed up in his *History of Greece from its Conquest by the Romans to the Present Time* (1877).

Among historians of less importance, John Mason Neale

John Mason
Neale
(1818-1866).

did for the Holy Eastern Church a service similar to that performed by Milman for the Latin Church; but he is more likely to be remembered as a hymn-writer than as a historian.   Charles Merivale was likewise a subordinate member of the group of ancient historians.   His principal work was a *History of*

Charles Merivale
(1808-1893).

the Romans under the Empire (1850-1862). Its worst defect is that the author is not quite equal to his subject.   Merivale was a respectable historian, but the successful treatment of the Romans under the Empire demanded a great one.

Among the writers of modern history the next in rank

James Anthony
Froude
(1818-1894).

after Macaulay and Carlyle is James Anthony Froude, the brother of Richard Hurrell Froude, famous for his connexion with the Oxford movement.   For a time J. A. Froude himself was a Tractarian, and he took orders

But Newman's drift to Rome forced him in the opposite direction. His first considerable book, *The Nemesis of Faith* (1849), records his change of mind and indicates how impossible it must always have been for him to rest permanently in the position of the Tractarians.

Leaving Oxford and the Tractarians, Froude fell under the spell of Carlyle. They were introduced to each other soon after this, but it was not till Froude's settlement in London in 1860 that they became intimate. Carlyle's influence upon his disciple was almost wholly good. The younger man had the good sense not to imitate his master's style, while he learnt from him clear, sharply-outlined, fearless judgment; and the mists of Tractarianism rolled away for ever.

The great work of Froude's life was his *History of England from the Fall of Wolsey to the Defeat of the Spanish Armada* (1856-1870). It was written under the direct inspiration of Carlyle. 'If I wrote anything,' says Froude, 'I fancied myself writing it to him, reflecting at each word what he would think of it, as a check on affectations.' He submitted the first two chapters, in print, to Carlyle; and the verdict, 'though not wanting in severity,' was on the whole favourable. The critics were divided. Froude was a man who usually either carried his readers wholly with him or alienated them. Those who loved clear, vigorous, pointed English, keen intelligence and life-like portraiture, were delighted with the book. Students, familiar with the original documents and able to criticise details, regarded it with very different eyes.

Both sides were right in their principal assertions, and both were prone to forget that there was another aspect of the case. On the one hand, it has been established beyond the reach of reasonable dispute that Froude was habitually and grossly inaccurate. It is indeed doubtful whether any other historian, with any title to be considered great, can be charged with so many grave errors. Froude is inaccurate first of all in his facts. He does not take the trouble to verify, he misquotes, he is not careful to weigh evidence. But moreover, he is inaccurate in what may be called his colour. He paints his picture in the light of his own emotions and prejudices, he is rather the impassioned advocate than the calm judge. He would not only have acknowledged this, but he would have defended himself; and there is something to be said for his view. Absolute impartiality is, in the first place, unattainable; and in the second place, so far as it is attained, it is not always an unmixed good. Pure disinterestedness is apt to mean absence of interest. It is certainly true that some of the greatest histories in the world are all alive with the passions of the writers. Those of Tacitus are so, and likewise those of Carlyle; and Herodotus had undoubtedly a partiality for Athens. Froude therefore is not to be wholly condemned on this score; but he ought to have remembered that the adoption of such a theory of history made it doubly incumbent on him to examine carefully the grounds upon which his opinions rested. His cardinal defect was a disregard of this precaution.

Froude moreover was given to paradox. It has been repeatedly pointed out that one of the great tasks of the century has been the whitewashing of scoundrels. De Quincey undertook Judas. Carlyle in his later days performed the service for Frederick. Froude in his justification of Henry VIII. was only following a fashion. Nevertheless, the twisting of facts, the exaggeration of all that tells on the one side and the slurring or suppression of arguments on the other, are grave faults in history. And these are the almost inevitable results of the indulgence in paradox and the advocacy of weak causes.

All the cleverness is unconvincing, and the detection of the sophistry brings discredit upon the whole work into which it is admitted.

This is the case of the *advocatus diaboli* against Froude. It is a re-statement of the main points in Freeman's indictment. But a history is a piece of literature as well as a record of facts ; and as literature Froude's work stands very high. In the first place, he is great in style. Not that his English is of the kind that calls attention to itself. It is seldom magnificent, but it is always adequate, and the reader never feels himself jarred by want of taste or befogged by obscurity either of thought or expression. It is wholly free from affectation. Froude concerned himself merely to express his meaning, and wrote a good style because he did not trouble himself about style. He answered impatiently those who inquired into the secret of his prose, telling them that he only wrote what he thought and let the style take care of itself.

Froude had moreover a great talent for the delineation of character. Whether his characters are always true to fact may be questioned ; but his Henry VIII., his Queen Mary and his Queen Elizabeth certainly leave the impression of living human beings, and the charm of his history is largely due to the vividness with which he paints them.

Froude never undertook another work on such a scale as the *History*. Perhaps he realised that the scale was too large. The plan of the *Short Studies on Great Subjects* (1867-1883) was in some respects better suited to him. In these essays he gives with unsurpassed vigour the thoughts of a powerful mind on themes of special interest; and as they do not pretend to be exhaustive the writer's weaknesses are not brought into prominence. *The English in Ireland in the Eighteenth Century* (1872-1874) was, next to the great *History*, his largest work. But Irish history has been and is the source of so much passion that the present generation is no favourable time for either writing or criticising such a work. Later, in 1889, the historical romance, *The Two Chiefs of Dunboy*, showed that his interest in the country still survived; and those who know Ireland are the readiest to acknowledge that Froude has not only written an interesting story, but has shown great insight into the country and its inhabitants.

But the principal work of Froude's later years was his biography of Carlyle, the first instalment of which was published in 1882, and the second two years later. No biography has ever raised a greater storm of indignation ; nor can it be denied that for this Froude was partly to blame. His method is ruthless, and in some cases its justice is questionable. At the same time, the condemnation passed upon him has been unmeasured ; and no small part of it has been due to the disappointment of worshippers of Carlyle at the discovery that if the head of their idol was pure gold the feet were miry clay. Froude has written, perhaps one of the least judicious, but certainly one of the most readable of English biographies.

The other works of Froude are of inferior consequence. Neither his *Julius Cæsar* nor his *Erasmus* is calculated to increase his reputation ; while the very interesting *Oceana* indicates, more clearly than any of his other writings, the source of his greatest errors—a habit of jumping to conclusions from insufficient premisses. Froude pronounces confidently upon the colonies on no better ground than a hurried visit and a few conversations with chance residents, who might not always be disinterested. Yet *Oceana* had more influence than many a better book. Like Seeley's *Expansion of England* it was partly the consequence, but also partly the cause of the great change in public opinion whereby the colonies, regarded thirty years ago as little better than a burden, have come to be considered the principal support of the greatness of England.

The historian generally prefers to work upon a subject removed to some distance from his own time, but the intense interest of a great armed struggle not infrequently makes it an exception. Thus, the Peninsular War found a contemporary historian in Napier, and similarly Alexander William Kinglake wrote the story of the next great European contest in which England was engaged after the fall of Napoleon. He had previously won a purer literary fame in the fascinating volume of travel, *Eothen*, published in 1844. The journey of which it is a record had been made about nine years earlier, and *Eothen* as finally published was the result of long thought and of fastidious care in literary workmanship. It is little concerned with facts and occurrences, attempting rather to reproduce the effect of the life and the scenes of the East.

Alexander
William Kinglake
(1809-1891).

The reputation acquired by this book opened up for Kinglake the larger subject of the Crimean War. He had accompanied the expedition from love of adventure, and chance made him acquainted with Lord Raglan, whose papers were ultimately intrusted to him. *The Invasion of the Crimea* (1863-1887) is open to several serious objections. It is far too long, and the style is florid, diffuse and highly mannered. Moreover, Kinglake is a most prejudiced historian. There is no mean in his judgment; he either can see no faults, or he can see nothing else. Raglan and St. Arnaud are examples of the two extremes. But frequently the historian supplies the corrective to his own judgment. If the battle of the Alma was won as Kinglake says it was, then it was won not by generalship but by hard fighting plus a lucky blunder on the part of the general.

On the other hand, Kinglake sustains the interest with great skill, especially in the battle volumes. Long as are the accounts of the Alma and of Balaclava, they are perfectly clear, and the impression left is indelible.

It has been already hinted that the chief defect in this great mass of historical work is the want of a philosophy of history. The unmanageable volume of material almost smothers the intellect. An attempt to make good the defect was made by Henry Thomas Buckle, in his *History of Civilisation* (1857-1861), with results not altogether satisfactory. Buckle was a man of vast reading and tenacious memory; but no knowledge, however extensive, could at that time have sufficed to do what he attempted. He soon discovered this himself, and what he has executed is a mere fragment of his daring design. Even so, it is larger than his materials justified. In accounting for Buckle's failure, stress has often been laid upon the fact that his education was private. This is a little pedantic. Grote, whose history has been accepted at the universities as the best available, was of no university. Mill, one of the men who have most influenced thought in this century, was of none either. Gibbon, perhaps the greatest of historians, has put on record how little he owed to Oxford; and Carlyle has told us with characteristic vigour how unprofitable he thought his university of Edinburgh. The men who did not go to a university have done good work; and the men who did go to one have declared that they owed little or nothing to the education there received. In the face of such facts it is impossible to account so for the failure of Buckle. The real reason, besides the cardinal fact that the attempt was premature, is that Buckle, though he had the daring of the speculator's temperament, had neither its caution nor its breadth. The

Henry Thomas Buckle (1821-1862).

great speculative geniuses of the world have been prudent as well as bold. No one is bolder than Aristotle, but no one is more careful to lay first a broad foundation for his speculations. Buckle did not use his great knowledge so. His account of the causes of things always rouses suspicion because it is far too simple. He never understood how complex the life of a nation is; and when he came to write he practically rejected the greater part of his knowledge and used only the small remainder. He was moreover a man of strong prejudices. He could not endure the ecclesiastical type of mind or the ecclesiastical view of things; and his account of civilisation in Scotland is completely vitiated by his determination to regard the Church, before the Reformation and after the Reformation alike, as merely a weight on the wheel, not a source of energy and forward movement.

Buckle then illustrates the tendency of the mind, noted by Bacon, to grasp prematurely at unity. This very fact, conjoined with the clearness and vigour of his style, was the reason of his popularity. When the inadequacy of his theories began to be perceived there came a reaction. But inevitably those theories will be replaced by others. To some extent they have been replaced already by the theories of two writers, Sir Henry Maine and Mr. W. E. Hartpole Lecky, of whom the latter belongs, however, rather to the period still current than to the Age of Tennyson.

The majority of Maine's works too were published after the year 1870, but as his most awakening and original book, *Ancient Law*, appeared as early as 1861, we may fairly regard him as belonging to the period under consideration. Sir Henry Maine was a great teacher as well as a great writer, and he had already acquired a considerable reputation before the appearance of his *Ancient Law*. But it was that book which established his name as an

Sir Henry Maine (1822-1888).

original thinker. It has two great merits. It is written in a most lucid, pleasant style, and it is decidedly original in substance. Maine's design is far less ambitious than Buckle's; but for that very reason his performance is more adequate. The most conspicuous distinction between the two is that the later writer shows in far greater measure than his predecessor the modern sense of the importance of origins. It was this that gave his work importance. To a great extent the task of recent historians has been to trace institutions to their source, and explain their later development by means of the germs out of which they have grown. In this respect Maine was a pioneer, and his later work was just a fuller exposition of the principles at the root of *Ancient Law*. His *Village Communities* (1871) and his *Early History of Institutions* (1875) are both inspired by the same idea. In his *Popular Government* (1885) he may be said to break new ground; but it is easy to see the influence on that book of the author's prolonged study of early forms of society. These later books are not perhaps intrinsically inferior to *Ancient Law*, but they are less suggestive, just because so much of the work had been already done by it.

Biography is another form of history, and it is not surprising that a period so rich in historical writings should also be distinguished in biography. If Boswell's *Johnson* is still supreme, the Age of Tennyson has produced several lives surpassed only by it. Two of the best of these lives, Carlyle's *Sterling* and Froude's *Carlyle*, were written by historians, and have been noticed along with their other works. Another remarkable book, the *Autobiography* of John Stuart Mill, is likewise best taken along with the more formal works of the philosopher. But even after these large deductions, and after a rigid exclusion of everything that is not, both in form and substance, of very high

K

quality, there remain at least two men of great distinction in literature, J. G. Lockhart and A. P. Stanley, who must be treated as first and chiefly biographers.

John Gibson Lockhart was a man of many gifts and accomplishments, a good scholar, a keen satirist and critic, a powerful novelist, an excellent translator. He was accomplished with the pencil as well as with the pen, and some of his caricatures are at once irresistibly amusing and profoundly true. His 'Scotch judge' and 'Scotch minister' would make the reputation of a number of *Punch*. His biting wit won for him the *sobriquet* of 'the Scorpion;' but notwithstanding his sting he won and retained through life many warm friends. He was trained for the Scottish bar, but attached himself to the literary set of *Blackwood*, in which Christopher North was the most striking figure. With him and Hogg Lockhart was concerned in an exceedingly amusing skit, the famous *Chaldee Manuscript*; but the joke gave so much offence that this 'promising babe' was strangled in the cradle. A good deal of more serious literary work belongs to the period before 1830,— the novels, a mass of criticism, and the *Spanish Ballads*. Then too was formed the connexion which opened to Lockhart the great work of his life. He was introduced to Scott in 1818. The acquaintance prospered. Scott liked the clever young man, Scott's daughter liked him still better, and in 1820 Lockhart married Sophia Scott. Largely through her father's influence he was appointed editor of the *Quarterly Review*, an office which he held until 1853, and in which he became to a very great degree, both by reason of what he wrote and of what he printed, responsible for the tone of criticism at the time.

Lockhart undoubtedly shared that excessive personality which was the blot of criticism, and especially of the

John Gibson
Lockhart
(1794-1854).

Blackwood school, in his generation. He has been charged with the *Blackwood* article on Keats, and with the *Quarterly* article on *Jane Eyre*, but he may now be acquitted of both these sins. It was however Lockhart who wrote the *Quarterly* article on Tennyson's early poems; but this, though bad in tone and excessively severe, is to a large extent critically sound. So far as they can be traced, Lockhart's criticisms are such as might be expected from his mind,—clear, incisive and vigorous. They are however often unsympathetic and harsh, because criticism was then too apt to be interpreted as fault-finding, and Lockhart could not wholly free himself from the influence of a vicious tradition.

But it is by his *Life of Scott* (1836-1838) that Lockhart will live in literature. He had in an ample measure the first of all requirements in a biographer, personal acquaintance with the man whose life he wrote. Almost from the time of his introduction, and certainly from the date of his marriage, Lockhart's relations with Scott were of the closest; and though he was not personally familiar with the facts of Scott's earlier life, he knew quite enough to understand the springs of the man's character. Moreover, in the autobiographical fragment and in the endless stores of family and friendly anecdote open to him he had ample means of making good the deficiency. For among Lockhart's advantages is to be reckoned the fact that he had not merely married into the family, but had married, as it were, into the circle of friends. The *Life of Scott* shows that the families of Abbotsford, of Chiefswood and of Huntley Burn (the last Scott's great friends the Fergusons) were for many purposes only one larger family.

There are certain dangers, as well as great advantages, to the biographer even in intimate friendship. Misused in one way, it lowers the biographer's own character; misused in another, it either lowers or unnaturally exalts that of his subject. Boswell, employing his materials with excellent effect for the purposes of his book, degrades himself. Froude, making a mistake of another sort, exaggerates all the less lovable characteristics of Carlyle; while there are multitudes who paint pictures not of flesh and blood, but of impossible saints and heroes. 'A love passing the love of biographers' was Macaulay's phrase for the excess of hero-worship. Lockhart has avoided all these errors. When his book was read the contradictory charges were brought against him, on the one hand of having exaggerated Scott's virtues and concealed his faults, and on the other of ungenerous and derogatory criticism. We may be sure that Lockhart's temptation, if he felt any, was rather to 'extenuate' than to 'set down in malice.' But, with a noble confidence in a noble character, he does not extenuate. To describe Scott as a mere money-lover would be untrue; yet many have felt that there is a fault in his relation to wealth, and Lockhart uses just the right words when he says, 'I dare not deny that he set more of his affections, during great part of his life, upon worldly things, wealth among others, than might have become such an intellect;' and he gives just the right explanation when he goes on to trace this defect to its root in the imagination. In his treatment of the commercial matters in which Scott was involved, Lockhart is equally judicial.

The tact of Lockhart deserves as much praise as his fairness of judgment. As regards part of his work, he was put to the test a few years ago by the publication of Scott's *Journal*. Lockhart had made liberal extracts from this journal, explaining at the same time that passages were necessarily suppressed because of their bearing upon persons then alive. A comparison of his extracts with the journal now accessible *in extenso* shows how skilfully he suppressed what was likely to give pain, while at the same time producing much the same general impression as the whole document leaves.

A biography, like a letter, may be said to have two authors, the man written about and the person who writes. Scott certainly gave Lockhart the greatest assistance, both by what he wrote and by what he was. At the beginning the delightful fragment of autobiography, towards the end the profoundly interesting *Journal*, and all through the free, manly, large-hearted letters, were materials of the choicest sort. Scott himself moreover, genial, cordial, of manifold activity, a centre of racy anecdote, was a person whom it was far more easy to set in an attractive frame than any mere literary recluse. Many could have produced a good life of such a man. Lockhart's special praise is that he has written a great one. Except Johnson, there is no English man of letters so well depicted as Scott. Lockhart's taste and style are excellent. The caustic wit which ran riot in the young *Blackwood* reviewer is restrained by the experience of years and by the necessities of the subject. Lockhart's own part of the narrative is told in grave, temperate English, simple almost to severity, but in a high degree flexible. In the brighter parts there is a pleasant lightness in Lockhart's touch; in the more serious parts he is weighty and powerful; and on occasion, especially towards the end, there is a restrained emotion which proves that part of his wonderful success is due to the fact that his heart was in his work.

Arthur Penrhyn Stanley ranks considerably below Lockhart, yet his *Life of Arnold* (1844) is inferior only to the few unapproachable masterpieces of biography. Stanley was a fluent and able writer in several fields, but in most respects his work is now somewhat discredited.

Arthur Penrhyn
Stanley
(1815-1881).

His *Commentary on the Epistles to the Corinthians* (1855) has been severely handled for inaccuracy and defective scholarship. His *Lectures on the Eastern Church* (1861) and *On the Jewish Church* (1863-1876), and his book of Eastern travel, *Sinai and Palestine* (1856) are delightful in literary execution, but they are popular rather than solid. Stanley neither was nor, apparently, cared to be exact. He trusted too much to his gift of making things interesting, and had an inadequate conception of the duty he owed to his readers of writing what was true. Other travellers who have followed his footsteps in the East have sometimes found that the scenes he describes, in charming English, are such as are visible only to those whose eyes can penetrate rocks and mountains. This constitutional inaccuracy is a blot upon nearly all his works, and his one permanent contribution to literature will probably prove to be the *Life of Dr. Arnold*. There is here, as Stanley's biographer justly says, 'a glow of repressed enthusiasm which gives to the work one of its greatest charms.' Stanley loved Arnold, and threw himself with unwonted thoroughness into the task of depicting him. For two years, we are told, he abandoned for it every other occupation that was not an absolute duty. The principal defect of the *Life* is that the plan—a portion of narrative, and then a body of letters—is too rigid and mechanical. But the narrative is exceedingly good, giving within moderate compass a clear impression of Arnold; and the letters are well selected and full of interest.

MINOR HISTORIANS AND BIOGRAPHERS.

Sir Archibald Alison was the son of a clergyman who won a name for a work on the *Principles of Taste*. Alison practised at the Scottish bar, became Sheriff of Lanarkshire,

and was knighted for his services to literature. His *magnum opus* is a *History of Europe during the French Revolution*, which he afterwards continued to the accession of
Sir Archibald
Alison
(1792-1867).
Napoleon III. It is laborious and honest, though not unprejudiced. Disraeli sneeringly said that 'Mr. Wordy' had proved by his twenty volumes that Providence was on the side of the Tories.

John Hill Burton, best known as the historian of Scotland, was an industrious man of letters, who wrote on
John Hill
Burton
(1809-1881).
many subjects,—*The Scot Abroad, The Book Hunter*, and *The Age of Queen Anne*, as well as the *History of Scotland*. The last is the work of a capable and careful writer rather than of a great historian. Burton is sensible and dispassionate, and he has collected and put into shape the principal results of modern research as applied to Scotland.

John Forster was a laborious but somewhat commonplace writer. He was the author of a *Life of*
John Forster
(1812-1876).
Goldsmith (1848) and a *Life of Sir John Eliot* (1864). But his most valuable works are two biographies of contemporaries, the *Life of Landor* (1869) and the *Life of Dickens* (1872-1874). Forster had little power of realising character, and the subjects of his biographies are never clearly outlined. His *Life of Dickens* has an importance beyond its intrinsic merits, because it is the most authoritative book on the great novelist.

Walter Farquhar Hook was a prominent clergyman, whose doctrine, that the English Roman
Walter
Farquhar Hook
(1798-1875).
Catholics were really seceders from the Church of England, caused a great stir when it was first promulgated. His vast design of the *Lives of the Archbishops of Canterbury* (1860-1876) was ultimately executed in twelve big volumes. The plan

was too large and the characters treated too multifarious for really good biography, but it is solid and valuable work.

Sir John William Kaye wrote two meritorious books of military history, *The History of the War in Afghanistan* (1851), and *The History of the Sepoy War in India* (1864-1876). The latter, which roused some controversy, was left unfinished at Kaye's death, and was afterwards completed by Colonel Malleson.

Sir John
William Kaye
(1814-1876).

Sir Francis Palgrave was in the early part of his life an active contributor to the *Edinburgh* and *Quarterly Reviews*, and a diligent editor of state documents. His *Rise and Progress of the English Commonwealth* (1832) threw much light on the early history of England. Palgrave was in his day one of the most earnest students of mediæval history.

Sir Francis
Palgrave
(1788-1861).

Philip Henry, Earl Stanhope, wrote the *History of the War of the Succession in Spain*, the *History of the Reign of Queen Anne*, and the *History of England from the Peace of Utrecht to the Peace of Versailles*. He took great pains with his work, but he does not reach distinction either of thought or style.

Philip Henry,
Earl Stanhope
(1805-1875).

Sir William Stirling-Maxwell is less widely known than he deserves to be, but this is partly due to the expensiveness of his works. He wrote *Annals of the Artists of Spain*, *The Cloister Life of Charles V.*, *Velasquez and his Work*, and a posthumous book, *Don John of Austria*. All his work is distinguished for learning and good taste.

Sir William
Stirling-Maxwell
(1818-1878).

Agnes Strickland was a popular writer whose work is readable rather than profound or original. Her principal books are the *Lives of the Queens of England*, followed up by *Lives of the Queens of Scotland*.

Agnes Strickland
(1806-1874).

Patrick Fraser Tytler, another historian of Scotland,
came of a family distinguished both in
Patrick Fraser   literature and in law.   His *History of Scot-
Tytler   *land* has been superseded in general favour
(1791-1849).   by Burton's, which has the advantage of
embodying more recent research.   Tytler however was
the abler man of the two, and he had a higher literary gift
than Burton.   Except where the narrative has to be re-
written in the light of later discoveries, his judgment is
always worth weighing.

CHAPTER VII.

THEOLOGY AND PHILOSOPHY.

THE early part of the nineteenth century was not very prolific in the department of speculative thought, but signs of movement may be detected in the third decade Each of the English universities became the centre of a very active intellectual society. The Cambridge men showed a bent towards general literature and philosophy, or to theology of a type cognate to philosophy. In the works of Whately Oxford gave signs of a philosophical revival; but she devoted herself mainly to theology, and the practical isolation of Whately, a hard and arid though a vigorous man, calls the more attention to her speculative poverty. The celebrated 'Oxford movement,' whose roots are in the twenties, though its visible growth dates only from the thirties, is of incomparably greater importance than this feeble revival.

Newman, the great artificer of the movement, rightly traces its inception to the influence of John Keble. But Keble's true literary form is poetry, and his principal contribution to poetry belongs to the preceding period. His prose works are not in themselves of great importance. As Professor of Poetry at Oxford he delivered lectures (in Latin) on critical subjects. In his character of pastor he preached many sermons, and a selection from them was published in 1847. The most famous of his pulpit utterances was

John Keble
(1792-1866).

one preached in 1833 on 'National Apostasy.' 'I have
ever considered and kept the day,' says Newman, with
regard to the delivery of this sermon, 'as the start of the
religious movement of 1833.' Finally, in 1863, appeared
Keble's latest work of importance, a *Life of Bishop
Wilson.*

Keble's influence was essentially personal, and was due
to his saintly life more than to anything he wrote, even in
poetry. The Tractarian movement took its rise in a longing
for saintliness, of which Keble furnished a living example.
He was not to any considerable extent an originator of
theory. Certain germs of theory about the Church, about
its relation to pre-Reformation times, about authority in
religion, were in the air, and they became absorbed in
Keble's system. But his was not a creative mind, and
his position at the head of the Anglo-Catholic movement
was little more than an accident. He was like a child
who by a thrust of his hand sends a finely-poised rock
thundering down a hill. In his literary aspects he is disappointing. A brilliant boy and a most blameless man,
he remains throughout too little of this world. The pale
perfection of his life is reflected in his works. He would
have been better had he been less good; he would have
been much better had he been less feminine.

In the ranks of the movement so initiated were included an unusual number of men who must be classed
among the 'might-have-beens' of literature; men of great
reputation eclipsed by premature death, men who never
wrote, or men whose writings disappointed expectation.
Nearly all its members had literary tastes, a fact not surprising when we consider how large a part imagination
played in its start and development. But Hurrell Froude,
one of the most daring-minded men engaged in it, died
early, leaving only inadequate remains as evidence of his

great gifts. W. G. Ward lived, but only to prove by his *Ideal of a Christian Church* that the power of writing good English was not among his endowments; and if the poetry of Keble is only second or even third-rate, that of Isaac Williams, a versifier of the movement, is of lower grade still. Manning was more the man of action than the man of letters; while the work of Dean Church and Canon Liddon, both of whom had marked literary talents, falls principally outside the limits of this period. There remain two remarkable men, one the very soul of the movement, the other its greatest recruit, who have attained, the first a great, the second a respectable place in letters. These are Cardinal Newman and Pusey, of whom the latter may be considered the exception to the rule that the Tractarians were by nature and instinct men of letters. Pusey was not; he was rather the technical theologian with no direct interest in letters at all.

John Henry Newman has been described by J. A.

John Henry
Newman
(1801-1890).

Froude, in language hardly too strong, as 'the indicating number' of the movement, all the others being, in comparison with him, but as cyphers. The story of Newman's inner life has been told with inimitable grace in the *Apologia pro Vita Sua*, and this is not only his greatest contribution to literature, but the best document for his life and doctrines. There are few studies more interesting than the contrast presented by this book on the one side, and the *Phases of Faith* by its author's brother, F. W. Newman, on the other. The younger Newman too has a mind prone to religion, but he decides to rest in reason, while his brother leans upon authority. Not unnaturally they drift very far apart; not unnaturally too the author of the *Phases of Faith* is amazed that it took his brother ten years to discover whither he was going.

Newman's education was private till he went to Oxford, where, in 1822, he won a fellowship at Oriel, then the great intellectual college of the university. He was at this time a Calvinist in his religious views, and held, among other things, that the Pope was Antichrist. At Oxford he came under the influence of Whately, who, he says, taught him to think. But the two men were essentially antipathetic and foredoomed to part, not the best of friends. Newman drew gradually closer to men of a very different stamp—R. J. Wilberforce, Hurrell Froude and Keble. His *Arians of the Fourth Century* was finished in 1832, and he took rest after the fatigue of writing it in a memorable journey with Hurrell Froude in the Mediterranean. During this journey he composed most of his verses printed in the *Lyra Apostolica*, and towards the end of it the exquisite hymn, ' Lead, kindly light.'

After his return, in 1833, Newman began, ' out of his own head,' the *Tracts for the Times*. They culminated in the celebrated *Tract XC* (1841), which raised such a storm of opposition that the series had to be closed. Contemporaneously with the *Tracts*, Newman was busied with other works in defence of the *Via Media*. To this class belong *The Prophetical Office of the Church* (1837) and the *Lectures on Justification* (1838). He was moreover building up a great reputation as a preacher; and, as if all this was not enough, he was for several years editor of *The British Critic*. The storm raised by his opinions, and especially by *Tract XC*, drove him into retirement at Littlemore in 1841. He called it his Torres Vedras, in the conviction that he, like Wellington, was destined to 'issue forth anew,' and to conquer. But the actual course was different. In 1843 he retracted his former strictures on Rome, and resigned his charge of St. Mary's. For two years more he lingered in the Church of England, fore-

seeing the inevitable end, but slow to take a step of such
importance without absolute assurance.   In 1845 he was
received into the Roman communion.   Here the history of
his spiritual development may be said to close.   'It was,'
he says, 'like coming into port after a rough sea.'   He
repudiates the idea that his mind was afterwards idle ;
but there was no change, no anxiety, no doubt.   He seems
to be unconscious that this individual peace may be dear
bought for the human race, and that the absence of doubt
is, to use his own favourite word, the 'note' of a low
type.

Among the voluminous works of Newman, in addition
to those of his Anglican period already mentioned, the
most important are *The Development of Christian Doctrine*
(1845), the *Apologia pro Vita Sua* (1864), *The Dream of
Gerontius* (1865), and the *Grammar of Assent* (1870).

Except the *Apologia*, no work of Newman's is more
valuable or more helpful to an understanding of him than
The Dream of Gerontius, subtle, mystical, imaginative.
Newman's great reputation for prose, and the supreme interest attaching to his life, seem to have obscured the fame
he might have won, and deserved, as a poet.   His poetry
is religious without the weakness, or at any rate the
limitedness, which mars so much religious verse.   He was,
in poetry as well as in theology, a greater and more mascu-
line Keble, one with all the real purity of Keble, but with
also the indispensable flavour of earth.   'I was in a
humour, certainly,' he says of the Anglican divines, ' to
bite off their ears ; ' and one loves him for it.   It is worth
remembering also that he taught the need of hatred
as well as love ; and though he explained and limited the
teaching, there is meaning in the very form of expression.   There was iron in Newman's frame and gall in his
blood.

Newman's mind was fundamentally imaginative, and in him imagination, though of an intellectual cast, was conjoined with an acutely sensitive organisation. Moreover, he had a tendency to solitude which powerfully influenced his development. Finally, along with his sensitiveness and power of imagination there went a subtle gift of logic, subordinate upon the whole to imagination, but clamorous until it had received what might at least plausibly pass for satisfaction. These characteristics together explain Newman's work.

There can be no dispute about the imaginative cast of Newman's mind. He had, besides the poet's, the philosopher's or speculative imagination. He pondered habitually over the secret of the universe. There is an often quoted sentence at the beginning of the *Apologia* which is vital to a comprehension of him. 'I thought life might be a dream, or I an angel, and all this world a deception, my fellow-angels by a playful device concealing themselves from me, and deceiving me with the semblance of a material world.' It has been said that no one has any genuine gift for philosophy who has never doubted the reality of material things. Newman evidently had the necessary 'note' of philosophy, but he had it with a morbid addition which, without careful control, might lead to strange and even disastrous results. If Newman had only known German he would have found in the German philosophers an idealism far more profound and more rational than any he was ever able to frame for himself. But in England the dominant philosophy was Benthamism, the dominant theology was equally hard, and Newman turned from both in disgust, took to the theological road-making of the *Via Media*, and finally found refuge in Rome, driven by the conviction that 'there are but two alternatives, the way to Rome and the way to atheism.'

Newman's sensitiveness produced a shrinking from intercourse and strengthened a love of solitude probably constitutional and not altogether wholesome. He was believed to be, and to have the ambition to be, the head of a party. In truth, he shrank almost morbidly from the idea of leadership, and it was in spite of himself that he gathered followers. Even the few friends with whom he lived in familiar intercourse came 'unasked, unhoped.' It would have been better for him had he been able to speak out more freely and to harmonise himself with the world around him. Instead, he fell back upon himself and upon a study of the Fathers, hoping to find the full truth in the primitive days of Christianity. This is a fatal error which, in theory, vitiates most theology, but from the effects of which a great deal of it is saved by inconsistency. Newman himself was afterwards led in his course towards Rome to recognise development in doctrine. The Fathers are doubtless excellent reading, but they are safe reading to him only who can read them in the light of the present day. It is vain to think of stopping the wheels of change even in theology. A creed which meant one thing in the first century, even though its verbal expression remain the same, means something widely different in the nineteenth. Newman unfortunately could conceive of modern thought only as a detestable and soul-deadening 'liberalism,' a halfway house to atheism, as Anglicanism was, in his mature view, a halfway house to Rome. Had he been more a real participant in contemporary life, his conceptions would insensibly have taken their bent from the 'liberalism' he hated ; and, little as he thought it, he had something to learn from that liberalism, just as it had something to learn from him.

Newman was moreover a logician, though he ultimately found refuge in a communion where the *science* of logic is little needed. The subtlety of his logic is unquestionable. The doubt which some feel is rather with regard to its honesty. This doubt however is only felt by those who fail to understand how behind and beneath and above his logic there spread and towered his imagination and his emotions. Newman was compelled by the law of his nature to find a foundation for his religion; he neither understood nor respected those who let it exist as a mere sentiment. 'I determined,' says he with reference to a time of crisis, 'to be guided, not by my imagination, but by my reason.' It was this resolve that kept him so long out of the Church of Rome. He is wholly, even transparently sincere. Nevertheless, in spite of himself, he *is* guided by imagination after all. The conclusion is at every point a foregone one; and his pause results, not in genuine reasons for the change, but in increased strength of feeling compelling it. This is what observers have noted in Newman's logic, and what has led them to doubt his sincerity. His dice are always loaded, but they are loaded against his own will. The absolute need for him to rest on authority makes it certain from the start that authority will win.

There is no way of using reason except by consenting to be wholly guided by it. Newman never consented. He always knew the general character of the answer he must receive, though he did not know the precise terms of it, whether those of the *Via Media* or those of Rome. This is the secret of Newman's power, in his argumentative works, over those who already fundamentally agree with him, and of his failure to move those who do not. For surely it is remarkable how little real effect followed from his secession, that blow under which, it has been said, the Church of England reeled. Newman, unlike both his friends and his enemies, was well aware that few would follow him to

Rome; and he paused for years because he believed, on the other hand, that his secession would shatter the party for which he had so long toiled. The character of the Oxford movement was changed by Newman's secession, because by that step many were awakened to the fact that his brilliant logic had no sound foundation in reason. Others had been awakened before. J. A. Froude in his *Nemesis of Faith* tells how his eyes were opened by a sentence in one of Newman's sermons: ' Scripture says the earth is stationary and the sun moves; science, that the sun is stationary and that the earth moves, and we shall never know which is true until we know what *motion* is.' Froude adds the common sense criticism that if Scripture uses the word motion in a transcendental sense it may equally use other words so, and we can never know what it means.

When we add to this Newman's impulsiveness we have a sufficient explanation of the aberrations of his reasoning. He tried to be and thought he was cautious; but he was mistaken. The pause he was accustomed to make before taking decisive action had only the appearance of caution; and the real impulsiveness of his nature is indicated by several things in his own narrative. For example, the phrase of St. Augustine, *Securus judicat orbis terrarum*, rings in his ears and recurs to his mind and produces more effect than volumes of argument. ' By those great words of the ancient Father, interpreting and summing up the long and varied course of ecclesiastical history, the theory of the *Via Media* was absolutely pulverised.' Was such a result ever before produced by such a cause? or was it that the the *Via Media* was in truth built of loose rubbish over shifting sand?

The fact is that Newman's talent for philosophy, though considerable, nay, almost great even in a strict use of the word great, was insufficient to construct a comprehensive system without better guidance than he could find. He was

> ' Wandering between two worlds, one dead,
> The other powerless to be born ; '

and, unable himself to bring about the birth, he turned back upon the dead old world, a conspicuous, though personally blameless and most attractive, specimen of the class of those who sink 'from the van and the freemen' back 'to the rear and the slaves.'

Great part of Newman's power and attractiveness depended upon his exquisite literary gifts. His mind grew up at Oxford, and few have shown so much of the *genius loci*. He is academical in the best sense. There is a polished scholarliness in all his work, and very little English prose can be ranked as superior to his. Yet it is perfectly simple. With the true scholar's instinct he strives for lucidity rather than magnificence. His writings frequently breathe passion, but there could be nothing less like what is commonly called 'impassioned prose.' Compare him with De Quincey or with Ruskin. They frequently betray a straining for effect, Newman rarely or never. His passages of eloquence come, like his friends, 'unasked, unhoped,' because the fervour of his own thought, or the pressure of circumstances, like the calumnies that provoked the *Apologia*, wrings them from him. Always clear, faultless in taste, capable of great elevation but never too high for the occasion, Newman's prose is as likely to be permanently satisfying as any of this century.

Edward Bouverie Pusey was, as regards his contributions to formal theology, superior to Newman ; but both as a man and as a writer he was indefinitely smaller. Pusey early won a great reputation for learning, and Newman considered his accession to the movement an event of the

Edward Bouverie Pusey (1800-1882).

first importance. He had great tenacity, and his adhe-
sion, once given, was sure. Notwithstanding suspicions
at the time of Newman's perversion, there never was the
least chance that Pusey would go over to Rome; the *Via
Media*, which had crumbled under Newman's feet, was
solid enough for him. He was not sufficiently imaginative
to push his way into the bog which, like another Chat's
Moss, swallowed up all the material Newman could collect.
On the contrary, for the forty years of his life after
Newman's secession, he went on diligently stopping the
holes which Stanley and others were 'boring in the bottom
of the Church of England.' And it is certainly a wonderful
tribute to the strength of Pusey's character that, never
quailing beneath the blow of Newman's perversion, never
yielding to the opposition which looked so formidable when
his party was small and feeble and despised, unretarded
and unhurried, he should have steadily pursued his course
and raised that party to a foremost place in the Church.
One or two events of his life make it matter of thankful-
ness that its temporal power was not equal to its spiritual
fervour. He did all he could to maintain the Anglican
exclusiveness of the universities; and he would, if he
could, have used the civil power to suppress opinions he
deemed dangerous.

Pusey's writings are purely technical theology, not
literature like those of Newman. Of their value diverse
opinions will long be entertained. They are oracles to the
High Church party; but it is well to consider what
opponents think, especially such as have some grounds of
sympathy. Pius IX. compared Pusey to 'a bell, which
always sounds to invite the faithful to Church, and itself
always remains outside.' In a similar spirit another great
Romish ecclesiastic, when questioned as to Pusey's chance
of salvation, is said to have playfully replied, 'Oh, yes,

he will be saved *propter magnam implicationem.*' These are just the criticisms of those who have attacked the Puseyite position from the point of view of free thought. They are also the criticisms implied in Newman's action. It is at least remarkable that critics from both extreme parties, together with the ablest of all the men who have ever maintained the views in question, should concur in the same judgment.

Samuel Wilberforce, Bishop of Oxford, deserves a passing mention, though he was more remark-

Samuel Wilberforce (1805-1873).

able as a man of affairs than as a man of letters. He was of the High Church, but was opposed to the extreme Tractarians. He was still more opposed to the advanced Liberals. He wrote an article in the *Quarterly Review* against *Essays and Reviews,* he framed the indictment against Colenso, and he was one of the chief opponents of evolution before it had been discovered that evolution is all contained in Genesis. His most formal literary work is the allegorical tale of *Agathos;* but his wit and power of expression find their best outlet in the letters which give to his *Life* a zest rare in ecclesiastical biography.

There is no other theological sect as compact as the Oxford school, but there are two others of considerable importance and distinguished by fairly well-marked characteristics. Both are imbued with that German thought of which Newman was so unfortunately ignorant; and one of them especially had what he would have considered a deep taint of the hated 'liberalism.' John Frederick Denison

John Frederick Denison Maurice (1805-1872).

Maurice was the chief of the first section, while Kingsley, who was more of a novelist than a theologian, and perhaps F. W. Robertson, may be regarded as affiliated to it. Maurice went to Cambridge, but was prevented by the Unitarian faith he then held from proceeding to his degree, and ultimately he graduated at Oxford. He became Professor of English Literature and History at King's College, London, but fell into trouble because his views on eternal punishment were unsound. At a later date Cambridge honoured him and herself by appointing him Professor of Moral Philosophy.

Maurice's theology was always a little indefinite, but it seems best described by the word broad. His friendship for the remarkable Scotch theologian, Thomas Erskine, of Linlathen, who, though not a Calvinist, thanked heaven for his Calvinistic training, is significant on one side; his position as a disciple of Coleridge on another. Coleridge made Maurice more orthodox than he had previously been, but also preserved him from narrowness. Thanks to Coleridge, reason fills a greater space in Maurice than it does in the Tractarians. From Coleridge also Maurice derived some of the mysticism, if not mistiness, which characterised his thought. The want of clear outline is one of his chief defects. Though always suggestive, he is often somewhat elusive; and perhaps it is for this reason that his influence seems to dissipate itself without producing anything like the effect anticipated from it. The practical outcome of the school of Maurice is poor in comparison with that of the school of Pusey. This however was not wholly Maurice's fault. The Oxford school has drawn strength from what, nevertheless, may ultimately prove to be its weakness,—the appeal to authority, so tempting to many minds for the relief it promises. Maurice is not chargeable with this fault to the same degree. But neither is he entirely free from a kindred fault. He too, like Newman, argues to a foregone conclusion. In Mill's opinion, more intellectual power was wasted in Maurice than in any other of his contemporaries, and it was wasted because all Maurice's subtlety and power of generalisation served only 'for proving to his own mind that the Church of England had known everything from the first.'

The principal theological works of Maurice are *The Kingdom of Christ* (1838), *The Doctrine of Sacrifice* (1854), and *The Claims of the Bible and of Science* (1863). He wrote also a not very valuable treatise on *Moral and Metaphysical Philosophy* (1848-1862). And finally he wrote a number of tracts on Christian Socialism, of which he was the originator.

The Christian Socialists made a well-meant but not very wise attempt to raise the condition of the working classes. The name is unfortunate. If the party had thought a little more carefully they must have seen that if their socialism was economically sound there was nothing specially Christian about it; while, if it was not sound, neither it nor Christianity was benefited by the addition of the adjective. The Christian Socialists had no more thought out their principles than they had considered the name they chose, and for want of solid ground-work they failed. Nevertheless, Christian Socialism has left a mark on literature, in the works of Maurice himself, in the novels of Charles Kingsley, and to some extent in the writings of John Sterling, who was for a time of the school of Maurice.

Frederick William Robertson owes his position entirely to the celebrated sermons which he preached at Brighton during the last six years of his life. They are not great in scholarship, nor even in eloquence, but they exhibit a character of many-sided attractiveness which was the real secret of Robertson's power.

Frederick William Robertson (1816-1853).

The other section of theologians made a much firmer stand for freedom of thought than Maurice. Their leader in the earlier days of opposition to Tractarianism was Dr. Arnold of

Rugby. Some of them were his pupils, and all were influenced
by his spirit. In many cases however they came to hold very
different ground from his, and supposing him to have lived
and to have remained stable in his opinions, he might
have regarded his disciples with as much disquiet and fear
as he regarded the Tractarians. One of his pupils was
A. P. Stanley, who entered the Church and remained in it;
another was Clough, the story of whose doubts and unrest
is written in his poems; and the author of *Literature and
Dogma* was a third. Outside the circle of Arnold's pupils but
in general sympathy with them were Mark
Pattison, a quondam follower of Newman,
and Benjamin Jowett, the celebrated
Master of Balliol, whose most important
literary work, the translation of Plato,
comes after 1870, but whose struggle for
freedom of opinion and whose persecution in its cause belong to the period under consideration. Jowett was Regius
Professor of Greek, and the animosity of those who detested
his opinions took the contemptible shape of withholding a
reasonable salary. They mistook their man and their means.
Jowett was no money-lover; his enemies could not starve
him out; and the effect followed which experience proves
to attend persecution when it cannot be made crushingly
severe. He became the hero of the more liberal-minded,
and he moulded almost as he pleased the best intellects of
the most intellectual college of the university.

Both Jowett and Pattison were writers in the celebrated
volume entitled *Essays and Reviews* (1860). This was a
collection of seven papers on theological subjects, united
only by a common liberalism of view. Few books, in the
main so harmless, have caused such a commotion. The
volume is valuable chiefly as a landmark. Some of the
opinions would still be considered heterodox, but they would

Mark Pattison
(1813-1884).

Benjamin Jowett
(1817-1893).

be received now, if not with satisfaction, at least with calmness. At that time however people were sensitive on the point of orthodoxy. Darwin had just been promulgating an obnoxious doctrine, and it seemed hard that the faith, in danger from without, should be assailed also from within; for six of the seven essayists were clergymen. Legal proceedings were taken against two of them, but they only let off harmlessly humours which, if suppressed, might have been dangerous. It was with respect to the Gorham controversy, ten years earlier, that a Frenchman ' congratulated Stanley on the fact that the English revolution had taken the shape of " *le père* Gorham." ' The truth underlying this remark applies to other things besides the Gorham case.

In 1862 the excitement was renewed by the publication of Colenso's book on the Pentateuch. It seems arid now, for there is nothing attractive in the application of arithmetical formulas to Noah's Ark; but it was just the kind of argument needed for the time and for the audience addressed. It is commonly objected that criticisms of the Bible are a wanton unsettlement of the faith of simple folk. One striking fact will demonstrate the need of some liberalising work. In 1864 the Oxford Declaration on Inspiration and Eternal Punishment was signed by 11,000 clergy; and according to Bishop Tait, afterwards Archbishop of Canterbury, the effect of this declaration was that 'all questions of physical science should be referred to the written words of Holy Scripture.'

The society in which such a thing as this was possible stood in crying need of an intelligent philosophy. The matter was all the worse because this incident came after the great English school, dominant during the first three quarters of the century, had grown and flourished, and was on the point of decay. This was the school which in the early years of the century had for its prophet Jeremy Bentham, and as inferior lights James Mill and the economists. During the third decade we see the thinkers who were in sympathy with these men gradually grouping themselves round John Stuart Mill, whose family connexions, as well as his own ability, made him a centre of the school. He was the son of the hard, dry, but able and clear-headed Scotch philosopher and historian, James Mill, who, almost from his son's cradle, set about the task of fashioning him in his own image. In some respects James Mill's success was wonderful. 'I started,' says J. S. Mill, 'I may fairly say, with an advantage of a quarter of a century over my contemporaries.' But even he was aware of the concomitant defects of the system. A want of tenderness on the part of James Mill led to the educational error of neglecting the cultivation of feeling, and hence to 'an undervaluing of poetry, and of imagination generally, as an element of human nature.' There are indications all through the younger Mill's life as of a warm-hearted, affectionate nature struggling to burst the fetters linked around him by his early education; and there is a touch of irony in the fact that in an early mental crisis John Mill found relief in the 'healing influence' of Wordsworth.

John Stuart Mill (1806-1873).

Among those who frequented James Mill's house were Grote and the two Austins, John and Charles, the latter a man of almost unequalled reputation for brilliant talents, who contented himself with extraordinary pecuniary success at the bar, and early retired with a fortune. The elder brother, John Austin, was rather an independent thinker who adopted many of the same views, than a disciple of James Mill. He never achieved what was expected of him.

John Austin (1790-1859).

S. Mill says that his error was over-elaboration : he wore himself out before his work was accomplished through incapacity to satisfy himself.   His writings are nevertheless full of redundancies ; but he did a great deal towards forming a terminology for scientific jurisprudence.   His works, *The Province of Jurisprudence Determined* (1832), and *Lectures on Jurisprudence* (1863), are, like nearly all the writings of his school, deficient in human interest.

Partly stimulated by and partly stimulating these men, John Mill began to think for himself and to initiate movements.   It was he who in the winter of 1822-1823 founded the Utilitarian Society, the name of which was borrowed from Galt's *Annals of the Parish*.   A little later he was brought, through the agency of a debating society, into contact with a wider circle.   The battles were originally between the philosophic Radicals and the Tory lawyers ; but afterwards they were joined by those whom Mill describes as the Coleridgians, Maurice and Sterling.   It was under the attrition of these friendships and friendly discussions that Mill's mind was formed and polished after it passed from under the immediate control of his father.   His interest from the start centred in philosophy.   Before 1830 he had begun to write on logic, but his first important publication was the *System of Logic* (1843).   For some years he edited the *London Review*, afterwards entitled the *London and Westminster*.   His *Political Economy* appeared in 1848.   In 1851 he married a widow, Mrs. Taylor, to whom he ascribes a share in some of his works scarcely inferior to his own.   Her influence is especially strong in the essay *On Liberty* (1859), though this was not published until after her death.

About this time Mill took up the question of parliamentary reform, and in 1861 published his *Considerations on Representative Government*. Nearly contemporaneous in composition, though eight years later in publication, was the *Subjection of Women;* while *Utilitarianism* (1862) was the result of a revision of papers written towards the close of Mill's married life. *Auguste Comte and Positivism* (reprinted from *The Westminster Review*) and the *Examination of Sir William Hamilton's Philosophy* both appeared in 1865. There remain to mention only the *Autobiography* and a collection of essays, both posthumous. During these later years Mill's life was for a time more public than it had previously been. In 1865 the electors of Westminster asked him to be their representative, and he was elected without the ordinary incident of a canvass. In the election of 1868 however he was defeated, and the constituency never had an opportunity of redeeming its error.

Mill's writings may be grouped under the heads of philosophical, economic, and political. The highly interesting but depressing and melancholy *Autobiography* stands outside these classes. Perhaps it is his best composition from the point of view of literature; and certainly it is the most valuable document for a study of the growth of his school. The three divisions are not mutually exclusive, for, strictly speaking, the first would embrace the other two. In it an attempt is made to lay down general principles which are applied in them.

Mill's theory is contained in his *Logic*, his *Utilitarianism*, and his books on Comte and Hamilton. It has become known by the name he gave it as Utilitarianism; and as Bentham was the founder and first leader of the school, so was Mill the successor to his position and authority. It is a modern form of the theory associated with the name of the philosopher Epicurus; and on that ground it has been subjected to moral censure. Perhaps ultimately, as directed against the principle, the censure is sound; but it cannot be fairly turned against individuals. Certainly no thinkers of their time laboured more strenuously for the good of the community than Mill and Bentham. In Bentham's exposition, the philosophy crystallised itself in the often-quoted phrase, 'the greatest happiness of the greatest number.' His contribution consists in the introduction of the idea of the greatest number. Whether that idea is logically consistent with a philosophy of pleasure may be questioned; but it was to Bentham's addition that the maxim owed its power and its practical influence on legislation. It was moreover this consideration, in addition to the fact that he breathed Benthamite ideas from the cradle, that attracted Mill. For he was a typically English philosopher. He never of his own choice dwelt long on purely metaphysical problems, nor did he succeed well when he was forced to attempt them. His attitude towards Hume's theory of cause, after Kant's criticism of it, is vividly illustrative of his speculative limitations. If Oxford is the place where German philosophies go when they die, apparently London in Mill's time was the place where German philosophies did not go at all; and even dead German philosophies are better than the English predecessors which they slew in the day of their vigour.

As a Utilitarian, Mill was more valuable for exposition than for the original elements of his thought. In all his writings he is clear in expression and abundant in illustration. This abundance, in truth, appears to the reader not wholly ignorant of the subject to be cognate to verbosity. It was however part of the secret of Mill's great influence. He forced people to understand him. He talked round and round the subject, looked at it from every point of view and piled example upon example, until it was impossible to miss his meaning. When we add wide knowledge, patient study, keen intelligence and a considerable, if not exactly a great talent for original speculation, Mill's influence as a philosopher is explained. He wielded, from the publication of his *Logic* till his death, a greater power than any other English thinker, unless Sir William Hamilton is to be excepted for the earlier part of the period.

These characteristics, combined perhaps with a greater share of originality, appear in the *System of Logic* as well as in the Utilitarian treatises. Its merit is proved by the fact that through many years of adverse criticism it has maintained its ground at the universities as one of the most useful books on the subject. The freshest section is that which is devoted to Induction. The *Examination of Hamilton* shows Mill to have possessed the gift of acute and powerful criticism of philosophy. He may not have succeeded in establishing his own position, but he certainly damaged very seriously the rival system of Hamilton.

Mill's *Political Economy* is, like his general philosophy, lucid, full and thorough. Though cautious here, as always, in the admission of new principles, Mill made considerable contributions to economics. The theory of international exchanges is almost wholly his, and many particular turns and details of economic doctrine are due to him. In a still greater number of cases he has been, not the originator, but the best exponent of economic theory. The caution and judiciousness of his reasoning were qualities peculiarly valuable in this sphere; and where the views of 'orthodox' political economy are accepted at all, Mill's opinions are treated with respect.

The time when Mill's authority was at its height was also the time when political economy was held in greatest honour as a science. The writers on it were numerous;

and though, with the exception of Mill, they were not individually very distinguished, their collective work was important. They developed the doctrines of Adam Smith and Ricardo and Mill; while the speculations of Malthus acquired through Darwin a new importance, until a reaction, brought about more by sentiment than reason, led many to the conviction, or the faith, that they could not possibly be sound. The doctrine of *laissez faire,* so influential on government during the third quarter of the century, was the work partly of the economists and partly of the practical politicians of the Manchester school. It was never followed out logically, and before the close of the period there were signs of a movement which has since led to an opposite excess. Of the men who did this work Nassau W. Senior (1790-1864), in the earlier part of the period, and J. E. Cairnes (1823-1875) in the later deserve individual mention. The former was a great upholder of the deductive theory of political economy. The latter, in his treatise on *The Slave Power* (1862), produced one of the most noteworthy special studies in economics, and also one of the most powerful arguments in favour of the action of the Northern States of America.

It was the practical aspect of the science that chiefly interested Mill in economics. It was this still more, if possible, that inspired him in his more specifically political works, the treatises on *Liberty,* on the *Subjection of Women,* and on *Representative Government.* In his schemes of reform Mill was, in his own time, considered extreme; he would now be thought moderate. The caution of his speculation is nowhere more clearly marked than in his *Liberty.* It pleads certainly for more power to the state than the Manchester School would have granted; but it does so only in order to preserve the real freedom of the individual. In the *Subjection of Women* Mill was a pioneer on a road which has been well trodden since; and, for good or ill, there has been steady progress towards the triumph of his ideas. In *Representative Government* he shows a faith, probably excessive, in political machinery; but, whether it can do all Mill supposed or not, such machinery is necessary, and his labour tended to make it better.

Over against Mill, with some points of resemblance, but more of difference, may be set William Whewell, who, in 1841, became Master of Trinity College, Cambridge, and who acquired an immense reputation both for encyclopædic knowledge and for brilliant wit. On the human side he was certainly more attractive than Mill. Like the latter, he was fascinated by the great performances and the boundless promise of science; and he is one of those whose task it has been to formulate a philosophy of science. To this task he devoted himself more exclusively than Mill, and he brought to it a greater knowledge of scientific processes and discoveries. Moreover, his point of view was different. Mill was a pure empiricist. Whewell held that empiricism alone could not explain even itself; and he therefore taught that there was necessary truth as well as empirical truth. This was at once the starting point of his controversy with Mill and the ground-work of his writings, the *History of the Inductive Sciences* (1837) and the *Philosophy of the Inductive Sciences* (1840). He is best known by his *Novum Organum Renovatum*, which was originally a portion of the second work.

Whewell's strong point is his great knowledge of the history of science. His inductive theory is somewhat loose. It amounts to no more than a succession of tests of hypotheses; and of these tests the most stringent, prediction and consilience of inductions, are open to the fatal objection

William Whewell (1794-1866).

that they are not and cannot be applied to all inductions. Mill's inductive methods also are more stringent in appearance than they prove to be in reality; but they at least point to an ideal towards which it is always possible to strive.

Of a widely different school of thought was Sir William Hamilton, Professor of Logic and Metaphysics in Edinburgh from 1836 to his death. Hamilton was a man of vast reading, and though it has been questioned whether his learning was as exact and profound as it appeared to be, there can hardly be a doubt that it was great enough to hamper the free play of his thought, and that it explains two of his characteristic faults. One is the excessive technicality of his diction. His style, otherwise clear and good, is overloaded with words specially coined for the purposes of the logician and metaphysician. The second fault is his inability to resist the temptation of calling a 'cloud of witnesses,' without making any serious attempt to weigh their evidence. Hamilton was a disciple of the Scottish school of philosophy, and a great part of his life was devoted to an elucidation of Reid, of whose works he published an elaborate edition in 1853. But Reid's principle of Common Sense, as an answer to the philosophic scepticism of Hume, is little better than an evasion; and Hamilton had not much to add to it. Besides the edition of Reid Hamilton published *Discussions on Philosophy and Literature* (1852); and after his death there appeared the *Lectures on Metaphysics and Logic* (1859-1861), by which he is best known.

Sir William Hamilton (1788-1856).

James Frederick Ferrier (1808-1864).   Hamilton had a great and not altogether a wholesome influence on James Frederick Ferrier, who in the domain of purely metaphysical thought was probably the most gifted

M

man of his time. Ferrier describes his own philosophy
as Scotch to the core. There is in it, nevertheless, a
considerable tincture from the German, and Ferrier deserves the credit of being one of the earliest professional
philosophers who really grappled with German thought.
He was also the master of a very clear and attractive
style, which makes the reading of his philosophy a pleasure
rather than a toil.

Henry Longueville Mansel, a pupil of Hamilton's, and
joint editor of his lectures along with
John Veitch, afterwards Professor of
Logic in Glasgow University, was the
ablest exponent of the Hamiltonian
philosophy in England. Mansel's power of acute and
lucid reasoning was shown in his *Prolegomena Logica* (1851),
and afterwards in his *Philosophy of the Conditioned* (1866).
Both were developments of Hamilton's principles, and they
have suffered from the general discredit of the Hamiltonian school. Mansel is better known now, by name
at least, on account of his *Limits of Religious Thought*,
(constituting the Bampton lectures for 1858), which was the
occasion of a controversy between him and Maurice.

Henry Longueville
Mansel
(1820-1871).

The other philosophical writers of the period were, with
one exception, of minor importance.
Harriet Martineau was a woman of
varied activity. She wrote political
economy, history and fiction; and her story, *Deerbrook*
(1839), is among the best and freshest of her works. She is
however most memorable, not as an original thinker, but
as a translator and expounder. She translated and condensed the philosophy of Comte, and did as much as anyone to make it known in England. She had the great
merits of unshrinking courage, perfect sincerity and un-
doubting loyalty to truth.

Harriet Martineau
(1802-1876).

Another miscellaneous writer of the Comtist school was
George Henry Lewes, who has been elsewhere
mentioned in connexion with George Eliot.
He was an active-minded, energetic man,
whose life touches literature at many points.
He too wrote novels, but they did not succeed. He
was a critic of no mean power. He took great interest
in and possessed considerable knowledge of science, and in
1859-1860 published a popular scientific work, *The Physi-
ology of Common Life*. But his best known book is the
Life of Goethe (1855). It is an able biography and pleasant
to read, though perhaps, considering the calibre of the
subject, rather lacking in weight. It is however no small
compliment to Lewes's work that it was for many years
accepted, both in Germany and in England, as the standard
biography of Goethe. Lewes's principal contributions to
philosophy were *A Biographical History of Philosophy* (1845-
1846), *Comte's Philosophy of the Sciences* (1853), and *Problems of Life and Mind* (1873-1879). In all of them Lewes
shows himself an unswerving Positivist. He accepts and
reiterates his master's doctrine that the day of metaphysics
is past, so that his philosophy is, in a sense, the negation
of philosophy.

George Henry
Lewes
(1817-1878).

In the sphere of political science, the man next in power
to Mill was Sir George Cornewall Lewis.
As Chancellor of the Exchequer in the
first administration of Lord Palmerston,
Lewis had the opportunity of making a
practical acquaintance with his subject; but his theories
were formed earlier. Extensive knowledge, combined with
clearness of intellect and independence of judgment, gives
value to his work. His *Inquiry into the Credibility of
Early Roman History* (1855) was remarkable for its attack
upon the theories of Niebuhr, which were in those days

Sir George
Cornewall Lewis
(1806-1863).

accepted with an almost superstitious reverence. But previous to this Lewis had written his most important book, *The Influence of Authority in Matters of Opinion* (1849), a well reasoned and well written argument, worthy of attention in these days when there seems to be a disposition to forget the limits beyond which the influence is illegitimate. Lewis teaches the wisdom and even the necessity of submitting to 'authority' where we cannot investigate for ourselves, and where all who are competent to form an opinion are agreed; but he is careful not to set up any absolute and indefeasible authority which might dictate to reason and against reason.

Towards the close of the period there are noticeable traces of a new school superseding both Utilitarianism and Positivism. This school, nourished upon German idealism, had its centre at Oxford, and the men who have done the principal work in it were pupils of Jowett. They belong however to the later period and come within our present scope only as an indication of tendency.

The root of thought in all these men is the idea of development, the great formative idea of the present century. This idea however had an English as well as a German growth. In England it is best known through Darwin. But while Darwin shows its scientific side, the most celebrated of recent English philosophers, Mr. Herbert Spencer (1820), makes it the basis of a philosophy. *The Synthetic Philosophy*, just completed, is distinguished for the vastness of its design, the accomplishment of which gives Mr. Spencer a place among the few encyclopædic thinkers of the world. His philosophy is interesting also because it concentrates and reflects the spirit of the time. No other thinker has so strenuously laboured to gather together all the accumulations of modern knowledge and

Herbert Spencer (1820-1903).

to unite them under general conceptions. The alliance between the Spencerian philosophy and physical science is unusually close; and Mr. Spencer in his illustrations shows an all-embracing range of knowledge, which becomes minute in those branches of science bearing directly upon the phenomena of life. The future only can determine the exact value of this knowledge, for there are grave differences of opinion between Mr. Spencer and some of the leading biologists, like Weismann; but it may at least be said of him that he is the first philosopher since Bacon ('who wrote on science like a Lord Chancellor'), or at latest Leibnitz, who has met men of science on something like equal terms within the domain of science. Mr. Spencer's unique interest is that he has attempted an exhaustive survey of all the facts relating to the development of life and of society. He does not go beyond that, to the origin of all things; for it is one of his cardinal principles that behind the Knowable there is dimly visible a something not only unknown but unknowable. We are compelled to regard every phenomenon as the manifestation of an infinite and incomprehensible Power. In this the philosopher finds the reconciliation of religion with science; a reconciliation for which the religious have seldom shown much gratitude, because they are forbidden to say anything specific about the Power whose existence they may, and indeed must, assume. On this point there is a quarrel between Mr. Spencer and the metaphysicians, who dispute the right of any man to assert the existence of an Unknowable. If we can assert its existence surely we know it at least in part; and if so may we not by investigation come to know it better?

The Spencerian philosophy is the most comprehensive and ambitious application of the principle of evolution ever attempted. Without showing anywhere that mastery of detail and that power of marshalling facts in evidence which give Darwin's great work its unequalled significance, the *Synthetic Philosophy* yet reaches at both ends beyond the limits Darwin set himself. Mr. Spencer begins by recognising three kinds of evolution, in the spheres of the inorganic, the organic and the super-organic; and all the parts of the *Synthetic Philosophy* find a place under one or other of these; but the treatment of the first part is omitted as less pressing and as adding too greatly to the magnitude of the scheme. After the *First Principles*, in which are laid down the limits of the knowable and the unknowable, there follows therefore the *Principles of Biology* (1864-1867), where the evolution of life, the gradual differentiation of functions and kindred topics are treated. Still within the sphere of the evolution of the organic we have next the *Principles of Psychology* (1855), where organisms exhibiting the phenomena of mind are examined from various points of view to determine so far as possible the nature of mind, its relations with the universe, the composition of its simpler elements, etc. From psychology we step to super-organic evolution in the *Principles of Sociology* (1876-1896), which is probably regarded by the majority as the most characteristic part of the Spencerian philosophy. It is certainly one of the most interesting; for it combines in an unusual measure the best results of ancient thought with full justice to modern individualism. Mr. Spencer is a consistent individualist, but a far-sighted one. He sees that 'the survival of the fittest,' and with it progress, are impossible unless 'the fittest' both wins and keeps advantage to himself. Unlimited altruism would be as bad as unlimited egoism, and would indeed foster egoism, for it would in the end mean the stripping of generosity to pamper greed. On the other hand, pure egoism is fatal to society; and the animal for whom gregariousness is an advantage must fail in the struggle if he is unfaithful to the social principle. Hence there arises a society which is a balance between the two principles. It demands sacrifices from the individual in return for benefits; but the law of its existence prohibits the extension of this demand beyond the point where the individual 'fittest' survives and prospers. If the demand goes beyond this the course is downwards; for, as society is composed of individuals, a society in which the strongest has no advantage is a society in which progress is impossible, but, on the contrary, deterioration is sooner or later certain. There is no room on Spencerian principles for any socialism which does not recognise difference of reward according to difference of capacity.

In the *Principles of Ethics* (1892-1893) Mr. Spencer attempts to apply the results reached in the earlier parts of his scheme to the enunciation of a theory of right living. It is here that an evolutionary system based upon science is felt to be least convincing. There is a gulf never satisfactorily bridged between ethical principles as gradually evolved out of the non-moral state, and the 'moral imperative' as it is felt by the human conscience. Hence, the man of religion insists, the necessity of being specific about that vague Power dimly seen behind the philosophy of evolution; and hence the necessity, in the view of the metaphysician, of regarding evolution from above as well as from below. We learn much by tracing things to their origin; but to learn all we must consider as well what they ultimately become. It is in fact the final form that gives importance to the question of origin. The temptation of evolution is certainly to underrate the significance of the later stages; and the higher we go the greater are the effects of such an error.

But whatever its faults the *Synthetic Philosophy* remains unequalled in the present age for boldness of con-

ception and for the solidity derived from its league with
science. No other philosophy is so eminently modern
in spirit and method; and whatever modifications may
prove to be required, thought at once so daring and
so patient can never be ignored.

CHAPTER VIII.

SCIENCE.

THE achievements of science as a rule hardly come within the purview of the critic of literature, for language is commonly used by science for a purpose other than that of literary expression, and even when science is popularised by writers like Mary Somerville the result is apt to be something not very valuable for its substance nor yet for its style. Nevertheless, all science may indirectly, and some of it does directly, influence literature. In point of fact, this influence has been one of the great features of the present century. We see it on the one hand as a force of attraction, on the other as a force of repulsion; for while some have been fired with the hope of human progress, others have been chilled by the fear of its materialising tendency. Both classes have been prone to exaggerate the mere mechanical results of science and to forget that its true aim is knowledge, not machines. It is however in the sphere of ideas that we must look for its effect upon literature. Whether we travel by railways or by stage-coaches, whether we transmit our messages by letter or by telegraph, matters little; but it matters much whether we are hopeful or despondent, whether we feel that there is no new thing under the sun, or are inspired by ideas that seem to open new worlds to our intellect. We must ask then, in the first place, what is the effect of science on the spirit of men and their view of life; and in the second place, what are the scientific ideas which directly and in themselves influence popular thought and colour literature.

It is obvious that there are certain departments of science which from their very nature can have little or no direct influence. The mathematical researches of men like Sir William Rowan Hamilton are far too technical, too difficult and too abstruse for popular apprehension. They remain a mere name, and not even their general import is understood. The same remark applies to the mathematical work of Augustus de Morgan, who, by the way, gave valuable hints for Hamilton's great work on quaternions. But De Morgan was a logician as well, and the author of the *Budget of Paradoxes* is worthy of remembrance in literature. In physics the case is somewhat different. The processes by which physicists like Joule and Faraday attain their results remain mysterious, but the general character of the results becomes known, their great importance is obvious, and they generate a confidence in the powers of man which in the present day goes far towards counteracting tendencies to pessimism.

There are however certain sciences whose influence upon life and thought is direct, because their results bear upon man's own position in the universe. Astronomy, through its relation to the Mosaic cosmogony, belongs to this class; but its force had been felt long before the opening of the period. It is especially the sciences of geology and biology that have changed men's minds, and it is they that have produced the most books which, apart from the scientific value of their contents, might claim to rank as literature.

Geology was at the opening of the period practically a new science. What had previously been done in it was trifling compared with what has been accomplished since.

and its bearing upon questions of universal interest was not even suspected by the multitude. Darwin in his brief autobiography relates an anecdote illustrative of the primitive state of the science in his youth. 'I,' says he, 'though now only sixty-seven years old, heard the Professor [of Geology in Edinburgh], in a field lecture at Salisbury Crags, discoursing on a trap-dyke, with amygdaloidal margins and the strata indurated on each side, with volcanic rocks all around us, say that it was a fissure filled with sediment from above, adding with a sneer that there were men who maintained that it had been injected from beneath in a molten condition.' Even more striking than any aberration of an individual is the general fact that the prevailing theory at that time in geology was the 'catastrophic,' and a science with an unlimited command of catastrophes is no more scientific in spirit than a theology with an unlimited command of miracles.

The first need of a science in this state is the accumulation of facts, and most of the older geologists of the time, like Sedgwick, Murchison and Buckland, bent themselves to this task. But the man who dealt the death-blow to the old uncritical view of geology was Sir Charles Lyell, whose *Principles of Geology* (1830-1833) marks an epoch in the science. Lyell's central doctrine is that the past history of the earth must be inferred by ordinary processes of observation and reasoning from the present, and that it is possible to interpret 'the testimony of the rocks' by means of principles which we still see at work. In other words, he was a 'uniformitarian.' The victory of his view established 'the reign of law' over the field of geology, and went far towards convincing men of its universality. Assuming no causes except such as he could point to in experience, Lyell showed how the geological

Sir Charles Lyell (1797-1875).

formations of the earth arose. According to Darwin, the effect of Lyell's work could formerly be seen in the much more rapid progress of geology in England than in France; and the *Principles of Geology* was most helpful to Darwin himself.

In his *Antiquity of Man* (1863) Lyell touched the verge of the problem of organic life. He did so in a spirit of open-minded conservatism. He had now to guide him the great light of the *Origin of Species*, and even before its publication he had had glimmerings of evolution. He saw that Darwin only extended to the animal and vegetable world his own central principle. But he felt a deep objection to tracing the descent of man through some ape-like creature, and hence, while *The Antiquity of Man* recognises the long history of the race upon earth, it contains no avowal of belief in his descent from inferior forms of life.

Another geologist, who was rather a popular expositor than a profound man of science, was Hugh Miller. Miller was bred as a mason, and it was in the quarries where he pursued his trade (quarrying being in his time and district associated with stone-cutting) that he laid the foundation of his geological knowledge. But Miller was more than a geologist. He threw himself energetically into the contest which culminated in the Scottish Disruption of 1843; and for the last sixteen years of his life he was editor of the bi-weekly paper, *The Witness*, which had been established by the leaders of the Free Church movement as the organ of their opinions. The sad close of Miller's life by suicide is well known. His health had been undermined by early hardships and by subsequent overwork, and an examination after death proved that the brain was diseased.

Hugh Miller (1802-1856).

A great deal of Miller's work was done for *The Witness*.

He was a most conscientious as well as a most able journalist, and he brought to his occupation a rare literary power. There was an imaginative and poetic strain in his nature which sometimes showed itself in the weaker form of fine writing, but often gave eloquence to his descriptions and fervour to his argument. This is the living part of him; for it is certainly not their scientific value that causes Hugh Miller's books to be still read.

Miller's most important works are *The Old Red Sandstone* (1841), *Footprints of the Creator* (1847), *My Schools and Schoolmasters* (1854), and *The Testimony of the Rocks* (1857). In their geological aspect they merely supply the raw material of science. Miller had not the previous training requisite to give his work the highest value. He knew little or nothing about comparative anatomy, and therefore could not himself deal with the fossils he discovered. In the view of modern experts his scientific value lies in his strong common sense and his keen powers of observation amounting almost to genius. His function is to stimulate others rather than to sway thought by great discoveries. A liberal in politics, he was something of a conservative in science. *The Footprints of the Creator* was written in answer to the *Vestiges of Creation*, and its author figures as one of the numerous reconcilers of the text of Genesis with the discoveries of geology. His value in literature is higher than in science, for he wrote a style always pleasant, and sometimes eloquent. *My Schools and Schoolmasters*, a volume of autobiography, is one of the best of its class in the language, and is the work by which Miller will be longest remembered.

Related to geology, and even more influential upon modern thought, has been the theory of biological evolution, represented within the present period by Robert

Chambers, Charles Darwin and Alfred Russel Wallace. Thomas Huxley too, though so much of his work is of a later date, demands mention for his long polemic on behalf of evolution, begun immediately after the publication of *The Origin of Species* and continued till his death. The work of Sir Richard Owen the great anatomist had an important bearing upon this theory, but he was neither a Darwinian nor are his scientific writings literature.

Robert Chambers stands by himself. He was of the best class of self-made men, and as a publisher perhaps even more than as a writer did service to literature. He had great talent for not only acquiring information but making it popular. His most remarkable book, the *Vestiges of the Natural History of Creation* (1844), was published anonymously, and, in fear of the outcry of orthodoxy, extraordinary precautions were taken to guard the secret of the authorship. For a long time the efforts were successful, and, though the secret gradually became an open one, it was not till 1884 that his responsibility for the book was authoritatively avowed. The *Vestiges of Creation* has been unduly depreciated since the time of Darwin. The gaps in the argument, and still more perhaps the untenable assumptions and mistaken assertions, are easy to detect now; but it is at least ungracious to insist upon them. Chambers was not an accomplished naturalist; on the contrary, Huxley charges him with 'prodigious ignorance.' He had not laboured as long, as patiently or as strenuously at the subject as Darwin; but at the same time his book is in an uncommon degree bold and suggestive. The best minds were already dallying with the idea of evolution, but in 1844 there nowhere existed in English such a concrete and clear presentation of it as Chambers gave.

Robert Chambers
(1802-1871).

Judged in relation to what was known and thought then, his work was a memorable, though, from lack of a sufficiently firm foundation, hardly a great one.

Charles Robert Darwin is the true father of evolution as applied in modern science, and of all the men of science of the century he most demands and deserves attention in connexion with literature. No recent doctrine, either in science or philosophy, has produced anything comparable to the revolution in thought caused by *The Origin of Species*. Its central ideas have been applied not merely in the department of biology, but everywhere in the world of thought,—in philosophy, in religion, in literature and literary criticism. We cannot refer all this to Darwin alone, for the conception of evolution can be traced for two thousand years or more; but it was Darwin who first planted it firmly in the human mind, and consequently he is the chief though not the sole cause of the revolution. Another element of his greatness, important in a criticism of literature, is that his works are themselves literature. Writing a perfectly plain style, he yet succeeds in so expressing his meaning that the manner is no inconsiderable part of his charm. Some of the less compressed works, like the *Naturalist's Voyage round the World* and the monograph on earthworms, are as fascinating and as difficult to relinquish as a skilful story of adventure; and if this cannot be said of *The Origin of Species* itself, the reason is that it is so packed with thought that the reader is compelled to pause over it.

Charles Robert Darwin (1809-1882).

Darwin, the son of a physician, was originally destined to follow his father's profession, and went to study in Edinburgh; but he liked neither the teaching nor the profession. In 1828 he went to Cambridge, and though he derived no great benefit from the regular studies of the place, the connexions he formed influenced the course of his life. He began the study of geology under Sedgwick, and he was on very intimate terms with Professor Henslow, through whom he became naturalist of the 'Beagle.' The voyage of this ship laid the foundations of his fame but permanently injured his health. In 1839 Darwin married, and in 1842 he settled at Down in Kent, where he lived an exceptionally retired and quiet life, compulsorily sequestered from society because of his health.

Darwin's literary life had begun before this. In 1839 his *Journal of Researches* (better known as *A Naturalist's Voyage round the World*) was printed as part of the narrative of the voyage of the 'Beagle,' and in 1845 a second edition was called for. It is full to overflowing of the results of observation set down in a delightfully easy narrative style. Darwin was not yet an evolutionist, though the materials are there out of which the evolutionist grew, and occasional remarks indicate that the subject was not foreign to his mind. *The Structure and Distribution of Coral Reefs* (1842) was another product of this memorable voyage. The theory maintained is that the reefs are the result of gradual subsidence, and form the last relics of submerged continents. Geologists were impressed by the boldness and originality of the speculation and by the great mass of facts with which, in Darwin's invariable way, it was supported. This was followed by two other publications on volcanic islands, and on the geology of South America. These writings won for Darwin a high position among men of science ; but it was not until the appearance of the second edition of the *Naturalist's Voyage* that he became widely known.

The highly characteristic and instructive story of the incubation and writing of *The Origin of Species* has been told by Darwin himself. He had been long haunted by the idea of a possible modification of species; and shortly after his return in the 'Beagle' he began to collect all facts bearing on the variation of animals and plants. His first note-book was opened in July, 1837. He read widely, conversed with breeders and gardeners, and addressed printed enquiries to such as seemed likely to give him information. He was led to the conclusion that 'selection was the keystone of man's success in making useful races of animals and plants;' but he could not understand how selection could be applied in a state of nature. The reading for amusement of Malthus on *Population* gave him the clue. In the fierce competition for life among animals and plants, favourable variations would tend to be preserved, and unfavourable ones to be destroyed. He read Malthus in October, 1838. But, to avoid prejudice, for three years and a half, till June, 1842, he refrained from writing even the briefest sketch of his theory. In 1844 the first sketch was enlarged. In 1856 he began to write out his views on a scale much more extensive than that finally adopted; and yet, even so, it was only an abstract of the materials collected. In 1858 Mr. Wallace, then in the Malay Archipelago, sent Darwin an essay which proved to contain exactly his own theory. On the advice of Lyell and the great botanist Hooker an abstract from Darwin's manuscript was published in 1858, simultaneously with Mr. Wallace's essay. The concurrence of ideas between Mr. Wallace and himself set Darwin vigorously to work. He undertook once more to make an abstract of the manuscript begun in 1856, and in 1859 published the celebrated *Origin of Species*.

The book owes much of its effect to this process of gradual expansion and gradual contraction. The reader is struck with three things in it: first, the great range, combined with sobriety, of speculation; secondly, the wonderful mastery of detail; and thirdly, the beautiful balance and proportion, the sufficiency without undue length of the arguments. Hardly any other pioneer in untravelled realms of thought has left such an impression of wholeness.[1] Neither could Darwin have done so without the long preliminary training. The *Origin* bears on almost every page the marks that it too is a product of selection. Darwin sifts his mass of examples and chooses those best suited for his purpose. The completeness of the book moreover is largely owing to the fact, noted by Darwin himself, that for many years he had made a memorandum, at the moment, of every fact, observation or thought *opposed* to his results; because he had found that such facts and thoughts were more apt to be forgotten than favourable ones. 'Owing to this habit,' he says, with truth, 'very few objections were raised against my views which I had not at least noticed and attempted to answer.'

No book of this century has roused such a tempest as *The Origin of Species*. A number of the younger men of science hailed the theory with eagerness, and one or two of the older were extremely friendly; but many were startled and were unprepared to accept views so novel. Still more, the exponents of orthodox religion were wild against the theory; and in the British Association meeting in 1860, at Oxford, Bishop Wilberforce, by an unmannerly attack, drew down upon himself a crushing rebuke from Huxley. Gradually a calmer temper prevailed, and the problems were discussed fairly on both sides, as questions of science, not matters of faith to be determined by an appeal to Genesis.

The time has not yet come for a final verdict upon *The*

[1] One early criticism was that the book was suspiciously *teres atque rotundus*.

Origin of Species; but even if Darwin's theory should in the end prove to need great modification, his book will still be one of first-rate importance. It has proved itself already the most stimulating book of the century. Those who oppose Darwin oppose him now with his own weapons: they are evolutionists, though they think some other scheme of evolution the true one. The change is vast from the almost universally prevalent belief in special acts of creation and fixed types to a belief, nearly as widespread, in the gradual development of all the variety of life from at most a few primordial forms. And this result has been, more than almost any result equally great, the work of one man.

This great book was followed by some of those special studies which Darwin had the gift of making almost as interesting as his discussions of central principles. This is partly because he makes all his work illustrative of those principles. No one was ever more steadfastly guided by a single idea; and hence his works have an unusually intimate connexion with one another. Thus, *The Fertilisation of Orchids* (1862) is a detailed study of a subject which occupies one or two paragraphs in the *Origin*. In *The Movements and Habits of Climbing Plants* (1865) Darwin broke new ground; for it was after the publication of *The Origin of Species* that he was led to notice these phenomena. The new material however served the purpose of the theory, and the author was 'pleased to find what a capital guide for observations a full conviction of the change of species is.' The book on climbing plants was the outcome of observations carried on in broken health. 'All this work about climbers,' says Darwin, 'would hurt my conscience, did I think I could do harder work.' In *The Variation of Animals and Plants under Domestication* (1868), on the other hand he was reverting to that department of investigation in which he had first seen clear light on the question of species. The most debated point in this book is the celebrated speculation of Pangenesis. Darwin advanced it, not as something proved, but because ' it is a relief to have some feasible explanation of the facts, which can be given up as soon as any better hypothesis is formed.' It throws light however on the essentially speculative character of his intellect to find that this admittedly doubtful hypothesis of Pangenesis is the part of the book on which he looks with the greatest affection,—' my beloved child,' as he phrases it.

The Descent of Man (1871) ranks next in wide importance to *The Origin of Species*. It is the application in detail of the same principles to the human race. That the application was inevitable was already evident in the earlier book; and it was this that brought upon the *Origin* the most virulent abuse. Just because it is so inevitable, *The Descent of Man* has not the unique interest of *The Origin of Species*. Once we are familiar with the view that all the species of animals have been produced by the accumulation of minute variations, there is no surprise in the idea that man and all his powers may have been so produced likewise. Nevertheless, Darwin differs on this point from the man who shares with him the honour of discovering the theory of evolution. Mr. Wallace, while arguing with Darwin that man has been evolved out of some lower form, holds that ' natural selection could only have endowed the savage with a brain a little superior to that of an ape,' and that in the higher human faculties there is evidence of the working of a supernatural power. The position is a strange one. If the whole creation moves harmoniously through all its grades by the action of one law, it will need overwhelming evidence to show that just at the end this law is superseded by another altogether unlike it. Either the supernatural governs the whole of life, or its introduction to explain one stage is gratuitous.

After *The Descent of Man* came *The Expression of the Emotions in Man and Animals* (1872) ; and that again was followed by *Insectivorous Plants* (1875). The former was originally intended merely to form a chapter in the *Descent;* but the materials grew, and the result is one of the most readable of books. The *Insectivorous Plants* embodies one of the most remarkable of Darwin's discoveries. Its richness is due to the patience and skill with which the facts were accumulated. Sixteen years passed between the time when Darwin first noticed that plants lived on insects and the appearance of the book. In the interval he had done many things ; but, whenever he had leisure, he was always adding to his store of facts relating to this class of plants ; and, as he justly says, 'a man after a long interval can criticise his own work, almost as well as if it were that of another person.'

Later, Darwin wrote on the fertilisation of plants, in order to demonstrate the importance of cross-fertilisation ; on the forms of flowers ; and on the movements of plants, —the last a kind of extension and generalisation of the book on climbing plants, endeavouring to co-ordinate all the movements of plants as variations of an inherent tendency of the parts to a revolving motion. The theory has not been accepted by botanists. Last of all, in 1881, appeared the monograph on *The Formation of Vegetable Mould through the Action of Worms.* This book is just the expansion and completion of a paper read by Darwin to a scientific society as far back as 1837. All that time the subject dwelt in his mind; and when at last leisure permitted, he developed it into what is perhaps the most purely delightful of all his books. In greatness it does not come into competition with some of them at all ; but the familiarity of the phenomena, the care with which they are examined, the skill of the arrangement and the charm of finding meaning in what had been so meaningless, have made the volume one of the most widely read of all Darwin's works.

That which distinguishes Darwin from other naturalists is the combination of extraordinary speculative power with great knowledge of detail and unlimited patience. These qualities have been combined in others as well, but never, within the field of natural history, in the same degree. More commonly they are found separate. The ordinary type of naturalist is the man who knows an immense number of facts about plants and animals, and who rests content with that knowledge. He may be master of everything about the great subject of scarabees, but it scarcely occurs to him to *explain* the scarabees themselves, still less to use them in explaining other creatures. On the other hand, the opposite type, the type which speculates only without first laying the foundation of fact, is likewise common enough. How ineffectual this is may be seen from the history of earlier speculations on evolution. The *Vestiges of Creation* and the theory of Lamarck are superseded, not so much because of deficiency in speculative power, as because the theories are not sufficiently buttressed by facts Even though Darwin's own theory should ultimately be, in one sense, as dead as that of Chambers, it will always remain one of the landmarks of thought.

Undoubtedly Darwin's intellect was fundamentally speculative. We have seen how in the book on *Variation under Domestication* his affection clung to Pangenesis, perhaps the most questionable part of its contents. He was restless under the sense of an unexplained fact, and thankful for even a provisional explanation. He notes the effect upon him of the discovery that science cannot remain content with facts alone. Geologising with Sedgwick in North Wales, he heard about a tropical shell which had been picked up in a neighbouring quarry. ' I told Sedgwick of the fact, and he at once said (no doubt truly) that it must have been thrown away by some one into the pit ; but then added, if really embedded there it would be the greatest misfortune to geology, as it would overthrow all that we know about the superficial deposits of the Midland Counties. . . . I was then utterly astonished at Sedgwick not being delighted at so wonderful a fact as a tropical shell being found near the surface in the middle of England. Nothing before had ever made me thoroughly realise, though I had read various scientific books, that science consists in grouping facts so that general laws or conclusions can be drawn from them.' It is this conception that he kept steadily before his eyes, and his glory lies in his success in drawing general laws from his facts.

The work of the other evolutionists, so far as it is not technical rather than literary, is almost accounted for when Darwin's is described. With respect to one indeed, Mr. Alfred Russel Wallace, an inevitable injustice is done whatever course be pursued. He is the co-discoverer with Darwin of the scheme of evolution associated with the name of the latter; and though the fame has gone to the elder man, it seems clear that if not Darwin then Mr. Wallace was destined to stir the mind of the age with this great conception. Mr. Wallace has been an extensive traveller ; he published, in 1853, a volume of *Travels on the Amazon*, giving an account of journeys in that region during part of which he was the companion of Mr. Henry Walter Bates, whose *Naturalist on the Amazon* (1863) is well known as one of the most interesting and

Alfred Russel
Wallace
(1822).

valuable books of travel and natural history in the language. It was however his observations in the Malay Archipelago that led Mr. Wallace to the theory of evolution, and perhaps he is best known by his book, *The Malay Archipelago* (1869).

CHAPTER IX.

CRITICISM, SCHOLARSHIP, AND MISCELLANEOUS PROSE.

IT was a maxim of Matthew Arnold's that the main effort of the mind of Europe in our time was a critical one. By this he meant something more than merely literary criticism; but he certainly included that. All will agree with him that one of the characteristics of recent times is the desire to understand the meaning and the historical order of the forms of literature. The great development of journalism has done much to foster critical work; for a critical view of individual men or of isolated works can be conveniently expressed within the compass permitted by the periodical form of publication. The quality of this periodical criticism is uneven. Much of it is worthless, but the fact that the best critics of the present century—Lamb, Carlyle, Macaulay, Lockhart, Ruskin and Matthew Arnold—have all written for periodicals, is proof sufficient that the best as well as the worst is to be found there.

One of the features of this journalistic criticism is its anonymity, and this doubtless encouraged the ferocity characteristic of the early school of the *Edinburgh*, the *Quarterly* and *Blackwood*. But the evil seems to have worked its own cure. It would be rash to assert that there is not incompetence and unfairness still; but at least the bludgeon school of criticism has passed away. The

cause is twofold : the fixing of an ethical standard, and
the discovery, which Matthew Arnold did much both by
precept and example to spread, that the rapier is the more
deadly weapon.   The critics of the early periodicals had
no tradition to guide them, and, like settlers in a new
country, they ran riot.

A good deal of uncertainty necessarily attaches to
anonymous writing, and all that is possible here is to
notice shortly a few of the more eminent names, avoiding
any minute discussion.   Some, like Carlyle, Macaulay and
Lockhart, have been mentioned elsewhere.   It was however under their influence, and under the gradually growing
influence of Lamb, Coleridge and Hazlitt, that the criticism
of this period grew up.   There has also to be taken into
account the spread of German thought, which gave to
criticism greater breath and a firmer foundation in principle, and conduced likewise to a more careful and patient
scholarship.   The Germans have not only themselves done
a great work in Shakespearian criticism, but they have
induced the English to do the same.   Still, an exclusive
following of the Germans would have led to mischief, and
fortunately for English criticism this tendency has been
corrected by the opposite influence of the French school.
Thanks largely to Matthew Arnold, and to the charm of
Ste. Beuve, whom he helped to make known in England,
the lucidity, good form and sanity of French criticism have
had their effect as well as the laborious learning and sometimes rash theorising of the Germans.

Shakespearian criticism might almost be said to be in
its infancy when the period opened.
John Payne Collier   The highest reputation was speedily
(1789-1883).   acquired by John Payne Collier, whose
History of English Dramatic Poetry (1831) was a really
valuable contribution to the study of the drama.   A later

work of Collier's however brought dishonour on his name, and threw doubt upon all his conclusions unless they could be proved from other authorities. His *Notes and Emendations to the Plays of Shakespeare* (1853) professed to give all the 'essential' readings of the Perkins Folio; but when the mystery which for a time hung over this folio was penetrated, it proved that the emendations in question were forgeries. Unfortunately these 'emendations' do not stand alone. Nearly all through Collier's work is tainted with falsehood. He attempted to vitiate the old ballads as well as Shakespeare, and perhaps even now his evil influence in retarding the progress of sound scholarship is not wholly annulled. Mrs. Anna Jameson was a better writer than Collier, and she enjoys an unclouded reputation. Her *Characteristics of Shakespeare's Women* (1832) still holds its ground as a fine example of the critical analysis of character. She wrote other books afterwards— *Sacred and Legendary Art, Legends of the Monastic Orders,* and *Legends of the Madonna*—but none so good as her Shakespearian criticisms. J. O. Halliwell-Phillipps did great service to the study of English literature in general, especially by his elucidation of the life of Shakespeare; and Alexander Dyce deserves mention for one of the most useful editions of Shakespeare's works. The palm for learning and research must however be assigned to the great Cambridge Shakespeare, published between 1863 and 1866, under the editorship of W. G. Clark and W. Aldis Wright. Charles and Mary Cowden Clarke likewise deserve to be remembered. The *Concordance* of the latter was until lately the standard work of its class, and must always remain an honourable monument of patience and thoroughness.

Mrs. Anna Jameson (1794-1860).

J. O. Halliwell-Phillipps (1820-1889).

In the sphere of general criticism, a man of great
reputation in the middle of the century
was Sir Arthur Helps, author of *Friends
in Council*, a collection of social and
critical dialogues and essays, published between 1847 and
1859. Many of these essays are essentially commonplace, and the book is so long drawn out that it would be
intolerable, but for occasional vivid and forcible passages
and epigrammatic expressions. Such, for example, are
the imaginary picture of the woman taken in adultery,
and the description of a great cathedral, with a thin con-
gregation lost in a little corner of it, a bad sermon and a
dull service : ' We look about, thinking when piety filled
every corner, and feel that the cathedral is too big for the
religion, which is a dried-up thing that rattles in that
empty space.'

Sir Arthur Helps (1813-1875).

There remain two writers, John Ruskin and Matthew
Arnold, who are as distinctly leaders of criticism in the
middle and later portions of the period, as Carlyle and
Macaulay were at the opening of it.

John Ruskin is an author whose multifarious activity
makes it somewhat difficult to classify him.
He has written on art, literature, morals,
economics, society, in short, on nearly everything. He has written verse as well as prose, and the
unwise enthusiasm of disciples has lately gathered together the rhymes of his youth. If however we regard
Ruskin's work as a whole, we see that its principal motive
is critical, and that his criticism is mainly directed to art.
This is the case with what still remains his greatest work,
Modern Painters. The first volume of this book, magni-
ficently illustrated, excellently printed, and written with
an elaborate splendour of style almost unexampled in
English, was published in 1843 with the simple inscrip-

John Ruskin (1819-1900).

tion. 'by a Graduate of Oxford.' The fifth and last volume did not appear until 1860. The *Modern Painters* is easily first among all the English works that treat of painting. Its full merit can hardly be appreciated until we realise how daringly original it was; and to realise this is difficult, because of the very success of Ruskinism. The young graduate of Oxford preached a new gospel, and set himself in opposition at once to the established canons of art-criticism, and to the established philosophy of his time. In the former convention reigned supreme. 'The man who in the pre-Ruskinian era was the high priest among connoisseurs was Sir George Beaumont; and Sir George, admirable man as he was in other respects, when he looked at a landscape, asked, not whether it was true to the facts of nature, but whether it accorded with the fictions of convention. "But where is your brown tree?" he asked of Constable when that painter gave in his adherence to the then revolutionary course of proclaiming that trees were green.' Ruskin too proclaimed that trees were green, and no one has done more than he to vindicate nature's right to be what she is. It was their championship of truth and their earnestness that drew him towards the Pre-Raphaelites, and made him their formidable and efficient champion in *Pre-Raphaelitism* (1851), as well as in many detached passages of his writings.

While Ruskin was elaborating and completing his *Modern Painters*, he was likewise engaged upon works bearing on the kindred art of architecture. His chief writings upon it are *The Seven Lamps of Architecture* (1849) and *The Stones of Venice* (1851-1853). His appointment in 1869 as Slade Professor of Fine Art at Oxford greatly stimulated his activity. His reputation had then reached nearly its highest point. He interpreted his duties seriously, and threw himself with ardour into the work.

Quite a number of his smaller publications—among them *Aratra Pentelici*, *The Eagle's Nest*, *Ariadne Florentina* and *Love's Meinie*—are the outcome of his tenure of the professorship. His second tenure of office, beginning in 1883, produced *The Art of England* and *The Pleasures of England*. He moreover made himself an art-guide to travellers in Italy; and hence his *Mornings in Florence* and *St. Mark's Rest*.

This great body of art-criticism is all bound together by a few fundamental principles; and it is perhaps his fidelity to principle, hardly less than the magnificence of his style, that has won for Ruskin a popularity denied to other critics of art. It will be useful to regard his critical work from two points of view: its rise in negation and opposition, and its issue in positive doctrine.

Ruskin, like every man who has had much to teach, begins by being a protestant. He finds that all is *not* for the best in the best of all possible worlds, and his effort is first to uproot what is bad, and secondly to encourage and foster what is good. The objects of his dislike have been so often denounced by him that all know what they are. Materialism, utilitarianism, a sordid industry merely concerned with the accumulation of wealth, and caring little either for its use or for the quality of the thing produced —these have been the objects of Ruskin's life-long hatred. The merits of his method of dealing with them must be touched on later; here it is enough to notice that the motive for his work on art is the pressing need to find some foundation, other than these, for the beautiful and good. Though Ruskin was not of the Oxford movement, he was stimulated by much the same sympathies and dislikes that produced it; and it is interesting to note how Pre-Raphaelitism in art, Ruskin's art-criticism, and the poetic and religious movements of the middle of the century, all show various forms of the same revolt against the deification of matter.

Starting with this opposition to mere material utility, Ruskin is careful always to define art so as to bring out its spiritual significance. ' All great Art,' he says, ' is Praise.' To him, art and religion, or art and morality, are not so much different things as different phases of the same thing. Beauty is measured, not by economic utility, or capacity to satisfy a material want, but rather by transcendental utility, or capacity to satisfy a spiritual want. In proportion as it embodies the conceptions of a great spirit, art is great. The artist ought to be faithful to nature, but mere imitation is not enough. Greatness consists in the something which the artist does not exactly add to nature, but rather educes from nature, the something which the gifted eye only can see, but which the gifted hand can make visible to others less splendidly endowed.

In his application of these principles Ruskin is sometimes capricious, sometimes, perhaps, presumptuous, and very often dogmatic. His caprice is visible in his changes of opinion. We find judgments pronounced in one edition of his works with the confidence of omniscience, and retracted in another with frank self-contempt, but with unabated confidence. The reasons for the one opinion seem, as a rule, just as convincing as the reasons for the other; and while all men may legitimately change their views, frequency of change ought to beget a certain amount of diffidence. That Ruskin's criticism is sometimes presumptuous follows from its extreme confidence. He discovers the meaning of every stone in a building, and of every line and colour in a painting, in a manner hardly granted to mere man ; for, after all, the most sympathetic of critics cannot enter into another man's mind, nor can the most learned completely realise a past age. This dogmatism, though irritating, is generally harmless enough; but it is not so when it results in underrating an artist like Michael Angelo, because he will not fit into the preconceived theory, and in undue exaltation of the comparatively little, because they sometimes furnish just the illustrations needed.

From the same root springs the cognate fault of the intensely subjective character of Ruskin's criticism. In a celebrated passage on the Jura in the *Seven Lamps*, after an eloquent description of the scene, the writer imagines it transported to some aboriginal forest of the New Continent. In an instant it loses all its impressiveness—to him. The reason is that the element of human association is lost; and he instantly jumps to the conclusion that this element is an essential part of the charm of nature to all. Few will dispute that such association is to many an important factor in the delight in nature. But this has not been a universal feeling. Some travellers, like Darwin on the Cordilleras or in the Brazilian forests, have felt, in the midst of untrodden solitude and unbroken desolation, a sense of the sublime nowhere else to be experienced.

That which, in spite of faults, gives Ruskin's art-criticism its superiority over all rivals is, in the first place, the fulness of knowledge whence it springs, and, in the second place, the magnificence of the style in which it finds expression. Ruskin's continental travels in early manhood gave him an acquaintance with the best models, such as could not otherwise be acquired. He was moreover himself an artist, capable of good and accurate, if not of great work, and aware of what is possible and what is not possible in art; and his steady confidence in the existence of an inner meaning and a serious purpose in all art worthy of the name saved him from the thinness of substance and the dilettante trifling too apt to be seen in writings of that class.

But it is, first of all, beauty of style that the name of Ruskin suggests. His prose has been lauded as the finest in the English language. The English language contains so much that the absolutely finest is not easy to discover; nor will men ever agree as to the relative merits of simple and of ornate styles. There is not a little to be said for Oliver Goldsmith, even as against John Ruskin. The latter writes what is known as 'poetic prose;' and in doing so, though he is no mere imitator, he follows in the footsteps of men like De Quincey, who sought to obtain by prose effects commonly associated with poetry. This was in part a reversion, but a reversion with a difference. The eighteenth century had evolved a clear, direct, simple structure of sentence, well adapted to appeal to the understanding. It was not unfitted too, as many passages in Addison and Steele and other acknowledged masters prove, for an appeal to the emotions. Nevertheless, this was its weak side; and just as the lucid, bright, highly intellectual verse of the eighteenth century gave place to poetry more emotional and more varied, so the prose of the eighteenth century had to receive its complement in a prose more ambitious in design, more complex in structure and richer in tone. It was romanticism overflowing, as it were, the bounds of verse. The change was not so much the introduction of something wholly new as the grafting of old tendencies on a new stock. The complex structure and involved harmonies and wealth of imagination which the new writers hungered for were to be found in the prose of Milton and of Jeremy Taylor. On the other hand, the type of sentence established by the eighteenth century writers was too sound to be set aside. It remained the basis, while the

o

older magnificence and daring were brought back and wedded to it.

Of this type of poetic prose Ruskin is the acknowledged master. Others, like De Quincey, have rivalled, and perhaps equalled his best passages. But excellent passages in De Quincey are much rarer than in Ruskin. The latter has built upon a broader foundation. All the field of nature and great part of the field of knowledge have been his. Ornate prose tends to be descriptive; and in his descriptions Ruskin has, over the mere literary man, the great advantage which the study of art gives. He had been educated to observe, and he naturally saw more than others who, even if they possessed equal sensibility, had less of this special culture.

Next in importance to his art criticisms must be ranked Ruskin's writings on social subjects. Here his interest has been keen and his energy great. Most of his special ideas have been denounced as Quixotic nonsense, and some of them, it must be added, deserve a description not much more flattering. Yet great is the merit of earnestness. Ruskin has always been fired by indignation against wrong and falsehood, and has always believed profoundly in the truth of his own gospel. He has had, both as a writer and as a man, the gift of fascination. Hence, even when his audience was scanty, it was enthusiastic; and few, whose ideas seem so unpractical, have succeeded in persuading so many to try them. The story of his inducing his Oxford pupils to engage in road-making is well known. The fact that the road was and is, as he laughingly admitted, one of the worst in the three kingdoms, does not weaken its testimony to his personal influence; though it may throw doubt on the wisdom of his guidance. In a similar spirit he founded the St. George's Guild. This however was no mere by-work. It was the direct outcome of his writings on social questions, and it was more remotely connected with his teaching of art. It was connected with the latter through his conviction that only to a people living wholesome lives is sound art possible. It was connected with his social writings because his studies for them convinced him that mere writing would do little to cure the evils he saw. Hence in the *Fors Clavigera* in 1871 he launched the scheme of the St. George's Guild. The idea was to restore happiness to England. ' We will try,' said he, ' to make some small piece of English ground beautiful, peaceful, and fruitful. We will have no steam-engines upon it, and no railroads; we will have no untended and unthought of creatures on it; none wretched, but the sick; none idle, but the dead. We will have no liberty upon it, but instant obedience to known law and appointed persons; no equality upon it, but recognition of every betterness that we can find, and reprobation of every worseness.' It is not surprising that plans so visionary have failed to regenerate society; it is surprising that men should have been willing to join in the effort to realise such a Utopia. The agricultural ventures of the Guild are an admitted failure; one or two of the efforts to plant village industries have had some measure of success, and seem capable of doing good within narrow limits.

Prominent among the faults of Ruskin's social writings is a disregard of practically unalterable facts. Railways and steam-engines may not be objects of beauty, but until they find swifter means of locomotion and production men will use them. To regulate their use and to reform abuse would be the ideal of the practical social reformer. Denunciation and banishment are the cures which occur to Ruskin. Similar faults mark his extremely eccentric political economy; as for example his condemnation of interest on capital and his ascription of property ' to whom proper.' This would be attractive if we could only find some one to tell us infallibly, or with some approach to infallibility, to whom it *is* proper. Historically, the stronger man has generally proved the person 'to whom proper.' The condemnation of competition and the praise of co-operation are open to a similar objection. They ignore the facts of human nature. There is doubtless room for valuable work in promoting co-operation and in regulating competition; but no worse service could be done to the human race than to supplant the latter. Fortunately, no effort is more hopeless: it is like that sin which Macaulay declared would be unspeakably shocking if it could be committed, but which, happily, Providence had not put within the reach of fallen humanity.

Ruskin's economic and social writings are certainly not to be valued for soundness of thought or for sobriety of judgment. They have however the beauty of style which characterises all his works, they are enriched with memorable sentences and weighty sayings, and they are inspired by a nobility of purpose which redeems even the most indefensible doctrine. Unworkable as his economic principles are, it is impossible to withhold admiration from the man who has so generously endeavoured to carry them out; and however numerous may be his crotchets, the laugh at them must be kindly when he has himself so genially led the laughter. It is moreover only just to say that, however unsound his own views may be, he was one of the first to point out the unsoundness of the old political economy. There is no answer to his contention that a science so abstract, a science which leaves out of account so many considerations essential to human welfare, has no right to pronounce authoritatively upon it. The modern economist would agree with Ruskin that we must reintroduce the factors eliminated before we can draw conclusions trustworthy for practice.

Matthew Arnold rose into prominence as a critic somewhat later than Ruskin, and he did his
work in a different sphere. He has the unusual distinction of being almost equally
celebrated in prose and in poetry. There are numerous
writers who have won a considerable, and some even a
great reputation in both; but generally, as in the case of
Scott, there is no difficulty in subordinating the one to the
other. In Arnold's case there is a difficulty, and though
the prediction may be ventured that he will in the end
take rank as a poet, he is probably best known at present
as a writer of prose.

Matthew Arnold
(1822-1888).

Matthew Arnold was educated at Winchester and Rugby.
He went up to Balliol College, Oxford, in 1841, and won
a fellowship at Oriel in 1845. In 1851 he became inspector
of schools. Besides his ordinary routine work as inspector
he discharged the important duty of visiting and reporting
upon the schools and universities of France and Germany.
From 1857 to 1867 he was professor of poetry at Oxford.
In his later years he made two visits to America, where
also he lectured. He afterwards published the addresses
under the title of *Discourses in America*.

The prose writings of Matthew Arnold may be classed
under three heads. They are all critical in spirit. In the
first division the criticism is of literature, in the second of
theology, in the third of society. As regards their chronology, the literary criticism is mainly the product of the
decade between 1860 and 1870, but from time to time all
through his literary career Arnold wrote criticism. In
theology the period of his greatest activity was from *St.
Paul and Protestantism* (1870) to *Last Essays on Church and
Religion* (1877). Social essays, including the educational
writings under this head, are interspersed all through, but
the period of greatest activity, as regards publication, was

from the *Mixed Essays* (1879) to the *Discourses in America* (1885). In respect of merit these writings can also be classified with confidence. The literary essays are unquestionably the most valuable, the social essays rank next, while the theological works have the least permanent worth.

Arnold's critical work may be said to begin in his poems, and these for the most part precede his prose writings. It may be doubted whether any English poet has written as much fine criticism in verse as Arnold. Besides the penetrating judgments on individual writers, like Goethe, Wordsworth and Heine, we have a discussion of the principles of art in the *Epilogue to Lessing's Laocoön* and, throughout, a critical view of life as well as of literature. The volume of poems published in 1853 contained moreover a critical preface in prose, short but highly suggestive. When therefore Arnold was appointed Professor of Poetry at Oxford, he was already a critic of proved capacity, and he fully justified his appointment by the lectures *On Translating Homer* (1861), certainly the most valuable ever delivered from that chair. But most of Arnold's critical work was originally written for periodicals; and the scattered essays, gathered up into volumes, are known to the world as the *Essays in Criticism* (1865) and the *Essays in Criticism: Second Series* (1888). These, with a few essays scattered through other volumes, constitute the body of Arnold's critical work. What is its spirit and method?

To comprehend Arnold as a critic we must grasp his conception of culture. His aim is to know the best that has been thought and said in all ages and by all nations. No criticism was ever less negative. He sees indeed that the pointing out of deficiencies, indirectly if not directly, is an essential part of criticism, but it is not the end in view. Again, Arnold's purpose is always practical. He was long

regarded as a dreamer, a 'superior person' sitting on a
solitary height and on the whole proud of the isolation.
On the contrary, it was just because he was at heart
essentially English, and therefore practical, that he acquired
this reputation. Two of his favourite dogmas in criticism
were the necessity of going back to and studying the
classics, and the equally crying necessity of going beyond
our own island and studying the mind of Europe. He was
never content unless he brought English opinion to the
test of foreign opinion. Hence his interest in knowing
how Milton appears to a French critic. For a similar
reason he frequently went to foreign writers for the subjects
of his own criticism. In the first series of *Essays in
Criticism*, the most characteristic and the most valuable, as
a whole, of his critical writings, the subjects are principally
foreign—the two de Guérins, Heine, Joubert, Marcus
Aurelius. He turns to these, not because he thinks them
better than the writers of his own country, but because he
thinks more good will come, both to himself and to
England, from an investigation of what is foreign and unfamiliar, than from an examination of writings illustrating
our own merits and charged with our own defects. The
impulse which determines his choice in criticism is revealed
in his *Letters*. He condemned Carlyle in England and Gambetta in France, each for 'carrying coals to Newcastle;'
Carlyle, because he preached earnestness to a nation that
already had enough of it, but was not equally endowed with
other good qualities; Gambetta, just because he evaporated
in words and failed to teach that very earnestness to a
nation that would have been all the better for more.

The same principle explains Arnold's insistence on the
study of the ancients. 'They can help to cure us of what is
. . . the great vice of our intellect, manifesting itself in
our incredible vagaries in literature, in art, in religion, in

morals: namely, that it is *fantastic*, and wants sanity.'
It was for this reason that he dwelt on things distasteful
to his countrymen, or to whomsoever he was addressing.
He was eager to carry the coals of Newcastle where they
were needed, the earnestness and practical sense of
England to France, the lucidity of France and her love of
ideas to England. This, combined no doubt with personal
taste, accounts for his devotion to French literature. No
one saw French weaknesses more clearly,—'France, famed
in all great arts, in none supreme.' But irrespective of the
relative merits of French and German writings, he thought
the Germans a bad model for the English to follow, and
the French a good one, because they, a race of Latin
culture, differ from us more than another branch of the
Teutonic stock can do. So too, in his eyes, the highest
value of the classics is just that they present us with
ideals unlike our own. 'We can hardly at the present day
understand what Menander meant when he told a man
who inquired as to the progress of his comedy that he had
finished it, not having yet written a single line, because
he had constructed the action of it in his mind. A modern
critic would have assured him that the merit of the piece
depended on the brilliant things that arose under his pen
as he went along.' The width of the difference measures
the value of the lesson to be learnt.

We can thus understand the seeming eccentricity, sometimes, of Arnold's choice of subjects, and also the superficial appearance of negation in his criticism. It is only
superficial; the essence of the criticism is always sympathy, agreement rather than difference, the recognition of
merit in preference to censure for defects. Carlyle had
already placed criticism on the basis of sympathy, but it
was shown in a different way. Carlyle had a large share
of the dramatic faculty, and an intense interest in the

individual soul. Arnold's genius was social, but not dramatic. He had no such mastery as Carlyle of the springs of individual character; but he set himself to understand the society in which the man lived, to grasp his idea, to look at things from his point of view, and so to explain what otherwise would be inexplicable. It is the fruitfulness of Arnold's method that has made the reading of the *Essays in Criticism* an epoch in the lives of many men who have now reached middle life.

Equally high praise must be accorded to the temper of this criticism. No writer was ever more uniformly urbane than Arnold. 'The great thing is,' says he, 'to write without a particle of vice or malice;' and he never forgets his own precept. He often gave rise to controversy, and was sometimes the object of vituperation; but, though he could write with cutting irony, the controversy was never on his side embittered, and he never replied in kind to the vituperation.

In his criticism Arnold laid little stress on rules, and those he did appeal to were wide and elastic. The one thing he greatly insisted upon was the necessity of unity of impression. No work of art could be called great that did not produce a deep and abiding impression as a whole, and not merely in its parts. In the details of criticism he trusted to no rules, but rather to a taste saturated with 'the best of what has been thought and said.' His sentiment is expressed in the well-known essay on the study of poetry, introductory to *Ward's English Poets*. 'There can be no more useful help,' says he, 'for discovering what poetry belongs to the class of the truly excellent, and can therefore do us most good, than to have always in one's mind lines and expressions of the great masters, and to apply them as a touchstone to other poetry.' He followed in practice his own precept, and determined to finish up with Shakespeare's *King Lear*, before writing this very essay, in order to have a proper taste in his mind while he was at work.

The rest of Arnold's works in prose are conceived in the same frame of mind, but deal with matter less tractable to the author. The social essays are of high quality. Arnold's campaign against Philistinism, his insistence on lucidity, not in literature alone but in all the relations of life, his championship of urbanity, his polemic against narrow sectarianism, whether religious, or social, or political—all this is important as well as interesting. The playfulness of Arnold's habitual mode of expression helped to conceal the real earnestness of his purpose. But in all this he had very much at heart the improvement of his countrymen. He was by nature and instinct a teacher; and, though he was too much an artist to obtrude it or let it spoil his work, there was a didactic purpose under nearly all he wrote, verse as well as prose. For this he sacrificed popularity. Knowing well that to say what is agreeable is a surer and easier road to favour than to say what is helpful, he yet chose the latter course.

The same purpose animates likewise Arnold's theological writings; but in this case the want of special equipment is more serious. It is unwise of anyone, without long years of special training, to undertake biblical criticism. The opinion of a great Hebraist as to the facts about the book of Isaiah is valuable; the opinion of anyone else is that of an amateur. The motive which animated Arnold however is easily understood, and for certain purposes his judgment is quite as worthy of respect as that of the most accomplished theologian. Arnold's position was peculiar. While retaining a great deal of religious sentiment he had thrown aside entirely the positive dogmas of religion. He was strongly attached to the religion of the Bible, Old Testament as well as New; and just because of this attachment he wished to remove the crumbling foundation of theological systems and find a safer basis for it. 'Our popular religion at present conceives the birth, ministry, and death of Christ, as altogether steeped in prodigy, brimful of miracle ;—*and miracles do not happen.*' Arnold's object was to set free Christianity, which had hardened in the mistaken fact, and to establish it on the living idea. Undoubtedly he was well qualified to form opinions on these fundamental questions. Neither the clergy, nor the churches, nor specialists in biblical lore, have any monopoly here, or any peculiar right to respect. The ultimate questions of religion are to be settled by a review of the whole of life, for which every man has his own special advantages as well as his own special limitations.

Arnold's style, in prose as in poetry, is one of the elements of his power. Though not free from mannerisms, it is easy, harmonious, scholarly and scrupulously pure. He is content to write about plain things in a plain manner. His great charm is the constant play of wit and humour, of irony and satire, over his prose. The wit and irony are, as a rule, lambent rather than piercing, but they are sometimes exceedingly keen. Occasionally he rises to a high pitch of eloquence. There are few passages of English prose more memorable than the celebrated apostrophe to Oxford, the 'home of lost causes, and forsaken beliefs, and unpopular names, and impossible loyalties.' Yet even there, when his feelings are most highly strung, the comic touch comes in : 'There are our young barbarians, all at play.' Arnold smiles at himself as he smiles at others, and by doing so takes all offence from his wit.

Two minor names, those of Dr. John Brown and

Dr. John Brown (1810-1882).

William Brighty Rands (1823-1882).

William Brighty Rands, are, perhaps, best included among the critics. The former is most widely known as the author of *Rab and his Friends*, a piece not easily surpassed for mingled pathos and humour. Brown wrote a style of very high merit. In the miscellaneous collection of his writings, which he entitled *Horæ Subsecivæ*, there is much to remind the reader of Lamb. Yet he was guiltless of imitation, and the resemblance exists because he had the same fine humour and the same sensitiveness of perception as the earlier writer. No one has written better than Brown about dogs; and his comprehension of them and his power of depicting them are seen even better in *Our Dogs* than in the famous essay on Rab, where the human figures divide the interest with the great mastiff. Brown's critical papers are few, but they show that he knew how to get at the heart of his subject.

Rands is a man much less known than he deserves to be. He wrote on many subjects, but generally under assumed names. His children's verse in *Lilliput Levee* (1864) is very good, and his opinions on 'life and philosophy' in *Henry Holbeach* (1865) are still better. This book is thoughtful, acute in criticism, and enriched with not a few memorable sayings. Perhaps the best essay in it is that on *Cavaliers and Roundheads*, where the description of the Tory or Cavalier mind, with no opinions, only dogmas, and a genial superstition which answers the purpose of religion, is admirable; and in another essay there is an even more delicious description of the minister of the Little Meeting, 'his heart amply supplied with the milk of human kindness, and his creed blazing with damnation.' Rich as English literature is, it is sensibly impoverished when work of this quality is forgotten.

The present period has been fruitful also in departments of scholarship cognate to literary criticism. Among scholars in the old sense of the term the most distinguished were John Conington at Oxford and H. A. J. Munro at Cambridge. The former had the more versatile literary gift, but the latter was far more 'high built' in learning, and his edition of Lucretius is admittedly one of the triumphs of English classical culture. In the same sphere the great statesman, W. E. Gladstone, deserves mention, less perhaps for the positive value of his *Juventus Mundi* and Homeric studies, than for the extraordinary energy which made such work possible amidst the distractions of party politics. More characteristic of the age has been the development of Anglo-Saxon and Middle English lore. Benjamin Thorpe and Joseph Bosworth both did valuable work in this sphere. The former edited Caedmon in 1832, and in the course of his long life supervised editions of nearly all the more important remains of Anglo-Saxon literature. Bosworth's name is identified with the Anglo-Saxon Dictionary, which, though now philologically rather antiquated, was in its time a bold undertaking. Sir Frederick Madden, a somewhat younger man, performed for a later period the work Thorpe did for the beginning of our literature. The accomplished Richard Chenevix Trench, for twenty years Archbishop of Dublin, was not only an agreeable poet, but did great service to the study of the English language. His *Study of Words* and *English Past and Present* have done more to popularise philology than, probably, any other books we possess.

The study of Eastern civilisation has been another special line of modern research. The explorations of Layard threw a flood of light upon Nineveh, and, in the still more remote East, Sir Henry Creswicke Rawlinson achieved the remarkable feat of deciphering the Persian cuneiform inscriptions. Curiously enough, the same thing was done independently and almost simultaneously by Dr Edward Hincks. Another portion of the East was studied by E. W. Lane, the greatest English Arabic scholar of his time, the best translator before Sir Richard Burton of the *Arabian Nights*, and author of one of the best books on life in the East, the *Account of the Manners and Customs of the Modern Egyptians*.

Among travellers who were not scholars, David Livingstone deserves mention for the greatness of his African discoveries, and McClintock as the chief in his time of Arctic explorers. But in the literary sense both were far surpassed by George Borrow, an author very hard to classify, but whom some would be disposed, for more reasons than one, to rank among the writers of fiction. Borrow did write stories, *Lavengro* (1851), and its sequel, *The Romany Rye* (1857), where facts of his own life are bewilderingly mingled with fiction; while it is strongly suspected that there is no small element of romance in the books of travel on which his fame chiefly rests. He had a remarkable gift for languages. Among other little-known tongues, he studied the Gipsy speech, and published a volume on *The Gipsies in Spain* (1841), and a word-book of the English Gipsy dialect. His best book however is *The Bible in Spain* (1843), an exceedingly readable account of his travels as colporteur in that country. Whether it be trustworthy as a record of facts or not, *The Bible in Spain* has at least induced some whose whole interest was in tracts and colportage to read a piece of good literature, and has delighted with entertaining adventures others who looked for nothing better than an enlarged specimen of the tract kind.

George Borrow
(1803-1881).

CHAPTER X.

POETRY FROM 1850 TO 1870: THE INTELLECTUAL
MOVEMENT.

WE have already seen that traces of change in the spirit
of poetry manifest themselves soon after the opening of the
present period. They appear in the works of men like
Bailey and Sir Henry Taylor, and they grow steadily
stronger in the successive volumes of Tennyson. We
have also seen that a spirit cognate to this manifests itself
in other departments of literature as well. It attains its
full growth, especially in poetry and art, about the middle
of the century; and so marked is the difference from the
previous four-and-twenty years that it has been called the
English Renaissance. The name is too ambitious and
grandiloquent, yet if we do not press it unduly it will be
useful in reminding us that literature had in nearly all
departments come to be dominated by new ideals. Nowhere do we see them more conspicuous than in poetry.
Their influence is visible in the rise of new schools; first,
the 'Spasmodic School,' stronger in passion than in intellect, and greater in promise than in performance; and
secondly, the Pre-Raphaelites, who were primarily artists,
but who were also men of letters. The first article of their
creed was to be true to nature; but they were far from
being realists as the word is now commonly understood.
More important than either of these were those whose task

may be described as that of wedding intellect to imagination. They were not a new school, for their leaders, Browning and Tennyson, had been active all through the first part of the period. But their power and their influence had now grown to maturity; both in their choice of subject and in their treatment they were swayed by the spirit of the time; and they were reinforced by some new writers who took a similar view of the functions of poetry.

The greatest of these new writers is Matthew Arnold, and his thought is so eminently representative of the generation that it may be well to consider him even before his seniors. It was as a poet that Arnold began his literary career. He won prizes for poetry at Rugby and at Oxford, and in 1849 he published his first volume, *The Strayed Reveller, and Other Poems. Empedocles on Etna*, also accompanied by other poems, followed in 1852, and another volume of poems the year after. A few additions to the pieces thus published were gradually made, and in 1867 appeared the *New Poems*. From that date Arnold wrote poetry sparingly. His career was therefore comparatively short, and the bulk of his verse is not great. He was frozen into silence by ' that dull indifference to his gifts and services which stirred the fruitless indignation of his friends.' But in poetry quality counts for more than quantity. Small in bulk as is his contribution, Gray has nevertheless a secure place among the immortals. Arnold's contribution is much larger than Gray's, and it has the same purity and beauty of finish.

Arnold was born just at the proper time to feel the forces of change working around him, and the sense of change is from the first deeply impressed upon his poetry. It is this, combined with his critical attitude of mind, that makes him specially the voice of the doubts and difficulties of his generation. The critical aspect of Arnold's verse has been already noted. It is critical of human existence as well as of other poetry. In *Obermann Once More*, in *Thyrsis*, in *The Scholar Gipsy*, in *Mycerinus*, in *Resignation*, in the lines *To a Gipsy Child*, and in numerous other pieces we see the workings of this critical spirit. We see too that he is most of all weighed down with the profound sense of change. He finds himself in a world where all things have to be made new, and where the power that promised to renew them remains unseen. This is the case with religion, for the conviction of the decay of Christianity in the dogmatic sense is as plainly visible in Arnold's verse as in his prose. It is the case also with politics and the social system. The French Revolution had shaken these, and had left to the next generation the task of rebuilding them. Its tremendous magnitude awes Arnold. He has none of that confident optimism which in Browning springs from breadth of intellect ; still less does he share that which, in the panegyrists of material progress, is begotten of narrowness. He thinks the conditions of the time unfavourable to spiritual growth. It does not afford that ' shelter to grow ripe,' and that 'leisure to grow wise,' which even Goethe found in his youth, exposed though he was in maturer years to ' the blasts of a tremendous time.'

This conception of the conflict, and especially of the unparalleled complexity, of modern life, is the dominant thought of Arnold. It is the warfare of so many elements that in his eyes distinguishes his own from all previous ages. In former times each civilisation stood by itself, not vitally affected by the puzzling elements of alien civilisations. The modern task is to fuse all together. The actress Rachel is typical, and as in her birth, and life, and death, and in her physical, mental and moral nature, there met and clashed ' Germany, France, Christ, Moses, Athens, Rome,'—so do they meet and clash in the lives of all

P

Arnold offers no solution of the problem. He points out the difficulty, he cherishes an ultimate hopefulness, but none of the answers to the riddle satisfies him.

The tone most characteristic of Arnold is in harmony with such fundamental conceptions. It is a tone of refined and thoughtful melancholy. This made him a supreme elegiac poet. *Thyrsis*, the memorial poem on his friend Clough, is generally ranked with the masterpieces in the same type of Tennyson and Shelley and Milton. But *Thyrsis* does not stand alone. *The Scholar Gipsy*, the *Obermann* poems, *Rugby Chapel*, *A Southern Night*, and several others of Arnold's finest pieces likewise belong to this class. The elegiac spirit is his special gift, and he shows it in a characteristic way. His poems are not elegiacs for the individual; they are not so even when, as in *Rugby Chapel* and *A Southern Night*, the subjects are most intimately related in blood to Arnold. He habitually looks beyond the individual to the race, and rather mourns 'the something that infects the world.'

Arnold was a student of Wordsworth, and was among the most discriminating admirers of that great poet. One of the best of the critical essays is devoted to him; and the finest selection ever made from the poetry of Wordsworth was made by Arnold. The skill of that selection proves that Arnold was capable of benefiting from Wordsworth without being tempted to follow him where his guidance would have been dangerous. He admired Wordsworth's calm, he admired him for his power to 'possess his soul,' he admired him as a student of nature. The calm and rest in himself were with Arnold rather an aspiration than a thing attained: it was part of his creed that in these latter days such calm was unattainable. But he followed Wordsworth as a student of nature. The love of nature was with Arnold an inborn passion, the strength

of which is proved not only by his poetry, but in one sense
even more convincingly by his familiar letters. Wordsworth gave him a point of view and strengthened his power
of vision. But Arnold writes his nature-poetry for a new
age under new conditions. The very fact that the calm of
Wordsworth is unattainable imparts to his verse a subdued
tone. He stands between Wordsworth and his other
favourite Senancour, sharing the spiritual force of the
one and the reflective melancholy of the other. Arnold's
best descriptions are tinged with this melancholy. The
'infinite desire of all which might have been' inspires
Resignation, one of the poems of his earliest volume. We
see it again in the lovely closing lines of *The Church of
Brou*. It determines Arnold's preference for pale colours,
soft lights and subdued sounds, for moonlight effects, and
for the hum of 'brooding mountain bee.' In the beautiful
Dover Beach it is associated with his sense of the decay of
faith. Even in the lyric rapture of the description of the
sea-caverns in *The Forsaken Merman*, the melancholy is
still present. To many it is oppressive, and perhaps it is
the absence of it from the song of Callicles in *Empedocles
on Etna* that has caused some sympathetic critics to pronounce that the finest of all Arnold's poems.

Arnold's longer pieces fall into two classes: the dramatic,
including *Merope* and *Empedocles on Etna;* and the narrative, best represented by *Sohrab and Rustum* and *Balder
Dead,* for *Tristram and Iseult* is as much lyrical as narrative.
As a dramatist Arnold was not successful. His *Merope*, a
play on the Greek model, is frigid; and fine as is *Empedocles on Etna*, its merits are in the thought and the beautiful verse rather than the dramatic structure. The truth
is that Arnold had neither the eye for fine shades of
character nor the interest in action essential to the drama.
His treatment of character has already been commented

upon in connexion with his prose. With regard to action, Arnold himself withdrew *Empedocles on Etna* shortly after its publication, on the ground that it was a poem in which all was to be endured and nothing to be done.

The same want of action appears in the narratives. The charm of these beautiful poems resides not in what takes place in them, but in the restful pictures they present. There is no breathless speed such as we feel in the narratives of Scott and Byron, but, on the contrary, the calm of a reflective spirit. *Sohrab and Rustum* (1853) and *Balder Dead* (1855) seemed to open out to Arnold a wider field of productiveness than any he had hitherto found. They took him outside himself, and gave variety to his poetry; and perhaps the thing most to be regretted in his literary history is that he wrote no more pieces of this class. Not that they are altogether the best of his poems; but blank verse so beautiful as his never cloys, and it seemed as if he might have found innumerable subjects suitable to his genius, subjects inviting quiet reflexion and not injured by the absence of rapid movement.

There are two features of special value in the work of Arnold. One is his unshrinking intellectual sincerity. The bent of his mind compelled him to endeavour to understand the world in which he lived. He found much in it that was unwelcome to him. His scepticism as to dogmatic religion was a source of great pain to himself. Life would have been far more smooth and easy if he had been able to believe more; and hence that sympathy with many things he did *not* believe which Newman noted in him. Yet he never shows the slightest sign of yielding to the temptation and playing false with his intellect. Wherever it leads him Arnold goes; and he has taught no higher lesson than that of unvarying trust in reason and loyalty to 'the high white star of truth.' It may be doubted whether any of his poetic contemporaries has pursued a path so undeviatingly straight. Even Browning is bribed by his feelings to play questionable tricks with his intellect.

The second feature is the style of Arnold. He presents one of the best examples in English of the classical spirit. He is always measured and restrained. He detested ' haste, half-work, and disarray,' and certainly his own example tended to discourage them. Lucidity and flexibility and sanity were the qualities he specially strove to embody in his work. It was because he found them in Goethe that he specially admired the great German poet. It was because of the absence of them that he uttered his most severe criticisms upon his countrymen both in the present and in the past.

Arthur Hugh Clough is in so many respects associated with Arnold that they are best taken together. But just because of the similarities there is the less need to dwell upon the inferior poet. Clough, who spent his early boyhood in America, was educated under Dr. Arnold at Rugby and at Balliol College, Oxford. At Oxford he was for a time carried away by the Tractarian movement, in his own words, ' like a straw drawn up the chimney by a draught.' In this he was influenced doubtless by his friendship for W. G. Ward. But Clough was not born for unquestioning belief, and the reaction shook his whole faith. The story of his separation from Ward is told in the beautiful allegorical poem, *Qua Cursum Ventus;* and in another of his finest poems, *Easter Day, Naples,* 1849, we see the position to which Clough ultimately came. To use Arnold's distinction, it is a faith which gives up the fact, but clings to the idea. Had Clough written much in the strain of these pieces he might have had some title to the name of a

Arthur Hugh Clough (1819-1861).

great poet. But he is seldom wholly satisfactory. He was prone to choose themes beyond his strength. Thus *Dipsychus* is a colourless and weak reproduction of *Faust*. The author has not sufficient force to deal with the battlings of a spirit with faith and doubt, pleasure and virtue, good and evil, and all the most complex problems of life. Defects fundamentally the same take a different shape in *Amours de Voyage*. Clough's presentation, in Claude, of the doubts, distrust and dilettantism of the century fails to give the sense of power. The poet is happier in his 'long vacation pastoral,' the *Bothie of Tober-na-Vuolich* (1848), with its glimpses of nature, its easy light touch, and its underlying seriousness. But the verse is unfortunate. The hexameter in English is an exotic, and has never yet been used in any long poem with complete success. The reader tires at last of what might otherwise have been a most successful story in verse.

The same movement visible in the poetry of Arnold and Clough may be detected still moulding and modifying the works of Tennyson. In the year 1850 *In Memoriam* appeared. It was the product of long meditation, and part is known to have been written as early as 1833. Nevertheless it is remarkable that just in the year when Browning published his *Christmas Eve and Easter Day*, and just about the time when Arnold's verse was exhibiting another aspect of the interest in religion, Tennyson too should have made his greatest contribution in this kind to literature. For while *In Memoriam* is of all great English elegies the most closely associated with the man to whom it is dedicated, still the treatment opens up the questions of death and immortality; and the passages of the poem which have clung to the popular memory are those in which the poet expresses his convictions or his hopes on these subjects. Perhaps the greatest weakness of *In*

Memoriam is its length. It is difficult if not impossible to dwell on the subject of death long, and to preserve perfect healthiness of tone. The other great English elegies are in the first place much shorter, and in the second place the writers find more relief to them than Tennyson does. The intensity of his friendship for Arthur Hallam kept him perhaps even too strictly to his subject.

In Memoriam is essentially a lyrical poem, and the years immediately before and after its publication are those in which Tennyson's lyrical genius was in fullest flower. *Maud* (1855) is a lyrical poem. The beautiful songs interspersed between the parts of *The Princess* belong to this period, and so does the grand *Ode on the Death of the Duke of Wellington*. The lyrics of these years are on the whole superior both in fervour of passion and in weight of thought to the earlier lyrics. Some of the songs, like ' Tears, idle tears,' are, as songs, almost overcharged with thought, yet they are beautifully melodious ; and Tennyson never wrote anything more full of exquisite sound than ' The splendour falls on castle walls.'

The *Ode on the Death of Wellington* is worthy of study, because it is the best specimen of a class of poems for which Tennyson was distinguished from first to last. He was always a patriot, and there is no feeling he expresses more fervently than that of pride in England. He contrasts her stability with the fickleness of France. He is proud of her freedom slowly won and surely kept. Patriotic ballads like *The Revenge* and *The Defence of Lucknow* are among the most prominent characteristics of his later volumes. His great success in the case of the *Ode* is due to the fact, first that his heart is stirred by the sense that ' the last great Englishman is low ;' and secondly, to the fact that he saw in Wellington an impersonation of all that he had admired in England. The picture he draws of the duke is identical in its great features with that he had painted of the nation, and it has the advantage of being concrete.

The passionate fervour of which Tennyson's lyric strain was capable is best illustrated from *Maud*, a poem which it is more easy to praise in parts than as a whole; for it must be admitted that the character of the hero is deficient in greatness and self-restraint; and the part which depicts his madness is poor. A good deal of at best exaggerated blame has likewise been meted out to the references to war in the course of the poem. But these faults are more than redeemed by such lyric outbursts as 'Come into the garden, Maud,' and 'O that 'twere possible.' The first is perhaps the most splendid, as it is one of the most justly popular, of all Tennyson's lyrics; while the second is among the most exquisite and delicately finished. These pieces have a deeper tone of feeling and more reality of passion than we find in Tennyson's earlier lyrics.

The *Idylls of the King* are the outcome of an interest in Arthurian legends that seems to have gradually developed. *The Lady of Shalott* proves that Tennyson's mind was dallying with the story of Arthur as early as 1833; and *Sir Galahad* and *Sir Launcelot and Queen Guinevere* attest the continuance of the interest in the volumes of 1842. Another piece, the *Morte d'Arthur*, published along with these, was afterwards embodied in the *Idylls*. It was professedly a fragment, and the epic of which it was described as the sole relic was spoken of disparagingly as 'faint Homeric echoes, nothing-worth.' Notwithstanding the disparagement, *The Passing of Arthur* is the gem of the *Idylls*; but the reference serves at least to direct attention to an actual difference between Tennyson's earlier and later work. Though the *Morte d'Arthur* is far from being a mere echo of Homer, there are numerous lines and phrases in it directly recalling Homer, and different in tone from the context. In the later *Idylls* the classical allusions seem to be one with the piece, they do not call attention to themselves but are transformed and made Tennyson's own.

There is no clear evidence before 1859 of an intention to treat the Arthurian story as a whole. In that year four of the idylls were published; but they were still fragments, and great gaps were left between. Gradually the gaps were filled, until in 1885 the poem was completed. Still, the connexion of the parts is loose. Each idyll is a separate story, related to the others because all are parts of one greater story. But the idylls have not the coherence required in the books of an epic. Tennyson was conscious of the want of unity, and he sought for a principle of con- nexion in allegory. At best the allegory is very indistinct; it appears chiefly in the parts later in order of publication; and we may suspect that it was an after-thought meant to supply a defect to which the author slowly awakened. The very name, *Idylls of the King*, serves as a warning not to expect too much unity. An 'idyll' is a short story, and the word therefore indicates the essentially episodic character of the whole poem.

The *Idylls* were, as they still are, Tennyson's greatest experiment in blank verse; and next to Milton's *Paradise Lost* they are the finest body of non-dramatic blank verse in the language. The form had gone out of fashion in the eighteenth century. Thomson, it is true, revived it, and the poets of the period of the Revolution followed his example. But through the early death of Keats, through that feeble- ness of will which robbed the world of an untold wealth of poetry in Coleridge, and through the fate that forbade Wordsworth to write long poems well, it remained true that no very great and sustained modern English poem was written in blank verse. The measure attracted Tennyson, and he soon mastered it. A number of pieces prior to the *Idylls* seem to be experiments in preparation for a bolder flight. The *English Idylls, Ulysses, Aylmer's Field, Sea Dreams* and *Lucretius* are specimens. The measure is used on a larger scale in *The Princess*. But Tennyson's supreme success was in the *Idylls of the King*. They cannot be said to rise higher than the best of the early poems; for the *English Idylls* include the *Morte d'Arthur*, and *Ulysses* is among the finest of Tennyson's poems. These pieces show the same exquisite grace, the same smoothness, the same variety of pause, the same skill in the use of adjuncts, such as alliteration. But there is necessarily more scope and variety in a long poem; and one of the finest features of Tennyson's verse is the flexibility with which it adapts itself to the soft idyllic tone appropriate to *Enid*, to the darkness of moral degradation in *The Last Tournament*, to the crisis of the parting of Arthur and Guinevere, to the spiritual rapture of *The Holy Grail*, and to the mysticism of *The Passing of Arthur*. Tennyson cannot equal the stateliness of Milton; but Milton is the only poet with whom, in respect of blank verse, he need greatly fear comparison.

When we come down to later years the principal change visible in Tennyson's work is the development of the dramatic element. The dramas proper have been the most neglected of all sections of his work; but 'the dramatic element' is by no means confined to them. They are rather just the final result of a process which had been long going on. Tennyson, as we have already seen, gradually put more and more thought into his verse. In doing so he felt the need of a closer grip of reality, and he found, as other poets have found too, that the dramatic mode of conception brought him closest to the real. This

is all the more remarkable because nothing could well be
more foreign to the dramatic spirit than his early work.
His youthful character sketches are not in the least
dramatic. Neither is there much trace of humour, a
quality without which true dramatic conception is impossible. The change begins to show itself about the
middle of the century. In *The Grandmother* and *The
Northern Farmer* we have genuine dramatic sketches of
character. The poet does not regard them from his own
point of view, he speaks from theirs. *The Northern Farmer*
is moreover rich in humour. Tennyson never surpassed
this creation, but he multiplied similar sketches. All his
poems in dialect are of a like kind. They are in dialect
not from mere caprice, but because the characters could
only be pointed to the life by using their own speech.
Other pieces, not in dialect, like *Sir John Oldcastle* and
Columbus, are likewise dramatic in their nature. Less
prominent, but not less genuine, is the dramatic element in
the patriotic ballads, such as *The Revenge*. The greater
part of the work of Tennyson's last twenty years is, in fact,
of this nature, and herein we detect the principal cause of
the change of which all must be sensible in that work as
compared with the work of his youth. The old smoothness
and melody are in great part gone, but a number of pieces
prove that Tennyson retained the skill though he did not
always choose to exercise it. It is the early style with
which his name is still associated, and probably the
majority of his readers have never been quite reconciled
to the change. But while we may legitimately mourn for
what time took away, we ought to rejoice over what it
added, rather than left. If there is less melody there is
more strength; if the delightful dreamy languor of *The
Lotos-Eaters* is gone, we have the vivid truth of *The
Northern Farmer* and *The Northern Cobbler*, and the tragic

pathos of *Rizpah*; if the romantic sentiment of *Locksley Hall* is lost, something more valuable has taken its place in the criticism of life in *Locksley Hall Sixty Years After*.

Tennyson's dramas then, surprising as they were when they first appeared, are merely the legitimate and almost the inevitable outcome of his course of development. Inevitable he seems to have felt them, for he persevered in the face of censure or half-hearted approval, perhaps it should be said, in the face of failure. A deep-rooted scepticism of his dramatic powers has stood in the way of a fair appreciation. The fame of his earlier poetry has cast a shadow over these later fruits of his genius; and the question, 'Is Saul also among the prophets?' was hardly asked with greater surprise than the question whether Tennyson could possibly be a dramatist. And, in truth, at sixty-six he had still to learn the rudiments of his business. *Queen Mary* (1875) is a failure. It is not a great poem, and still less is it a great drama. The stage is overcrowded with *dramatis personæ* who jostle each other and hide one another's features. *Harold* (1876) showed a marked advance; but *Becket* (1884) was the triumph which justified all the other experiments. It is a truly great drama, and, though not yet recognised as such, will probably rank finally among the greatest of Tennyson's works. The characters are firmly and clearly delineated. Becket and Henry, closely akin in some of their natural gifts, are different in circumstances and develop into very different men. Rosamond and Eleanor are widely contrasted types of female character, the former a little commonplace, the latter a subtle conception excellently worked out. All the materials out of which the play is built are great. No finer theme could be found than the mediæval conflict between Church and State; and Tennyson has seized it in the true dramatic way, as concentrated in the single soul of Becket, torn between his duty to the Church and his duty to the King, whose Chancellor and trusted friend he had been and to whom he owed his promotion.

The minor dramatic pieces are of inferior worth, and in some of them, as for example, *The Promise of May* and *The Falcon*, Tennyson showed a certain infelicity in his choice of subjects. But their failure leaves unimpaired the interest of the dramatic period. It seemed an almost wanton experiment on the part of Tennyson. But he was an artist all his life, and here too he was only obeying the inherent law of development of his art. Instead of wantonness, there is deep pathos in the old man's perseverance under unfamiliar conditions, and there can only be joy at his final success. There is surprise too that he who, from his earlier work, would have been judged one of the least dramatic of poets, should have so decidedly surpassed a poet so markedly dramatic as Browning.

Tennyson wrote up to the very close of his long life. His last publications were *The Foresters* and *The Death of Œnone*. They show some decline of power. *Demeter* too (1889) was probably a little below his level. But previous to that, though there had been change, there had been nothing that can be called decay. For the long period of sixty years and upwards Tennyson had written, and with rare exceptions he had written greatly. From the death of Wordsworth to his own death he was almost universally looked upon as the first poet of his time. No one else has wielded so great an influence. In no other poet's work is the record of change during the period so clearly written. In part he made the age, in still larger measure it made him. The hesitancy of his early work was typical of the spirit of the time. The gradual awakening, the deeper thought, the larger subjects, the more varied interests of the intermediate period, were typical too. In this last period, while Tennyson was as faithful as ever to the law of his own development, he did not move precisely with the time. Another race was rising and other palms were to be won.

Browning could not go through the same phase of development, for in him the intellectual element from the first was even abnormally prominent. Yet in Browning too the influence of the time is felt. *Christmas Eve and Easter Day* (1850) handles topics to which he is perpetually recurring; but in it they are seen in a new light. The poet had heard the noise of the Tractarian controversy, and in *Christmas Eve* he passes in review the three principal phases of contemporary opinion regarding religion,—the evangelical, represented by the Nonconformist Chapel, the Catholic, represented by Rome, and the critical, represented by the German professor in his lecture-room. It is significant that while Browning can accept neither of the two former, he prefers both to the third. Both are intellectually indefensible, yet in both the vital thing, love, is present, while it is not to be found in the lecture-room. Both ' poison the air for healthy breathing,' but the critic ' leaves no air to poison.' There is throughout the poem an unquestionable bias towards finding as much true as will by any means pass muster with the intellect. Long afterwards, in *La Saisiaz* (1878), Browning handled the same problems in a more boldly speculative spirit, though still with the same bias. The difference is largely due to time; for before the date of *La Saisiaz* Browning had adopted a method more philosophical than artistic. But partly, perhaps, it was due to his wife, who was alive when *Christmas Eve* was written, and dead long before *La Saisiaz*.

In the period between these two poems the same problems were frequently in Browning's mind, and no section of his work is richer in thought and poetic beauty than that which expresses them. In *Karshish*, with its vivid realisation of the mind of a thoughtful heathen longing for a faith, in *A Death in the Desert*, where the St. John is rather a man of the age of Strauss than of the first century, in *The Pope* and in *Rabbi Ben Ezra*, we have Browning's deepest treatment of the problems which interested him most, and we have not that sacrifice of poetry to philosophy which mars *La Saisiaz*. We may say that about this time Browning discovered the vital interest of his generation, and discovered also where his own strength lay. The effect is seen in the uniform excellence of his work. The publications of the twenty years between 1850 and 1870, taken as a whole, certainly surpass what he had done before or what he did afterwards. *Men and Women* (1855) has been probably the most popular and the most widely read of all his writings; *Dramatis Personæ* (1864) is even richer in poetry, but has been commonly felt to be more difficult in thought; while *The Ring and the Book* (1868-1869) is by almost all competent judges pronounced his masterpiece.

The plan of *The Ring and the Book*, whereby the same story is told ten times over from ten different points of view, is defensible only on the ground that it succeeds. Nearly half the poem is hardly worth reading; yet the other half so splendidly redeems it that *The Ring and the Book* ranks among the great poems of modern times. The pictures of Caponsacchi, of Guido, of Pompilia and of the Pope are all great. Guido has the interest, unique in this poem, of appearing twice; and there is no better illustration of the subtlety of Browning's thought than the difference between the Count, plausible, supple and polished, pleading for his life, and the man Guido, stripped of all but bare humanity, condemned to death, first desperately petitioning, then tearing off the veil of hypocrisy and uttering his terrible truths both about himself and the messengers who bear his sentence. Pompilia is Browning's most perfect female character; but, though a beautiful creation, she illustrates one of the defects in his dramatic art. She speaks Browning's speech, and she thinks his thought. Simple child as she is, there is a depth of philosophy in her utterances that is not in strict keeping with her character; and she, like all Browning's men and women, uses the abrupt vivid language of the poet. Notwithstanding his almost passionate repudiation of the idea, Browning is a self-revealing poet; and nowhere does he reveal himself more than in the Pope, the greatest character in *The Ring and the Book*. In him the resemblance to Browning himself does not matter, it rather adds a new interest. The mind can conceive and picture nothing higher than its own ideal best; and the Pope is Browning's ideal man, great in intellect, in morals and in faith. In two other cases, *Rabbi Ben Ezra* and *A Death in the Desert*, Browning has given similar glimpses of his own ideal, but they are less full than the view we get in *The Pope*.

To Browning's middle period belong likewise many of his love-poems, and these are unique in the English language. Others, like Shakespeare and Burns and Shelley, have given a more purely captivating expression to the ardour of love; no one else has so worked out its philosophy. Not that Browning's poems are deficient in feeling; the expressions of his own love for his wife, 'O lyric love' and *One Word More*, would suffice to refute such a criticism. But he prefers to take an aspect of passion and to explain it by the way of thought. He is analytical. The best example is *James Lee's Wife*, which goes through a whole drama of passion, and might be described, like Tennyson's *Maud*, as 'a lyrical mono-drama.' This, for good or evil, is another method from that of 'Take, oh take those lips away,' or 'I arise from dreams of thee,' or 'Of a' the airts.' There is both gain and loss in Browning's way of treatment. On the one hand, the lyric strain is less pure. If poetry ought to be 'simple, sensuous and impassioned,' and it has been generally thought that lyric poetry in particular should be so, then is Browning's less in harmony with the ideal. On the other hand, because his is a new way Browning impresses the reader with his originality; and because it is a thoughtful way he has a wide range. Moreover, it is a purifying and ennobling way. No poet free, as Browning is, from the taint of asceticism has ever treated the passion of love in a manner so little physical as he. There are in his works errors of taste that cause a shudder; but they are not here.

It was likewise during this period that Browning was at his dramatic best. Nearly all his best pieces are dramatic in conception, though sometimes, as in the love-poems, we are confined to single aspects of character. Not to speak of the great figures of *The Ring and the Book*, there is ample variety in *Men and Women* and in *Dramatis Personæ*. There are few figures more clearly drawn or more easily remembered than *Andrea del Sarto*; and *My Last Duchess* is equally fine. In these two pieces Browning has succeeded better than elsewhere in keeping himself in the background. *Fra Lippo Lippi* has likewise the stamp of dramatic truth, and is rich in humour; and *Bishop Blougram* is at once an excellent character, and, though a satirical conception, the mouthpiece of some serious thought.

In the last twenty years of his life Browning, on the whole, appears at his worst. We have seen how the development of Tennyson, though not unattended with loss, carried with it much compensating gain. There are some indications that Tennyson felt the influence of his great contemporary. The metrical effects of his later poems, as well as the studies of character, are sometimes suggestive of Browning. It would have been well if Browning had in turn borrowed a few hints from Tennyson; but unfortunately he went steadily along his own course, bringing into ever greater prominence characteristics that rather needed repression. He should have nourished the artistic rather than the intellectual element. Instead, the former dwindled and the latter grew; and some of his later writings may be not unfairly described as merely treatises in verse. Such is *Fifine at the Fair* (1872); such is *La Saisiaz* (1878); such are many parts of *Ferishtah's Fancies* (1884), and of the *Parleyings with Certain People of Importance* (1887). Such too is *Prince Hohenstiel-Schwangau* (1871); for there the dramatic conception of Louis Napoleon is smothered beneath the arguments of the Saviour of Society. In all of these the philosophy overloads the poetry, a state of matters all the less satisfactory because the philosophy itself is not so sound as that of the earlier periods.

There is nevertheless some fine work belonging to this late period. The translations from the Greek are interesting; but their value is outweighed by that of the beautiful romance of *Balaustion*, in which they are set, and by the discussion of the principles of art in *Aristophanes' Apology* (1875). Still better is *The Inn Album* (1875), remarkable for the magnificent character of the heroine, and for some of the most powerful reasoning to be found in Browning's works. His last volume, *Asolando* (1889), will always have a special interest for its publication coincidently with his death; and it illustrates how his favourite ideas remained fixed to the end. There is nothing more characteristic of him than the thought that evil is necessary to the evolution of good. We can trace this all through his work. It is present in *Sordello*, where we find evil described as 'the scheme by which, through ignorance, good labours to exist;' and the poet even modifies the prayer, 'Lead us not into temptation,' because, if we are strong enough to overcome it, the temptation will only do us good. It is indeed Bishop Blougram whom he causes to speak of 'the blessed evil;' but Browning could consistently have used the phrase himself. Nowhere is this doctrine, at first so strange, yet so suggestive, more fully and clearly expressed than in the poem *Rephan* in *Asolando*. Earth is superior to Rephan just because evil blended with good is better than 'a neutral best,' and it is progress to move from the sphere where wrong is impossible to one where through the risk of evil, and often through evil itself, a higher good may be attained.

Browning's last word to the world, the epilogue to *Asolando*, is most distinctive of his style and tone of thought. He held throughout a steady optimism, all the more cheering because it is the optimism of a man of wide knowledge of the world, and one who has looked evil in the face. The note is never clearer than in the epilogue, where he describes himself as

'One who never turned his back but marched breast forward,
  Never doubted clouds would break,
Never dreamed, though right were worsted, wrong would triumph,
  Held we fall to rise, are baffled to fight better,
      Sleep to wake.

No, at noonday in the bustle of man's work-time
  Greet the unseen with a cheer!
Bid him forward, breast and back as either should be,
  Strive and thrive! Cry, "Speed,—fight on, fare ever
      There as here."'

Elizabeth Barrett Browning was an author at an earlier date than her husband. As early as 1826 she published a

poetical *Essay on Mind,* along with other pieces; but her
first work of any note was *The Seraphim*

Elizabeth Barrett
Browning
(1806-1861).

(1838). Her introduction to Browning
took place in 1846. She was prepared
to admire him, for she already admired
his work, and had expressed her opinion of it in *Lady
Geraldine's Courtship.* An accident in girlhood had made
her a confirmed invalid; but in spite of this the two
poets fell in love, and were married in the autumn of the
year when they first met. They left England and settled
at Florence for the sake of Mrs. Browning's health; and
there, in 1861, she died.

There are two points of special and peculiar interest
in connexion with Mrs. Browning. She has only one
possible rival, Christina Rossetti, for the honour of being
the greatest poetess who has written in English; and her
marriage with Browning formed a union without parallel
in literature. Moreover, in relation to Mrs. Browning's
works, sex is not a mere accident. She is a woman in all
her modes of thought and feeling, and she is so especially
in her very finest work. Her greatest contribution to
literature, *Sonnets from the Portuguese,* derives its unique
interest from being the expression of the woman's love;
and *A Child's Grave at Florence* could hardly have been
written but by a woman and a mother.

Mrs. Browning's influence upon her husband was remarkably slight; his influence upon her was of mixed
effect, but good predominated. The questionable element
is seen when we compare *The Seraphim* with poems like
Casa Guidi Windows (1851) and *Aurora Leigh* (1857).
The Seraphim, a lyrical drama, though immature, is of
high promise. It is, above all, right in tone and method;
for the writer, Mrs. Browning, was not really a thinker;
woman-like, she felt first, and the attempt to translate her

feeling into thought was an error. She was by nature prone to this error, and Browning strengthened her innate ambition. But she never succeeds where thought is suffered to predominate. *Casa Guidi Windows* is sadly wanting in force and concentration; and the ambitious metrical romance of *Aurora Leigh* would be much improved by being compressed within half its bulk. It is moreover always the thought, the social discussions, the parts meant to be especially profound, that are wrong; the poetic feeling is sound and just, and its expression is often excellent. Minor influences of Browning may be traced in his wife's rhymes and rhythms; but while his effects, though often grotesque and uncouth, are striking and memorable, hers are feeble and commonplace.

But if Browning inspired his wife with a false ideal, he, on the other hand, lifted the shadow from her life, and gave her courage and hope, and the measure of health without which her work could not have been accomplished. Her best poems are related to him directly, like the *Sonnets from the Portuguese,* or indirectly, like *A Child's Grave at Florence;* for there her own child is an influence.

Beyond question, the *Sonnets from the Portuguese* (1850) are Mrs. Browning's most valuable contribution to literature. They are valuable even beyond their intrinsic merits. Good as they are, these sonnets have neither massiveness and subtlety of thought on the one hand, nor melody and charm on the other, sufficient to secure a place beside the greatest poetry. But they are the genuine utterance of a woman's heart, at once humbled and exalted by love; and in this respect they are unique. The woman's passion, from the woman's point of view, has seldom found expression at all in literature, and this particular aspect of it never. Hence, while it would be absurd to say that these sonnets are, as pieces of poetry, equal to the sonnets of Wordsworth or of Milton, it is not so unreasonable to question whether their removal would not leave a more irreparable gap in literature.

Mrs. Browning is on the whole happiest as a sonnet-writer. The sonnet form restrained that tendency to diffuseness which was her besetting sin, and so the fetters proved, as they so often do, to be the means whereby she moved more freely. Her purpose however frequently required the use of other forms. Thus, she sometimes aimed at romantic effects. She did so with no great success in *Lady Geraldine's Courtship*, a kind of *Lord of Burleigh* from the other side, spoilt by excessive length. *The Rhyme of the Duchess May* is much better. *The Romaunt of Margret* altogether fails to catch the weird effect aimed at, while *The Lay of the Brown Rosary* succeeds. But apart from the *Sonnets from the Portuguese* and some of the miscellaneous sonnets, her truest note is pathos. *Bertha in the Lane*, a simple story, sentimental but not weak, is an example of one aspect of it; *A Child's Grave*, already mentioned, of another; and, perhaps highest of all, *The Cry of the Children* of a third.

Mrs. Browning had a dangerous facility of composition, and much that she wrote is poor. Few poets gain more by selection. A small volume of pieces judiciously chosen would convince the reader that he was listening to the voice of a true and even a great poet; but his sense of this is lost in the flatness and weariness of the five superfluous volumes.

There remains one very remarkable poet, Edward Fitz-Gerald, whom it is difficult to place. Formally, he ought to be classed merely as an interpreter of other men's thoughts; but in reality he is an original poet of no mean rank, and his friendship with Tennyson, together with the strong intellectual quality of his principal work, gives him an affinity to the group

Edward
FitzGerald
(1809-1883).

now under discussion. His first noteworthy publication was a fine prose dialogue, *Euphranor* (1851), but his principal work was the translation of poetry. He translated six dramas of Calderon (1853), the *Rubáiyát* of Omar Khayyám (1859), *Salámán and Absál* (1856), and the *Agamemnon* of Æschylus, which, having been first privately printed, was published anonymously in 1876.

Probably no other translator ever showed equal originality. As a rule, the reader of a version of poetry, even if he be unacquainted with the original, feels a sense of loss. Pope's Homer is 'a pretty poem;' but not only is it not Homer, we feel that it is not worthy of the great reputation of Homer; and there is not one of the numerous versions of *Faust* but falls far short of the force and suggestiveness of the original. It is not so with FitzGerald. To some extent in the case of all his poems, but eminently in the case of the *Rubáiyát*, we feel that we are in the presence of a man of native power; and some Persian scholars hold that in this instance the order of merit is reversed, and that Fitz-Gerald is greater than Omar.

That his success was partly due to an inborn gift for rendering verse is proved by FitzGerald's high, though not equal felicity, as a translator of poets so different as Æschylus, Calderon, and Omar Khayyám. But partly also it was due to a very liberal theory of translation, outlined by himself in the prefaces to Calderon and the *Agamemnon*. In the former he says, 'I have, while faithfully trying to retain what was fine and efficient, sunk, reduced, altered, and replaced much that seemed not; simplified some perplexities, and curtailed or omitted scenes that seemed to mar the general effect, supplying such omissions by some lines of after-narrative; and in some measure have tried to compensate for the fulness of sonorous Spanish, which Saxon English at least must forego, by a compression which has its

own charms to Saxon ears.' The extent to which he allowed
himself liberties may be partly gauged by the differences
between the first and fourth editions of the *Rubáiyát*. In short,
FitzGerald was more properly a paraphrast than a translator.
He got into his mind a conception of the central meaning
of the work and of the author's character where, as in the
case of Omar, that was of importance as a key to the
meaning; and he then, without troubling himself about
exact equivalence of word or phrase, or even of whole sections, proceeded to create a similar impression in the new
language. Hence his work is wholly free from the impression of cramped movement so common in translations.

With reference to Omar, FitzGerald had first to decide
whether his quatrains were to be interpreted literally, or
as the utterances of a mystic Sufism, in which the wine so
frequently sung of really meant Deity, and all the sensual
images covered a spiritual meaning. Fortunately, he de-
cided for the former alternative; and whatever the real
Omar may have been, FitzGerald's Omar is an epicurean.
The original Omar has been compared to Lucretius; as
FitzGerald represents him he is far more suggestive of
Horace. His touch is lighter than the elder Roman's; and
he has no system, nor any ambition to frame one. Rather
it is his conviction of the futility of systems that makes him
what he is. He is a thoughtful man, questioning the
meaning of life, finding no answer except in the philosophy
of 'eat, drink, and be merry, for to-morrow we die,' and
drawing thence the inevitable melancholy it must impart
to the reflective mind.

> 'There was the Door to which I found no Key;
> There was the Veil through which I might not see;
> Some little talk awhile of ME and THEE
> There was—and then no more of THEE and ME.'

Herein lies the charm of his epicureanism, and herein too

its kinship with that of Horace. In both, the moral, *carpe diem*, is the advice of men who, in spite of themselves, must live for more than the day.

Thanks to the deeply human element in his philosophy, Horace after nineteen centuries is one of the most modern of poets. He has been emphatically the guide of the man of the world, whose experience, as it broadens, more and more convinces him of the poet's truth. FitzGerald's Omar has the same modern tone, perhaps in a degree even higher. His necessitarianism is modern, his scepticism is modern, and the difficulties in which it arises are modern too. His stinging quatrains answer a theology familiar enough to the readers of Burns, and seem to breathe the spirit of the Scotch poet's satires on the Kirk:

> 'Oh Thou, who didst with pitfall and with gin
> Beset the Road I was to wander in,
>   Thou wilt not with Predestined Evil round
> Enmesh, and then impute my Fall to Sin !
>
> 'Oh Thou, who Man of baser Earth didst make,
> And ev'n with Paradise devise the Snake :
>   For all the Sin wherewith the face of Man
> Is blacken'd—Man's forgiveness give—and take !'

Except perhaps in America, FitzGerald is not yet appreciated as he ought to be. When he is so appreciated he will rank only under the greatest of his time, and his chief work will be classed little below their best.

CHAPTER XI.

CONTEMPORARY with the great poets, who seem to feel first
of all the imperative necessity of understanding and interpreting the intellectual movement of the age, were
others, some of them great too, in whose work passion
takes a prior place to intellect. Of these the most talented
group were the Pre-Raphaelites, and the greatest man was
Dante Gabriel Rossetti. The celebrated founder of the Pre-

Dante Gabriel
Rossetti
(1828-1882).

Raphaelite Brotherhood was a man who had
the rare fortune to be highly distinguished
in two arts. Other artists—Thomas Wool-
ner and William Bell Scott and Sir Joseph
Noel Paton are contemporary examples—have been poets
also; but no one has attained a level at once as high and
as equal in both as Rossetti. He has also been influential
upon others in a degree rare even among men of as great
calibre; and finally, he was only the greatest of a family
all highly gifted in literature.

Rossetti, though English by birth, was more Italian
than English by blood, and he was brought up in an
atmosphere largely Italian. Both his literary and his
artistic talents showed themselves early. The literary
organ of the Pre-Raphaelites, *The Germ*, received some of
his earliest writings; but he had begun to compose even

earlier, the two well-known pieces, *The Blessed Damozel* and *My Sister's Sleep*, having both been written in his nineteenth year. The greater part of his poetry was composed in early manhood. On the death of his wife, in 1862, Rossetti, in the transport of his grief, buried the MSS. in her coffin. They were exhumed in 1869 and published under the simple title of *Poems* in 1870. After his wife's death Rossetti for a long time wrote little poetry, though he continued his artistic work. In later years the complete breakdown of his health checked his production. He suffered from insomnia and attempted to cure it by the use of chloral, with the usual result. Nevertheless, some very fine pieces, notably *The King's Tragedy*, are of late composition. The later poems were gathered together in the *Ballads and Sonnets* of 1881. Rossetti was also a translator, and in 1861 had published, under the title of *The Early Italian Poets*, the collection now known as *Dante and his Circle*. He likewise occasionally wrote prose, his most considerable work being a story, poetical in spirit, entitled *Hand and Soul*.

Mr. W. D. Howells (quoted in Sharp's *Dante Gabriel Rossetti*) says it will always be a question whether Rossetti ' had not better have painted his poems and written his pictures; there is so much that is purely sensuous in the former and so much that is intellectual in the latter.' There is certainly an element of truth in this judgment. The sensuousness was the cause of the celebrated attack entitled *The Fleshly School of Poetry*, which was met by Rossetti's effective rejoinder, *The Stealthy School of Criticism*. The poet showed that the attack was in great measure unjust, but he would not have sought to deny that there was sensuousness in his poetry. He would have held, on the contrary, that poetry not only might legitimately be, but ought to be, sensuous. This concep-

tion influenced Rossetti's whole style of poetical portraiture. We see its effect in the fine description of a girl
in *A Last Confession*, beginning, 'She had a mouth made
to bring death to life.' It is all so written that from it the
painter could easily put the portrait on canvas.

But with respect to the allegation of sensuousness, the
question for criticism is one of degree. There are two
aspects of it, the moral and the artistic, which, though not
entirely distinct, are best treated apart. Rossetti's answer
was most successful upon the moral side, though even in
this respect there remained one or two pieces not easily
justified. From the artistic point of view, it must be said
that the sensuousness is sometimes so great as to blur the
intellectual outlines. We see this particularly in the
sonnets, which many regard as Rossetti's best work in
poetry. He certainly does put into the sonnet a fulness of
melody and a wealth of colour not surpassed and perhaps,
in their conjunction, hardly equalled in the language. But
when we ask if the idea of the sonnet stands out with due
clearness, the answer must be in the negative. In the best
sonnets of Milton and Wordsworth, and in a less degree in
those of Drummond of Hawthornden, of Mrs. Browning
and of Christina Rossetti, the idea is precise and definite.
Dante Rossetti is a poet who 'deals in meanings,' but he
sometimes darkens, if he does not altogether bury, the
meaning under a wealth of sonorous words. The fault of
over-elaboration, which is chargeable also against the
pictorial art of the Pre-Raphaelites, is visible here. We
see it in other aspects too. The sense of spontaneity is
lost; the poet seems to be perpetually aiming at a mark
just beyond his reach; and there is an excessive addiction
to some of the subordinate artifices of verse. Among
these Rossetti's favourite is alliteration; and the reader is
not infrequently troubled with the suspicion that a word is

used, not because it is the best, but because it begins with a particular letter.

A defect kindred in origin, but more serious, is shown in Rossetti's treatment of nature. One of his best poems of this class is *The Stream's Secret*. The poet certainly wrote it ' with his eye on the object,' for the stream in question was no figment of the brain, but the Penwhapple in Ayrshire. All the more for that reason it illustrates the difference between inspiration and conscientious study. Rossetti did not feel natural beauty like Wordsworth, and his descriptions have not the easy grace of the true poet of nature. He deliberately set out to make a poem, with the result that he produced a fine piece of skilled workmanship.

Next perhaps to Rossetti's reputation as a writer of sonnets stands his reputation as a balladist; and it may be questioned whether the order ought not to be reversed. Rossetti's art was far too elaborate for a ballad of the genuine old type. Even in *The White Ship* there is a note which distinguishes it not only from the true popular ballad, but from such approximations as the ballads of Scott. But poetry ought to be valued for what it is, not for conformity with what may possibly be a misleading standard; and Rossetti's ballads are noble poetry. He imbibed enough of the ballad spirit to check his habitual faults, and of all his compositions the ballads are the simplest and most natural. The universal favourite, *The King's Tragedy* is a grand story told with great fire and energy. So, too, *Rose Mary* is a powerful and beautiful poem, less uniform however than *The King's Tragedy*, for the lyrics between the parts are at best second-rate. It is in pieces like these, and in some of the more clearly-thought sonnets, like *Lost Days*, that Rossetti proves himself the true poet. The more deeply sensuous sonnets, and such characteristic pieces as *The Blessed Damozel*, are representative rather of the dangers and defects of his poetry.

Less great but hardly less interesting than her brother was Christina Georgina Rossetti, who, like him, wrote for *The Germ*, though she published no volume of poems for many years afterwards. Though her course extends far beyond the limits of the period, the poetical work for which she is most memorable was chiefly done within it, and her closest connexions belong to it too. Her first published volume was *Goblin Market, and other Poems* (1862); her second, *The Prince's Progress, and other Poems* (1866). Then, after some prose tales, came the book of nursery rhymes, *Sing-Song* (1872). From this time onwards, except for *A Pageant, and other Poems* (1881), Miss Rossetti's books were chiefly of a devotional character; but one of them, *Time Flies* (1885), contains some of the finest of her verse.

The religious poems form a most important section of Christina Rossetti's works. She is one of the most profoundly devotional of modern writers. Unlike Arnold and Clough, she is not a poet of doubt but of faith; unlike Browning's, her creed is rather a creed of feeling than of intellect. But while she is not touched with the doubt of the age she is touched with its sadness. Her devotional pieces have sometimes, as in *Advent*, the ring of conquering faith, but more often they have in them something of a wail. What Dr. John Brown called the 'inevitable melancholy' of women seems to find a voice in Christina Rossetti; and though she is bound by her faith to an ultimately optimistic view, her habitual tone of mind is gloomy. 'Vanity of vanities' is the title of her finest sonnet, and it is also the conclusion she draws from the life of this world.

One of the praiseworthy points of Christina Rossetti's work is that, while invariably imaginative, it never fails to be clear. In this respect she far surpasses her brother. The marks of the artist's chisel are, as we have seen, too conspicuous in his work; in hers they are invisible. Yet few writers are more carefully artistic than she. Less ambitious in her aims than Dante Rossetti, her work impresses the reader with its adequacy to those aims. Herein she has an advantage over Mrs. Browning also. The latter has produced a far greater body of work, and at her best writes with far more strength than Miss Rossetti; but on the other hand Miss Rossetti is free from those astonishing lapses into bathos or triviality or mere bad taste which disfigure Mrs. Browning's poetry. The two poetesses meet most closely in their respective series of sonnets—*Monna Innominata* and the *Sonnets from the Portuguese*. These are among the masterpieces of each, for both were peculiarly happy in the sonnet form; Christina Rossetti because she was an artist by nature, Mrs. Browning probably because the form compelled her to be an artist. The comparison is unquestionably in favour of Mrs. Browning. The *Sonnets from the Portuguese* are richer and deeper than *Monna Innominata*. They record a love actually felt; and they are the product of an intellect wider, though perhaps less fine than Christina Rossetti's. But as regards the form, it is by no means clear that the advantage lies with the elder writer. Mrs. Browning's sonnets are sometimes laboured in expression; Christina Rossetti's have an inimitable ease, all the more delightful because in modern poetry it is rare. Her beautifully pure style is one of her greatest merits; and it is also one of the most striking points of contrast between her and her brother. A sonorous richness is characteristic of his style, a fine simplicity of hers. This simplicity, and the fineness of touch and delicacy of taste which accompanied it, served her well in those poems of the supernatural where her imaginative flight is highest. She is a mistress in the fairy realm, and in its own class *Goblin Market* is unsurpassed.

Another school which sprang up about the middle of the century, taking its rise in the longing for something deeper and more satisfying than had been recently in vogue, was that nicknamed 'the Spasmodic.' The name was fixed upon the school by the extremely clever satirist of it, William Edmondstoune Aytoun, himself a poet of a very different family, that of Scott. Aytoun is best known from his *Lays of the Scottish Cavaliers* (1848), narratives of martial exploit and tragic sorrow written in animated but excessively rhetorical verse. He was also, in conjunction with Mr. (afterwards Sir) Theodore Martin, the author of the *Bon Gaultier Ballads* (1845), one of the most amusing collections of comic verse of this century. His satire of the Spasmodic School is contained in *Firmilian* (1854), a mock-serious piece purporting to be by a member of the school. It was at the time customary to say that Aytoun had killed the Spasmodic School. If he had done so he would hardly have deserved well of literature. But though it is true that the Spasmodic Poets shot up like a rocket only to come down like the spent stick, both the rise and the fall were due partly to whims of popular taste, while the main cause of the fall lay in defects of the writers which satire did not make and could do little to remedy. On the whole, *Firmilian* was more likely to have helped the school than to have hurt it if it had contained in itself the seeds of long life. But the name 'spasmodic' was only too accurately descriptive of more than its style,—unfortunately so, for both the chief members, Sydney Dobell and Alexander Smith, possessed talents for poetry in some respects very high.

Sydney Dobell had the misfortune to be born a member of a narrow and intense religious sect, in which his talents caused him to be regarded as the destined instrument for some grand design of providence. He outgrew the sect, but never quite outgrew the education it had given him and the ideas it had instilled. From about 1850 he devoted himself chiefly to literature. His writings are *The Roman* (1850), *Balder* (1853), *Sonnets on the War* (1855), in which he collaborated with Alexander Smith, and *England in Time of War* (1856). But his health failed, and though he lived eighteen years longer he wrote little more of consequence.

Sydney Dobell (1824-1874).

'He never weeded his garden,' wrote Dr. John Brown of him, 'and will, I fear, be therefore strangled in his waste fertility.' This is the central truth about Dobell. Few poets are so uneven, perhaps hardly any poet capable of rising so high has ever sunk so low. Many passages are mere fustian, some are outrages against all taste ; but others have a sublimity not often surpassed.

At the beginning Dobell gave promise of development which, if fulfilled, would have led him very high indeed. In the short interval between *The Roman* and *Balder* the youthful author had grown surprisingly. *The Roman,* a fervid poem carrying on a Byronic tradition of interest in Italy, has all the faults of youth. It is too long, and it is bombastic. Its chief merit is width of sympathy ; and it also contains here and there hints that promise in the future reach of thought. In *Balder* we see this promise redeemed. It is far more forcible than *The Roman* and it is loaded with thought. *Balder* was a poem of vast design. It was to be in three parts, of which only one was ever published. The purpose was, in the words of the author's preface, to trace ' the progress of a human being from Doubt to Faith, from Chaos to Order. Not of Doubt incarnate to Faith incarnate, but of a doubtful mind to a faithful mind.' The design therefore bears a certain general resemblance to that of *Paracelsus*. *Balder* is not equal to that great poem. It is even more difficult while less profound, and it is especially far less of a unity. It is, strictly speaking, paradoxical to regard as a whole what proclaims itself as a part; but a part of a great design may have completeness in itself, and this *Balder* has not.

Again, if we regard the poem in the light most favourable to it, as a collection of passages in verse, we have to admit the most amazing inequalities. Few passages in literature are more hideous than the description of the monster on which Tyranny rides; but, on the other hand, the best passages may challenge comparison with all but the greatest poetry. Even this comparison has been sometimes made. The description of Chamouni has been said to rival the great hymn of Coleridge, and that of the Coliseum the celebrated stanzas of Byron on the same subject. The comparison, especially with Coleridge, is unkind to Dobell. At his best he cannot rival one of the most poetic minds in all literature in one of its highest flights. Nevertheless, both passages are exceedingly good. The subjects moreover are characteristic. Magnitude and massiveness are congenial to Dobell, and almost necessary to draw out his best. ' Alone among our modern poets,' says Dr. Garnett, ' he finds the sublime a congenial element.' It is in such passages as those named, and in Balder's magnificent vision of war, that Dobell shows the grand material of poetry that was in him.

For this reason it might have been expected that Dobell's

next volumes, *Sonnets on the War* and *England in Time of War*, would have been more uniformly good. *The Roman* proves that he had the fire of patriotism in his veins, and many passages of his verse show that this fire was not all spent, as most of Byron's was, to warm other nations than his own. Of all the poets then living, Dobell had the largest share of Tennyson's patriotic fervour and of his love for warlike themes. Nevertheless, the *Sonnets on the War* are of but moderate merit; and though *England in Time of War* contains some powerful pieces, it has all the inequality of Dobell's earlier poetry. Dobell had learnt little of the art of self-criticism, and whether he had the capacity to learn must remain doubtful. He afterwards wrote a few fine poems, such as *The Magyar's New-Year-Eve* and *The Youth of England to Garibaldi's Legion*, but broken health prevented him from undertaking any great work. He remains therefore a poet great by snatches. A selection, including the passages already mentioned, *An Evening Dream*, with its stirring ring of heroism, the fascinating ballad, *Keith of Ravelston*, and some others, might be made, which would greatly raise his reputation. The volume would not be large, but the contents would be excellent.

Next in importance among the Spasmodic Poets to Dobell was Alexander Smith. He was the son of a pattern-designer of Kilmarnock, Ayrshire, and in his now little known but quietly pleasing novel, *Alfred Hagart's Household*, he has embodied a good deal of autobiographic matter. He was also the author of a thoughtful and well-written volume of essays, *Dreamthorp*. But he is first and chiefly a poet. His earliest volume was *A Life Drama* (1853), which excited a degree of interest rarely roused by the first work of a young author. It was warmly praised and loudly

Alexander Smith
(1829-1867).

condemned; and the result of the controversy that raged over it was to make the author for a short time one of the most prominent writers in the kingdom. But his fame speedily declined, and *City Poems* (1857), though it contains some of his best work, was coldly received. *Edwin of Deira* (1861) was somewhat more successful, but was far from reviving the interest which had centred in *A Life Drama*.

The present generation, which has been unjust to Dobell, has dealt still more hardly with Alexander Smith. The Nemesis of excessive praise is unjust depreciation, and both have been Smith's lot. He has been denied the title of poet altogether; but he is a poet, and even a considerable one. He shares both the defects and the excellences of Dobell, never sinking so low, and, on the other hand, never rising as high. His execution is unequal, he rants, he uses metaphor to excess, he is by no means free from affectation. But though the *Life Drama* is crude and unequal, there is plenty of promise in it. There was ground to hope that the spirit from which it proceeded was like a turbid torrent which would by-and-by deposit its mud and flow on strong and clear. To those who hoped thus *Edwin of Deira* was disappointing. A good deal of the mud had been deposited, the execution was more perfect, but there was less strength and less volume of thought than might have been expected. It is in his minor pieces and in occasional lines and passages that Smith shows best. There is rare beauty in the melancholy close of the lyric *Barbara* in *Horton*. The picture of the sphinx, 'staring right on with calm eternal eyes,' has the true touch of imagination; and so has the image of the wind smiting 'his thunder-harp of pines.' *Glasgow* in the *City Poems*, is a strong as well as a beautiful piece. There can be no question of the imaginative power of this picture of the city in its cloud of smoke pierced by sunlight:

' When sunset bathes thee in his gold,
In wreaths of bronze thy sides are rolled,
   Thy smoke is dusky fire ;
And, from the glory round thee poured,
A sunbeam like an angel's sword
   Shivers upon a spire.
Thus have I watched thee, Terror ! Dream !
While the blue night crept up the stream.

There remain two or three considerable poets whom it is
difficult to classify.   Coventry Patmore
Coventry Patmore
(1823-1896).
cannot be placed in either the Pre-
Raphaelite or the Spasmodic School,
and though he has some points of affinity with the poets
of the intellectual movement, they are not close enough to
justify ranking him with them.   Patmore is especially the
poet of domestic love.   His greatest work, *The Angel in the
House* (1854-1856), was meant to be a poem on married
life.   In the opening the poet congratulates himself that
he, though born so late, has had the good fortune to discover 'the first of themes sung last of all.'   As he proceeded however he found his mistake, and never carried
out his design; but it imparted the characteristic tone
of quiet domestic affection to his verse.   He may be described as the Wordsworth of the home.   He is seldom
if ever great, but his verse at its best has a simple sweetness, with an occasional dignity, that is exceedingly pleasing.
It is unfortunate that against the merits of the better
passages of *The Angel in the House* there has to be set the
weakness of the letters of Jane.   Patmore's purpose was to
fit the thought to the character ; but merely weak thought
and merely weak character have no right to a place in poetry
such as this.   There is no dramatic realisation and no
humour to justify them.

The Unknown Eros (1877) is a work strangely different

from *The Angel in the House;* it is more lyrical and more ambitiously imaginative; and for this very reason it brings into greater prominence Patmore's weaknesses. There is a frequent sense of effort. The meaning is often obscure, and there are here and there, as in the earlier poem, surprising lapses of taste. The poem recalls Drummond of Hawthornden, not only by the rhythm, but also by a certain 'preciosity' of diction and imagery.

The second Lord Lytton, best known in literature by his pseudonym of Owen Meredith, must also be ranked among 'the unattached' of literature. He had a distinguished diplomatic career which more than once interrupted his pen. But, except for the intervals caused by his various ambassadorships and his eventful tenure of the Viceroyalty of India, Lytton was, from 1855 to his death, a diligent writer. In 1855 *Clytemnestra and other Poems* appeared, while *Marah* was a posthumous work. The greater part of Lytton's writings is poetical, and their total bulk is very great. It is indeed too great for his fame, and most of his poems would be improved by condensation. Lytton presents a singular example of heredity, which, in his case, showed itself in a manner damaging to his reputation. We have seen how the first Lord Lytton veered with every turn of the popular taste. The second Lord Lytton changed his style, chameleon-like, with almost every poet he happened to be reading. The consequence is, in the first place, that his own style is not easily discovered; and in the second place that he has been accused of plagiarism with more show of reason than almost any other man of equal literary rank. It is not merely that he echoes successively the pensive sentiment and melancholy reflectiveness of Arnold, the rich diction of Tennyson, the headlong abundance of Browning, the lyrical sweetness of Shelley,

The second
Lord Lytton
(1831-1891).

or that he in a snatch or two almost paraphrases
Byron. In *Lucile*, his indebtedness to George Sand is
far more extensive. It is true he avowed that he had
taken from her the story of the piece; but the story is
the principal part of it, and no writer ought to borrow quite
so much from another. The fault is a serious one, and it
is reason sufficient for the belief that Owen Meredith
will never take a high place in poetry; yet his endowments
were almost great, his taste was purer than his father's,
and had he been more independent-minded he might
have stood high in the second class of the poets of the
century.

J. B. Leicester Warren, Lord de Tabley, was a man
of richer poetic gifts, who might have done
very great work had he met with popular
encouragement. He began his poetic career
as early as 1859, but his first volume of
importance was *Præterita*, issued under the
pseudonym of William Lancaster, in 1863. For the next
ten years he was an active writer. Partly his own taste
and partly admiration for *Atalanta in Calydon* induced him
to attempt the classical drama; and his two experiments,
Philoctetes (1866) and *Orestes* (1867), rank among the
most finished of their class. They secured the warm approval of the best judges, but they did not become popular.
He tried novels, also without winning popularity; and
after two more experiments in verse—*Rehearsals* (1870)
and *Searching the Net* (1873)—he almost disappeared from
the ranks of authors for twenty years; for the *Soldier of
Fortune*, though bulky, can hardly be considered important.
It was the reissue in 1893 of his best pieces under the
title of *Poems Dramatic and Lyrical* that first made Lord
de Tabley's name widely known. So marked was the success of this collection that it was followed two years later

J. B. Leicester
Warren,
Lord de Tabley
(1835-1895).

by another, which was less successful because it was the result of a less rigid selection.

These volumes represent Lord de Tabley at his best, and that best is very good indeed. Such pieces as the *Hymn to Astarte*, the *Woodland Grave* and *Jael*, would do honour to any poet. There is intense dramatic power in the last-named piece, and a rich magnificence of style in the others. A tendency to sameness may sometimes be detected. He has, for example, one favourite colour, and the whole world is seen by him bathed in an amber light. There are also here and there echoes of contemporary poets, such as Browning, and still more, Swinburne, whose fulness of sound attracted De Tabley. But he is an essentially independent poet, and had he been encouraged to write he would doubtless have grown increasingly independent. Few losses in contemporary literature are more serious than that occasioned by his almost complete silence between 1873 and 1893, just the years when, by reason of his age, his work ought to have been best. He was a great man unrecognised, and the failure to recognise is sometimes severely punished.

Most of Lord de Tabley's contemporaries by birth belong rather to the subsequent period than to the Age of Tennyson. Even Swinburne did so, though before 1870 he had, by the publication of *Atalanta in Calydon* (1865), enriched English literature with one of its most perfect dramas on the Greek model, and by the *Poems and Ballads* (1866) had 'raised a storm, and founded a school.' The fact that he founded a school makes him rather the poetical leader of the present generation than a member of the preceding one. In some ways Lord de Tabley has more affinity to this later band than to those who were under the dominion of Carlyle and Browning and Tennyson. He certainly shows the workings of a new spirit, and seems to feel the old ideals insufficient; but his twenty years of literary eclipse serve to fix him chronologically rather among the older men. For a different reason William Morris, a man just one year older than De Tabley, also belongs, as a poet, to this period. Morris was a man who played many parts in life, and he played them not concurrently, but rather successively. In his characters as high priest of domestic art and as prophet to the Socialists he is identified with the closing quarter of the century; while his greatest achievements in poetry belong to the third quarter. *The Defence of Guenevere and other Poems* (1858) was his first volume of verse. Then after nine years came *The Life and Death of Jason*, followed almost immediately by *The Earthly Paradise* (1868-1870). Morris afterwards translated the *Æneid* and the *Odyssey*, and he also did much to make familiar in England the spirit of Icelandic literature. His *Sigurd the Volsung* (1876) is certainly the finest English poem inspired by Scandinavia, and perhaps his greatest work.

William Morris (1834-1896).

Morris is the most prominent example in these later days of that revival of the mediæval spirit which was initiated by the Romanticists of the latter part of last century, which attained its fullest flower in Scott, and which shows itself in such varied aspects in Rossetti's poetry, in the Pre-Raphaelite painters, and in the Oxford theologians. Morris exhibits it in a way quite his own. Chaucer more than any one else is his master in poetry. To him Morris reverted for the model of his verse, and the old poet's influence is seen in the disciple's mode of conception as well as in many turns of expression. One thing however Morris could not learn, though Chaucer was eminently qualified to teach it, and that was the true narrative spirit. Morris chose the narrative form, but the interest of his poetry rarely lies in the story. He does not himself care greatly for the story. He is never passionate; he is too calm to enter deeply into the feelings or to be absorbed in the fortunes of his characters. The charm of his poetry resides rather in leisurely and restful beauty of description. In this respect it ranks high, but seldom attains absolute mastery. Nearly all of Morris is readable and enjoyable, but few of his lines linger in the memory, and perhaps the only one frequently quoted is that in which he describes himself as 'the idle singer of an empty day.' Morris was more than this, but it may be questioned whether there is enough either of the substance of thought in his verse or of melody and pure poetic beauty to keep it long alive.

MINOR POETS.

Sarah Flower Adams is sure of at least a small niche in the temple of the English poets were it but for the beautiful hymn, 'Nearer, my God, to thee.' Her *Vivia Perpetua* is an ill-constructed drama, partly redeemed by fine passages.

Sarah Flower Adams (1805-1848).

William Allingham was an Irish poet, of much taste, but of no great power. His inspiration is strangely fitful and uncertain, and after his removal to London, in consequence of the success of his earlier verses, it seemed almost wholly to desert him. He was for a time editor of *Fraser's Magazine*.

William Allingham (1824-1889).

John Stuart Blackie, for many years Professor of Greek in Edinburgh University, was a very vigorous miscellaneous writer. He translated Æschylus, the *Iliad* and *Faust*. He was very successful in the lighter lyrical strain, and appears at his best in his rollicking and amusing university songs.

John Stuart Blackie (1809-1895).

Robert Barnabas Brough was the author of *Songs of the Governing Classes* (1859), a small col-

Robert Barnabas
Brough
(1828-1860).

lection of pieces, chiefly satirical, and remarkable for their vigour, point and sincerity. Strength of feeling, clearness of intellect and wit are his characteristics. Brough was generally very much in earnest, but in his *Neighbour Nellie* he showed that he could touch lighter themes very charmingly.

Charles Stuart Calverley, the scholarly and witty author of *Verses and Translations* (1862) and *Fly*

Charles Stuart
Calverley
(1831-1884).

Leaves (1872), had a faculty for more serious things, but, partly from indifference, partly because of the accident which made great effort in his later years impossible, he never wrote anything worthy of his talents. What he has left however is the very best of its kind. He is one of the most skilful of translators; and his parodies and satiric verse are excellent.

Mortimer Collins, poet and novelist, had a very happy knack for the lighter kinds of lyrical verse,

Mortimer Collins
(1827-1876).

half playful and half serious. Under pressure of circumstances he wrote too much, and the failure to 'polish and refine' tells against a great deal of his work.

William Cory, originally Johnson, for many years one of the masters of Eton, was the author of

William Cory
(1823-1892).

a small volume of poems entitled *Ionica* (1858), which, after long neglect, won, in its third edition of 1891, the attention due to thoughtfulness and scholarly expression. Cory's best pieces, such as *Mimnermus in Church*, soar beyond the range of the minor poet, and show that it only needed quantity to insure him a considerable place in literature. But he wrote few such pieces, and indeed little verse of any kind after *Ionica*.

Sir Francis Hastings Doyle succeeded Matthew Arnold in the chair of poetry at Oxford. Doyle is distinguished for the spirit and the martial ring of the ballads in which he celebrates deeds of daring. *The Red Thread of Honour, The Private of the Buffs,* and *Mehrab Khan* are pieces that take high rank among poems inspired by sympathy with the heroism of the soldier.

Sir Francis
Hastings Doyle
(1810-1888).

Sir Samuel Ferguson has been called the national poet of Ireland, on the score of *Congal,* an epic published in 1872. He is really more remarkable for his shorter pieces, some of the best of which deal with subjects not specially Irish. He was an active contributor to the *Dublin University Magazine* at the beginning of the period.

Sir Samuel
Ferguson
(1810-1886).

Adam Lindsay Gordon divides with Charles Harpur and Alfred Domett (Browning's ' Waring ') the honour of being laureate of the Antipodes. Wildness in youth drove him to Australia. It is probably true that but for the stirring and adventurous life there he never would have written anything of note; nevertheless, what we find in his verse is rather the spirit of the English hunting field and of English adventure the world over, than much that is distinctively Australian.

Adam Lindsay
Gordon
(1833-1870).

David Gray, author of *The Luggie,* a poem on a small stream which flowed near his home, was cut off too soon to do much in literature. His verse however is pleasant, and it might have acquired power. It retains a pathetic interest on account of the author's fate. He was drawn by the hope of fame from his native village to London, caught a cold there, and died while his poem was in process of printing.

David Gray
(1838-1861).

Dora Greenwell is chiefly remarkable as a writer of

Dora Greenwell
(1821-1882).

religious verse, the best of which is to be
found in *Carmina Crucis*. She also wrote
prose of considerable merit.

Robert Stephen Hawker, a clergyman who spent his life

Robert Stephen
Hawker
(1803-1875).

in the remote parish of Morwenstow, in
Cornwall, is best known for his *Cornish
Ballads* (1869). The spirited and stirring
Song of the Western Men, printed as early
as 1826, and accepted by Scott as a genuine old ballad, is
the most celebrated of all his compositions. Hawker
wrote also *The Quest of the Sangraal* (1863), a poem dis-
playing a mysticism which must have been deep-seated in
the author's character; for it led to his reception, just
before he died, into the Roman Catholic Church.

Jean Ingelow is one of the best of recent poetesses, and

Jean Ingelow
(1820-1897).

has also acquired a considerable, though a
less conspicuous name as a writer of fiction.
She is best as a lyrist, and some of her
poems are touched with a very fine and true pathos. She
likewise excels in the modern ballad form.

Edward Lear, author of the *Nonsense Rhymes* (1861)

Edward Lear
(1812-1888).

stands high in the very peculiar and difficult
kind of writing indicated by the title of his
book. There are other writers of humorous
verse, like Lewis Carroll, who possess greater qualities, but
the *Nonsense Rhymes* are unique for rich whimsical inven-
tiveness. Lear was an artist as well as a writer, and illustrated his own books.

Gerald Massey is a minor poet of unusual range. His

Gerald Massey
(1828-1907).

attachment to the Christian Socialists gives
a clue to his work; but in him the enthusiasm of humanity is concentrated in an
intense patriotism. Massey's martial verse is fine, but not

quite excellent. *Sir Richard Grenville's Last Fight* suggests comparison with Tennyson's *Revenge;* and the comparison illustrates the difference between good art and consummate art. Neither is Massey the equal of Doyle on this side; but he is far more varied and copious.

The Honourable Mrs. Norton was a grand-daughter of Richard Brinsley Sheridan, and inherited some of the family genius. Her poetic gift was not great, but her verse is spirited, and has frequently a ring of genuine pathos. Her sister, Lady Dufferin, also wrote verse, which, though less brilliant than Mrs. Norton's, is on the whole of a more poetic quality.

The Honourable
Mrs. Norton
(1808-1877).

Adelaide Anne Procter, daughter of Barry Cornwall, was a pleasing writer of the type of Mrs. Hemans, that is to say, feminine in the less flattering sense. There is a certain grace in her verse, but it is altogether destitute of weight and power of thought. Most of her poems were originally contributed to Dickens's papers, *Household Words* and *All the Year Round.*

Adelaide Anne
. Procter
(1825-1864).

William Caldwell Roscoe was at once lyrist, dramatist and critic, but failed to achieve greatness in any of these lines. If Roscoe had lived longer he might possibly have justified the opinion of his friends; but his actual performance, though graceful, is not weighty.

William Caldwell
Roscoe
(1823-1859).

William Bell Scott was a poet-painter, related to and in general sympathy with the Pre-Raphaelites, but never a member of the brotherhood. Scott's verse is characterised by mysticism; but mysticism in verse demands very skilful expression, and Scott's power over language was not sufficient. Perhaps his best poem is *The Sphinx,*

William Bell Scott
(1811-1890).

Menella Bute Smedley wrote both prose and verse well, and occasionally with distinction. Though an invalid, she published several volumes of poetry, and contributed to her sister, Mrs. Hart's *Child-World* and *Poems written for a Child*. Miss Smedley, like so many female writers, is in many of her poems markedly patriotic, and, though sometimes too rhetorical, she is, when stirred, successful in pieces of this type.

Menella Bute Smedley (1820-1877).

George Walter Thornbury, historian of the buccaneers, was also a poet who, in his *Songs of the Cavaliers and Roundheads* (1857) showed considerable skill in rapid and spirited narrative. The best of his later poems are gathered up in *Legendary and Historic Ballads* (1875).

George Walter Thornbury (1828-1876).

Aubrey de Vere, an Irish poet, has written, in the course of his long career, a good deal of pleasing and thoughtful verse. His sonnets are especially good, as were also his father's, but they would be still better if they were more terse. Much of his verse is religious, and the mystical tone of mind, indicative of the tendency which led him, as it led Hawker, into the Roman Catholic Church, is the one most distinctive of him.

Aubrey de Vere (1814-1902).

CHAPTER XII.

THE LATER FICTION.

AFTER the turn of the century fiction passes through a change similar to that of which we have seen evidence in poetry. The increased tendency to analysis, the greater frequency of the novel of purpose, and the philosophic strain conspicuous in George Eliot, all point to the operation of the forces which stimulated the intellectual movement in verse. The novelists, on the whole, take themselves more seriously than their predecessors—not always to their own advantage or that of their readers. Dickens, in his later days, is more of a reformer than at the opening of his career; and Charles Reade and Kingsley likewise make a conscious attempt to benefit society. In the case of the greatest novelist yet to be discussed this tendency to seriousness of aim grew till it injured her art. George Eliot was always serious in mind, but there is a great difference in treatment between *Scenes of Clerical Life* and *Daniel Deronda*.

Mary Ann Evans, who adopted the *nom de plume* of George Eliot, was the daughter of an estate agent. After the death of her mother in 1836 she was charged with the care of her father's house. But she continued to study, her subject at this period being language, German and Italian, Latin and Greek. Her father moved in 1841 from

George Eliot
(1819-1880).

Griff, near Nuneaton, to Coventry. There Miss Evans came under influences which affected her whole life. Intercourse with certain friends named Bray, and the reading of books like Hennell's *Inquiry concerning the Origin of Christianity* overthrew her hitherto unquestioning orthodoxy, gave to her thought a permanent bent, and introduced her to literature. A project for translating Strauss's *Leben Jesu* into English had been for some time entertained ; the person who originally undertook the work had to abandon it ; and Miss Evans took her place. *The Life of Jesus* was published in 1846. Miss Evans afterwards translated also Feuerbach's *Essence of Christianity* (1854), the only book ever published under her own name.

The death of her father in 1849 left her without domestic ties, and in 1850 or 1851 she accepted the position of assistant editor of the *Westminster Review*. In 1854 she took the most questionable step of her life. She went to live with George Henry Lewes, not only without the ceremony of marriage, but while he had a wife still living. All that can be said in defence has been said by herself ; but there are several passages in her works which show that she was permanently uneasy, and was not fully convinced that what she had done was right either towards herself or towards society.

Apart from the moral and social aspects of the question, the influence of Lewes upon George Eliot's literary career seems to have been mixed. On the one hand, it must be said that he acted with a delicate generosity for which his general character hardly prepares us. He encouraged her efforts, recognised her genius, avowed that all he was and all he did himself were due to her, and voluntarily sank into the second place. It is at least possible that without such fostering care the genius of George Eliot would not have run so smooth and successful a course. Further, the

s

very difficulties due to the relation add a deeper note to her voice. There is often a solemn, almost tragic tone in her utterances about domestic life which might have been absent had all been smooth between the world and herself.

On the other hand, Lewes, loyally as he effaced himself, could not but foster tendencies in her mind which were strong enough without his encouragement. He was a philosopher, imbued with the tenets of positivism; and she was naturally prone to be fascinated by abstract thought. Not that she was ever exactly original in philosophic speculation: the danger would have been less had she been so. But she hungered for philosophy, took the results proclaimed for absolute truth, and wove them into the fabric of her own work. From the *Scenes of Clerical Life* to *Daniel Deronda* and *Theophrastus Such* her writings became more and more loaded with philosophy. The two last-named books are decidedly overloaded; and even *Middlemarch*, the most massive, and probably on the whole the greatest outcome of her genius, would be still greater were it somewhat lightened of the burden.

Blackwood, the nurse of so much genius, in January, 1857, contained the first part of what became the *Scenes of Clerical Life*. *Adam Bede* appeared in 1859, *The Mill on the Floss* in the following year, and *Silas Marner* in 1861. *Romola* (1863) was the outcome of a journey to Italy in 1860. After *Felix Holt* (1866) George Eliot attempted poetry, and visited Spain to gather materials for *The Spanish Gypsy* (1868). Her only other long poem, *The Legend of Jubal*, was published with other pieces in 1874. *Middlemarch* was issued in eight parts in 1871 and 1872. *Daniel Deronda* (1876) was her last novel; and the *Impressions of Theophrastus Such* (1879) was her last work. In 1878 Lewes died; and in April, 1880, George Eliot married Mr. J. W. Cross, but survived the union less than a year, dying December 22, 1880.

George Eliot's place is certainly among the great novelists. At the lowest, she is classed after Scott, Dickens and Thackeray (and a few might add Jane Austen); at the highest, she is placed above them all. She carried by storm the intellect of one of the most thoughtful and weighty of critics, Edmond Scherer, who in his *Études sur la Littérature Contemporaine* devoted three essays to her, which have been admirably translated by Professor Saintsbury. In the last of these Scherer goes so far as to say that for her 'was reserved the honour of writing the most perfect novels yet known.' In spite of the note of exaggeration this judgment is significant. Only a writer, not merely of genius, but of great genius, could have drawn it from a critic so sober-minded; a foreigner, unbiassed by the predilections of patriotism; a man of wide knowledge, well aware of all that his sweeping assertion implied.

Most writers, even the greatest, have loaded themselves with a weight of literary lumber. George Eliot carries less of such *impedimenta* than many, but it will be well nevertheless to put aside at once such works as are neither in her special field nor in her best manner. Under this head fall the heavy and laboured volume of essays entitled *Impression of Theophrastus Such*, and also the poems. The latter, thoughtful, and occasionally eloquent, nevertheless prove that the writer had not the gift of verse. Richard Congreve described *The Spanish Gypsy* as 'a mass of positivism.' The description is accurate; and perhaps the fact that it is so is, to others who are not positivists, a heavier objection than it was to him. *The Legend of Jubal*, though better, is not great poetry.

Leaving these works then aside, the novels of George

Eliot fall pretty clearly into three groups, which conform to the divisions of chronology. In the first we have at one extreme the *Scenes of Clerical Life*, and at the other *Silas Marner*; in the second *Romola* stands alone; in the third, *Felix Holt*, the weakest if not the least readable of all, is transitional; while *Middlemarch* and *Daniel Deronda* illustrate her later manner respectively in full flower and in decay.

Each of these groups has found special admirers among critics. George Eliot herself was disposed to prefer *Romola* to all her other works; but she seems to have been swayed by the consideration that it had cost her more than any other book. *Romola* has been praised also as a marvellous picture of Florentine life in the fifteenth century. Only men who are profoundly versed in Italian character, literature and history are entitled to pronounce upon the question; and they are few in number. But if the statement be true the fact is wonderful, for George Eliot had only spent about six weeks in Florence before she wrote the book. In any case it smells of the lamp, and we may therefore suspect that it will give less permanent pleasure than most of her novels. Tito Melema is admitted to be a masterpiece of subtle delineation; but for the most part the picture of Romola, her home and her associates, is laboured to a degree almost painful.

Of the two other groups, if we take them as wholes, there can be little hesitation in assigning the palm to the earlier. The excellence here is evener, the artistic skill finer, the style more uniformly pleasing. The evenness of quality is proved by the fact that each work in turn has been praised as the author's best, or at least as equal to her best; whereas there can be no reasonable doubt about the pre-eminence of *Middlemarch* in the last group. The artistic excellence, again, of *Silas Marner*, perhaps the most faultless (which does not necessarily mean the best) of English novels, is as conspicuous as are the artistic defects of *Middlemarch*. And as to style, nearly all readers have felt how the fresh, easy grace, the flexibility of language, the lightness of touch, gradually disappear from the works of George Eliot; and how in her later books passages of genuine eloquence, masterly dialogue or description or reflexion, are mingled with leaden paragraphs wherein the author seems to be struggling under a burden too great for her strength.

The early novels then have the advantage of grace, spontaneity, and the charm exercised by a great writer when the great work is done without apparent effort. Like a giant wielding a club, George Eliot seems to execute the heavy tasks imposed by *Adam Bede* and *The Mill on the Floss* with an ease possible only because there is a reserve of strength behind. But some of these early products of genius, and among them the most charming of all, could hardly be repeated. Has child-life ever been as delightfully represented in literature as in the first part of *The Mill on the Floss?* But one secret of the charm is that the book, especially in this part, is autobiographical. Again, in the *Scenes of Clerical Life* and in *Adam Bede* the writer moves easily among characters with whom she had been familiar from girlhood. The religious enthusiasm of Dinah Morris is partly a reminiscence of her own early feelings, and partly a picture of her aunt Elizabeth; while in Adam Bede, as afterwards in Caleb Garth, may be seen the features of her own father. In those early years George Eliot skimmed the cream of her experience. Like Scott, she began to write novels rather late. Her powers were therefore mature, and in her first books she combines the perfect freshness of a new writer with the weight and the range of an experienced one.

Thoughtfulness and serious purpose were from the start conspicuous in the writings of George Eliot. It is the overgrowth of these qualities, to the detriment of the artistic element, that mars her later works. *Daniel Deronda* is ruined by its philosophy and its didactic purpose. The style is ponderous and often clumsy, and the question of heredity is made too prominent. *Middlemarch* too shows signs of failure on the part of the artist. More than almost any other great novel, it sins against the law of unity. The stories of Dorothea and Casaubon and Ladislaw, of Lydgate and Rosamond, of the Garths, and of Bulstrode, are tacked together by the most flimsy external bonds. They all illustrate a single thesis; but it is for this, and not for their natural connexion, that they are chosen. The keynote of the whole novel is struck in the prelude; and, as in the case of the young Saint Theresa and her brother, we see throughout 'domestic reality,' in diverse shapes, meeting the idealist and turning him back from his great resolve. But even want of unity will be pardoned, provided the details are conceived and presented in the manner of an artist, as they are in *Middlemarch*. Some of George Eliot's books contain fresher pictures than we find here, but none contains more that dwell in the mind, and in none is her maturest thought so well expressed. *Middlemarch* gives us one of the rarest things in literature, the philosophy of a powerful mind presented with all the charm of art. For this reason it at least rivals the best work of her first period.

George Eliot was the last of the race of giants in fiction. Some good novelists remain to be noticed, but none who can without hesitation be called great. Those who did respectable work are so numerous that the task of selection becomes exceedingly difficult; and moreover, as we draw near the dividing-line, it proves sometimes doubtful whether a man should be included in the present period, or viewed as belonging to that still current. It is safe to say however that of all forms of literature, fiction is the one in which a rigorous law of selection is the most necessary. Many popular writers must be passed over in silence. Mrs. Henry Wood, notwithstanding the success of her *East Lynne,* can be barely mentioned; and little more is possible in the case of Dinah Maria Craik, best known as the author of *John Halifax, Gentleman,* a pleasing but somewhat namby-pamby story, ranked by some unaccountably high. Mrs. Craik never shocks, never startles, nor does she ever invigorate. She is one of those writers who appeal to the taste of the middle class, not perhaps as it is now, but as it was a generation ago.

Mrs. Henry Wood (1814-1887).

Dinah Maria Craik (1826-1887).

Three detached novels, by men who cannot be classed as writers of fiction, may be named for the sake of their authors—*Eustace Conway* (1834), by F. D. Maurice, and *Loss and Gain* (1848) and *Callista* (1856), by J. H. Newman. Maurice's story was written when, a young man, he was still groping his way; but Newman's deliberately and when the bent of his mind had been long taken. His novels are among the symptoms of the passing of theological interest into general literature, but they have in themselves no value.

Charles Kingsley was also by profession a theologian, and his disastrous controversy with Newman remains as a proof of the interest he took in the movement Newman sought to serve by *Callista.* But fortunately Kingsley did not allow this interest to dominate his books. Tractarianism is indeed one of the themes of his earliest novels, *Alton Locke* (1850) and *Yeast* (1848), but socialism, to which his

Charles Kingsley (1819-1875).

attention had been turned by the personal influence of Maurice, is a far more prominent one. *Yeast* pictures the condition of agricultural labour, *Alton Locke* that of labour in crowded cities. Both books are immature, sometimes rash, and on the whole not well constructed; but they have the merits of vigour, earnestness and knowledge at first-hand; for Kingsley had personally taken part in the labour movements in London which resulted in Chartism. *Hypatia* (1853) is an ambitious novel, at once historical and philosophical, impressive in parts, but on the whole heavy. Kingsley, a man whose physical nature and instincts were quite as well developed as his intellect, is happiest where he can bring to play the experiences of his life, and where he can describe scenes familiar to him. About his best work there is always a breath of the moor, of the fen or of the sea; for he had lived by them all and had learnt to love them. This is shown by his verse as well as his prose. His *Ode to the North-East Wind*, his *Sands of Dee*, and the images scattered everywhere through his poems, prove how the features of the scenery and of the weather had sunk into his mind. So do such novels as *Westward Ho!* (1855) and *Hereward the Wake* (1866). The former, a historical romance, the scene of which is laid in the time of Elizabeth, is generally considered Kingsley's best work; and it is only a small minority, to which the writer happens to belong, who find it dreary. The power of some of the descriptions must be acknowledged; but whether *Westward Ho!* will live is a question on which there may be difference of opinion. *Hereward the Wake*, generally ranked much lower, is certainly uneven and in parts dull. But it has two great merits: it reproduces in a marvellous way the impression of the fen country; and, by vivid flashes, though not constantly, the reader seems to see before his eyes the very life of the old vikings.

Kingsley's work was most varied. Besides his novels, his professional work, such as sermons, and his lectures as Professor of History at Cambridge, we may mention his beautiful fairy-tale, *The Water Babies* (1863), with its exquisite snatches of verse, ' Clear and Cool,' and ' When all the world is young.' His poetry, if it were as copious as it is often high in quality, would place him among the great. But it was only occasional. Besides short pieces, he was the author of a drama, *The Saint's Tragedy* (1848), somewhat immature, and of *Andromeda* (1858), one of the few specimens of English hexameters that are readable, and that seem to naturalise the metre in our language. It is however noticeable that Kingsley's success is won at the cost of wholly altering the character of the measure. *Andromeda* is true and fine poetry, but its effect is not that of ' the long roll of the hexameter.' There is a very great preponderance of dactyls. This is the case with almost all English hexameters ; and the fact goes far to prove that the hexameter, as understood by the ancients, a fairly balanced mixture of dactyls and spondees, is not suited to the genius of English.

Henry Kingsley, the younger brother of Charles, was a novelist likewise, but one of considerably less merit. He passed some years in Australia, and his experiences there supplied materials for one of his best stories, *Geoffrey Hamlyn*. That by which he is best known is however *Ravenshoe* (1862). His novels are extremely loose in construction, and he is no rival to his brother in that exuberance of spirits which gives to the writings of the latter their most characteristic excellence.

Henry Kingsley
(1830-1876).

Senior to both the brothers, alike in years and as a

writer, was Anthony Trollope. Coming of a literary family (both his mother and his elder brother wrote novels), he proved himself, from 1847, when he published *The Macdermotts of Ballycloran*, to his death, one of the most prolific of novelists. No recent writer illustrates better than he the function of the novel when it is something less than a work of genius. The demand for amusement is the explanation of the enormous growth of modern fiction. But pure amusement is inconsistent with either profound thought or tragic emotion, while, on the other hand, it requires competent literary workmanship. Anthony Trollope exactly satisfied this demand. He wrote fluently and fairly well. He drew characters which, if they were never very profound or subtle, were at any rate tolerably good representations of human nature. He had a pleasant humour, could tell a story well, and could, without becoming dull, continue it through any number of volumes that might be desired. Perhaps no one has ever equalled him at continuations. What are commonly known as the Barsetshire novels are his best group. There are some half-dozen stories in the group, yet four of them, *Barchester Towers*, *Doctor Thorne*, *Framley Parsonage*, and *The Last Chronicle of Barset*, extending over a period of ten years (1857-1867), must all be classed with his best work. Perhaps it was the touch of the commonplace that made it possible for him thus frequently to repeat his successes. Trollope's description of his own methods of work in his *Autobiography* shows that he worked himself as a manufacturer works his steam-engine, and with the same result, so much of a given pattern produced *per diem*. His monograph on Thackeray proves him capable of comparing his methods with the methods of a man of genius, by no means to the advantage of the latter.

Anthony Trollope (1815-1882).

Among the minor writers a few, typical of different classes, may be briefly mentioned. James Grant wrote some historical works as well as many novels well spiced with adventure. His best book is perhaps *The Romance of War* (1845). It follows the fortunes of a regiment through the Peninsula ; but while the plan gives it a good groundwork of reality and an abundance of stirring scenes, it is inartistic. George John Whyte-Melville was similarly fond of adventure, but, though he was a soldier who had seen service in the Crimea, he is specially identified with sporting rather than with military novels. His best work is descriptive of fox-hunting, a sport to which he was passionately devoted. He also wrote historical novels, of which the best known is *The Gladiators*. Both of these writers relied for their effect upon the feeling of interest produced by the situations in which they placed their characters. So, but in a totally different way, did Wilkie Collins. He was a master of sensational narrative. He excelled in the skilful construction and the skilful unravelling of plot, and in his own domain he is among the best of recent writers. His best known book is *The Woman in White*, while perhaps that which best deserves to be known is *The Moonstone*. In neither is there a single character worth remembering ; the story is everything. The novel of society, again, is represented by George Alfred Lawrence, the author of *Guy Livingstone*, who repeats many of the faults of Bulwer Lytton, and has not the genius which in Lytton's case partly redeems the faults.

George John Whyte-Melville (1821-1878).

Wilkie Collins (1824-1889).

George Alfred Lawrence (1827-1876).

There remains one man of genius, Charles Reade, who towers over all these men of talent. Reade was mature in

years before he began his literary career with a group of
dramas, of which *Gold,* acted with moderate
success in 1853, was the best. His easy
circumstances as the son of an Oxford-
shire squire, and fellow of Magdalen College, exempted
him from the necessity of pushing his way in the world.
In literature he had one great ambition and one great gift,
and unfortunately the two diverged. His talent lay in
prose fiction, while his ambition drew him towards the
stage. It was the advice of an actress that caused him to
turn *Masks and Faces,* a drama written in collaboration
with Tom Taylor, into the prose story of *Peg Woffington*
(1853), and so to find his true vocation. But he remained
unsatisfied, and through his whole career he continued to
make experiments in the drama, never with much success
except in the case of *Drink* (1879), founded on Zola's
L'Assommoir. So strong was his predilection, that he
desired that in the inscription on his tombstone the word
'dramatist' should be put first in the specification of his
pursuits.

Charles Reade
(1814-1884).

Those who study Reade can have no difficulty in detect-
ing the cause of his failure in the drama. He is fertile of
incident, but he has not the art of selecting a few striking
scenes rising out of one another and leading rapidly up to
a catastrophe. His copiousness finds room in the freer
field of prose fiction, and his want of skill in selection is
less noticeable there. Accordingly he soon won as a
novelist the popularity he never secured as a playwright.
Christie Johnstone (1853), one of his best stories, was the
successor of *Peg Woffington,* and after *It is Never Too Late
to Mend* (1856) he took his place as one of the first writers
of fiction of the time.

Charles Reade was a man of strong individuality, intense
in all his opinions, and bent on making them known.

Hence he gives us perhaps the best examples of the novel with a purpose. Dickens had done much work of this description, but Reade went beyond him. Many of his novels are devoted to special questions. Thus *It is Never Too Late to Mend* deals with prison administration, *Hard Cash* with lunatic asylums, and *Put Yourself in his Place* with trade-unions. Moreover, Reade was by no means the man to approach these questions with a few *a priori* impressions only in his head. He was thorough, and he made an elaborate study of each before he wrote about it. Every incident reported in the newspapers, every trial in the courts of law, every fact wherever recorded, he made it his business to master. He cared less for theories, at least for the theories of other people: he made his own, and loved them. But his survey of the evidence was as nearly exhaustive as it could be. No other writer of fiction ever left such an apparatus of note-books, newspaper cuttings, etc., all digested and systematically arranged. It has been commonly held that Reade's work was injured by this laborious method; and no doubt the opinion is in part sound. Yet his merits as well as his defects are closely related to his method. His variety and his inexhaustible resource are due to the enormous accumulation of his facts. He loved to illustrate the saying that truth is stranger than fiction, and he held that no man's invention could supply incidents equal to those which patient investigation would reveal. There is no novelist with respect to whom it is so dangerous to say, ' this is unnatural or impossible.' Probably the seeming impossibility is a hard fact, disclosed by some forgotten trial or recorded in some old newspaper.

While however this backbone of reality gives strength to Reade's novels, his devotion to fact sometimes leads him to forget unity and proportion. The violence of his convictions was apt to overbalance his judgment. He is at his best in his calmer and less didactic moods. For this reason *The Cloister and the Hearth* (1861) is his masterpiece. In a historical novel, of which the scene is laid in the fifteenth century and the hero is the father of Erasmus, there is ample scope for Reade's love of investigation, and he has with great skill woven into the narrative the results of wide reading and patient study. The works of Erasmus are appropriately laid under contribution. But Reade has here no thesis to defend, no abuse to attack. The book is consequently better balanced than the novels of the class already mentioned; and the adventures are diversified with touches of pathos and with scenes of domestic life in the Dutch home, such as are hardly to be found elsewhere in Reade's works. The delineation of character also is subtler. In many of Reade's novels the characters are wholly subordinate to the purpose of the story. It is not Mr. Eden who interests us in *It is Never Too Late to Mend*, but rather his theories and methods.

There is no rival among Reade's novels to *The Cloister and the Hearth;* but several of them nevertheless are of high quality. *Christie Johnstone*, a remarkably clever and successful study of the fisher population of the east of Scotland, is perhaps the freshest and least laboured of all his works; and *Griffith Gaunt*, an analysis of the workings of the passion of jealousy, is the subtlest as a psychological study; while *It is Never Too Late to Mend* stands pretty near the head of its own class, the novel of purpose. Except the greatest of the writers already dealt with, and one other, Mr. George Meredith, who belongs rather to the next period, there was no contemporary writer who could do work equal to any one of them.

We have now traced the course of literature through a

period of forty years, distinguished for their fertility and for the variety of the talent displayed in them. In the prominence given to history, in the drift of philosophic speculation, in the prevalence of the novel of purpose, and in the spirit of the later poetry, we see the influence of social problems clamouring for solution. The Age of Tennyson has been essentially an age of reconstruction. It inherited from the preceding generation a gigantic task, which it has earnestly and laboriously striven to accomplish. What measure of success has been won is still doubtful; how long the literary expression of the effort will remain satisfying may be doubtful too. It is said to-day that we no longer read Carlyle; it may be said to-morrow that we no longer read Tennyson or Browning either. But there is substance in the work of all these men, and of all the leaders of the period. If they are no longer read it is because their thought has penetrated the life of the time; and we may be sure that they will revive and have a second vogue when they are old enough to be partly forgotten.

CHRONOLOGICAL TABLE.

1831. Disraeli : *The Young Duke.*
Ebenezer Elliott : *Corn Law Rhymes.*
Peacock : *Crotchet Castle.*
Scott : *Count Robert of Paris.*
Scott : *Castle Dangerous.*

1832. John Austin : *The Province of Jurisprudence Determined*
E. L. Bulwer (Lord Lytton) : *Eugene Aram.*
Disraeli : *Contarini Fleming.*
Samuel Warren : *The Diary of a Late Physician.*
Bentham died.
Crabbe died.
Scott died.

1833. Robert Browning : *Pauline.*
Carlyle : *Sartor Resartus* (finished 1834).
Hartley Coleridge : *Poems.*
Disraeli : *The Wondrous Tale of Alroy.*
Lamb : *Last Essays of Elia.*
Lyell : *Principles of Geology* (completed).
J. H. Newman : *Arians of the Fourth Century.*
Newman and others : *Tracts for the Times* (begun).
Tennyson : *Poems.*

1834. E. L. Bulwer (Lord Lytton) : *The Last Days of Pompeii.*
Landor : *The Citation and Examination of William Shake-
    speare.*
Marryat : *Peter Simple.*
Marryat : *Jacob Faithful.*
Henry Taylor : *Philip van Artevelde.*
S. T. Coleridge died.

1834. Charles Lamb died.
       Malthus died.
1835. Robert Browning: *Paracelsus.*
       E. L. Bulwer (Lord Lytton): *Rienzi.*
       Dickens: *Sketches by Boz* (finished 1836).
       Thirlwall: *History of Greece* (finished 1847).
       Wordsworth: *Yarrow Revisited, and other Poems.*
       Mrs. Hemans died.
       James Hogg died.
1836. Dickens: *Pickwick* (finished 1837).
       Landor: *Pericles and Aspasia.*
       Lockhart: *Life of Sir Walter Scott* (finished 1838).
       Marryat: *Mr. Midshipman Easy.*
       Marryat: *Japhet in Search of a Father.*
       W. Godwin died.
       James Mill died.
1837. Robert Browning: *Strafford.*
       Carlyle: *History of the French Revolution.*
       Dickens: *Oliver Twist* (finished 1838).
       Disraeli: *Henrietta Temple.*
       Disraeli: *Venetia.*
       Hallam: *Literature of Europe* (finished 1839).
       Landor: *The Pentameron.*
       Thackeray: *The Yellowplush Papers* (finished 1838).
1838. Thomas Arnold: *History of Rome* (last volume, 1843)
       E. Barrett (Browning): *The Seraphim.*
       E. L. Bulwer (Lord Lytton): *The Lady of Lyons.*
       Dickens: *Nicholas Nickleby* (finished 1839).
       Maurice: *The Kingdom of Christ* (enlarged 1842).
       Newman: *Lectures on Justification.*
1839. Bailey: *Festus.*
       E. L. Bulwer (Lord Lytton): *Cardinal Richelieu.*
       Carlyle: *Chartism.*
       Carlyle: *Critical and Miscellaneous Essays.*
       Lever: *Harry Lorrequer.*
       Thackeray: *Catherine* (finished 1840).
       John Galt died.
       W. M. Praed died.

1840. Robert Browning: *Sordello.*
E. L. Bulwer (Lord Lytton): *Money.*
Dickens: *The Old Curiosity Shop* (finished 1841).
Frere: *Translation of Aristophanes.*
Thackeray: *The Paris Sketch Book.*
Madame D'Arblay died.

1841. Robert Browning: *Pippa Passes.*
Carlyle: *Heroes and Hero-Worship.*
Dickens: *Barnaby Rudge.*
Lever: *Charles O'Malley.*
Hugh Miller: *The Old Red Sandstone.*
Newman: *Tract XC.*
Thackeray: *The Great Hoggarty Diamond*
Warren: *Ten Thousand a Year.*

1842. Robert Browning: *Dramatic Lyrics.*
E. L. Bulwer (Lord Lytton): *Zanoni.*
Dickens: *American Notes.*
Macaulay: *Lays of Ancient Rome.*
Marryat: *Percival Keene.*
Henry Taylor: *Edwin the Fair.*
Tennyson: *Poems.*
Wilson: *The Recreations of Christopher North.*
Wordsworth: *The Borderers.*
Thomas Arnold died.

1843. Robert Browning: *A Blot in the 'Scutcheon.*
Carlyle: *Past and Present.*
Dickens: *Martin Chuzzlewit* (finished 1844).
Horne: *Orion.*
E. L. Bulwer (Lord Lytton): *The Last of the Barons.*
Macaulay: *Critical and Historical Essays* (collected).
Mill: *A System of Logic.*
Ruskin: *Modern Painters* (finished 1860).
Thackeray: *The Irish Sketch Book.*
Southey died.

1844. Barnes: *Poems of Rural Life, in the Dorset Dialect.*
E. Barrett (Browning): *Poems.*
Robert Browning: *Colombe's Birthday.*
Disraeli: *Coningsby.*

1844. Kinglake: *Eothen.*
Stanley: *Life of Arnold.*
Thackeray: *Barry Lyndon.*
Thomas Campbell died.

1845. Robert Browning: *Dramatic Romances and Lyrics.*
Carlyle: *Cromwell.*
Disraeli: *Sybil.*
Thomas Hood died.
Sydney Smith died.

1846. Dickens: *Dombey and Son* (finished 1848).
Grote: *History of Greece* (finished 1856).
Newman: *The Development of Christian Doctrine.*

1847. Charlotte Brontë: *Jane Eyre.*
Emily Brontë: *Wuthering Heights.*
Disraeli: *Tancred.*
Helps: *Friends in Council.*
Landor: *Hellenics.*
Tennyson: *The Princess.*
Thackeray: *Vanity Fair* (finished 1848).
Trollope: *The Macdermotts of Ballycloran.*

1848. Clough: *The Bothie of Tober-na-Vuolich.*
Mrs. Gaskell: *Mary Barton.*
Charles Kingsley: *Yeast.*
Macaulay: *History of England,* vols. i. and ii. (last volume, 1860).
Mill: *Political Economy.*
Thackeray: *The Book of Snobs* (reprinted from *Punch*).
Emily Brontë died.
Marryat died.

1849. Matthew Arnold: *The Strayed Reveller, and other Poems*
W. E. Aytoun: *Lays of the Scottish Cavaliers.*
Charlotte Brontë: *Shirley.*
Clough: *Ambarvalia.*
Dickens: *David Copperfield* (finished 1850).
Lytton: *The Caxtons.*
Ruskin: *The Seven Lamps of Architecture.*
Thackeray: *Pendennis* (finished 1850).
T. L. Beddoes died.

1849. Hartley Coleridge died.
     Maria Edgeworth died.
1850. Beddoes: *Death's Jest-Book*.
     E. B. Browning: *Sonnets from the Portuguese*.
     Robert Browning: *Christmas Eve and Easter Day*.
     Carlyle: *Latter-Day Pamphlets*.
     Dobell: *The Roman*.
     Charles Kingsley: *Alton Locke*.
     D. G. Rossetti and others: *The Germ*.
     Tennyson: *In Memoriam*.
     Wordsworth: *The Prelude*.
     Francis Jeffrey died.
     Wordsworth died.
1851. E. B. Browning: *Casa Guidi Windows*.
     Carlyle: *Life of Sterling*.
     Ruskin: *The Stones of Venice* (finished 1853).
     Joanna Baillie died.
1852. Matthew Arnold: *Empedocles on Etna*.
     Dickens: *Bleak House* (finished 1853).
     Thackeray: *Esmond*.
     Moore died.
1853. Matthew Arnold: *Poems*.
     Charlotte Brontë: *Villette*.
     Dobell: *Balder*.
     Mrs. Gaskell: *Cranford*.
     Charles Kingsley: *Hypatia*.
     W. S. Landor: *The Last Fruit off an Old Tree*.
     Lytton: *My Novel*.
     Charles Reade: *Peg Woffington*.
     Charles Reade: *Christie Johnstone*.
     Alexander Smith: *A Life Drama*.
     Thackeray: *The English Humourists of the Eighteenth Century* (printed).
1854. Hugh Miller: *My Schools and Schoolmasters*.
     Milman: *History of Latin Christianity*.
     Patmore: *The Angel in the House* (Part I.).
     Thackeray: *The Newcomes* (finished 1855).
     Susan Ferrier died.
     Lockhart died.

1854. John Wilson died.
1855. Matthew Arnold: *Poems.*
    Robert Browning: *Men and Women.*
    Mrs. Gaskell: *North and South.*
    Charles Kingsley: *Westward Ho!*
    Lewes: *Life of Goethe.*
    Herbert Spencer: *Principles of Psychology*
    Tennyson: *Maud.*
    Charlotte Brontë died.
    Samuel Rogers died.
1856. Dobell: *England in Time of War.*
    Froude: *History of England* (finished 1870).
    Charles Reade: *It is Never Too Late to Mend.*
    Sir W. Hamilton died.
    Hugh Miller died.
1857. E. B. Browning: *Aurora Leigh.*
    Buckle: *History of Civilization* (vol. ii. in 1861).
    Hugh Miller: *The Testimony of the Rocks.*
    Alexander Smith; *City Poems.*
    Thackeray: *The Virginians* (finished 1859).
    Trollope: *Barchester Towers.*
1858. Carlyle: *Frederick the Great* (finished 1865).
    George Eliot: *Scenes of Clerical Life* (serially, 1857).
    Lytton: *What will He do with It?*
    William Morris: *The Defence of Guenevere.*
1859. Barnes: *Hwomely Rhymes.*
    Darwin: *The Origin of Species.*
    Dickens: *A Tale of Two Cities.*
    George Eliot: *The Mill on the Floss.*
    Edward FitzGerald: *Rubáiyát of Omar Khayyám.*
    George Meredith: *The Ordeal of Richard Feverel.*
    Mill: *Liberty.*
    Tennyson: *Idylls of the King* (part)
    De Quincey died.
    Henry Hallam died.
    Leigh Hunt died.
    Macaulay died.
1860. George Eliot: *The Mill on the Floss.*

1860. *Essays and Reviews* (various authors).
    Swinburne: *The Queen Mother*.
    Swinburne: *Rosamond*.
    Thackeray: *The Four Georges* (printed).
    Sir W. Napier died.

1861. Matthew Arnold: *On Translating Homer*.
    George Eliot: *Silas Marner*.
    Maine: *Ancient Law*.
    May: *Constitutional History of England* (finished 1863).
    Mill: *Representative Government*.
    Charles Reade: *The Cloister and the Hearth*.
    D. G. Rossetti: *The Early Italian Poets*.
    Thackeray: *The Adventures of Philip* (finished 1862).
    Trollope: *Framley Parsonage*.
    E. Barrett Browning died.

1862. Alfred Austin: *The Human Tragedy*.
    Colenso: *The Pentateuch and the Book of Joshua Examined*
        (finished 1879).
    George Meredith: *Modern Love, and Poems of the English
        Roadside, with Poems and Ballads*.
    Mill: *Utilitarianism*.
    Christina Rossetti: *Goblin Market, and other Poems*.
    Henry Taylor: *St. Clement's Eve*.
    Buckle died.

1863. George Eliot: *Romola*.
    Freeman: *History of Federal Government*.
    Kinglake: *The Invasion of the Crimea* (finished 1887).
    Lyell: *The Antiquity of Man*.
    George Macdonald: *David Elginbrod*.
    Margaret Oliphant: *Chronicles of Carlingford* (begun).
    Thackeray died.
    Whately died.

1864. Robert Browning: *Dramatis Personæ*.
    Dickens: *Our Mutual Friend* (finished 1865).
    Newman: *Apologia pro Vita Sua*.
    Herbert Spencer: *Principles of Biology* (finished 1867).
    Tennyson: *Enoch Arden*.

1864. Landor died.
1865. Matthew Arnold: *Essays in Criticism* (collected).
    Lewis Carroll: *Alice's Adventures in Wonderland.*
    Grote: *Plato and the other Companions of Socrates.*
    Lecky: *History of Rationalism.*
    Lightfoot: *St. Paul's Epistle to the Galatians.*
    George Meredith: *Rhoda Fleming.*
    Ruskin: *Ethics of the Dust.*
    Ruskin: *Sesame and Lilies.*
    Seeley: *Ecce Homo!*
    Swinburne: *Atalanta in Calydon.*
    Swinburne: *Chastelard.*
    Aytoun died.
    Mrs. Gaskell died.
1866. Matthew Arnold: *Thyrsis.*
    Lord de Tabley: *Philoctetes.*
    Mrs. Gaskell: *Wives and Daughters*
    Charles Kingsley: *Hereward the Wake.*
    Charles Reade: *Griffith Gaunt.*
    Christina Rossetti: *The Prince's Progress, and other Poems.*
    Ruskin: *Crown of Wild Olive.*
    Swinburne: *Poems and Ballads.*
    Keble died.
    Whewell died.
1867. Matthew Arnold: *New Poems.*
    Bagehot: *The English Constitution.*
    Lord de Tabley: *Orestes.*
    Freeman: *History of the Norman Conquest* (finished 1876).
    Froude: *Short Studies on Great Subjects* (last series, 1883).
    William Morris: *The Life and Death of Jason.*
    Thackeray: *Denis Duval.*
    Trollope: *The Last Chronicle of Barset.*
    Alex. Smith died.
1868. Robert Browning: *The Ring and the Book* (finished 1869).
    George Eliot: *The Spanish Gypsy.*

1868. Lightfoot: *St. Paul's Epistle to the Philippians.*
William Morris: *The Earthly Paradise* (finished 1870).
Milman died.

1869. Matthew Arnold: *Culture and Anarchy.*
Blackmore: *Lorna Doone.*
Lecky: *History of European Morals.*
George Macdonald: *Robert Falconer.*
Mill: *The Subjection of Women.*
Tennyson: *The Holy Grail, and other Poems.*
Wallace: *The Malay Archipelago.*

1870. Matthew Arnold: *St. Paul and Protestantism.*
Dickens: *The Mystery of Edwin Drood.*
Disraeli: *Lothair.*
Huxley: *Lay Sermons.*
Newman: *Grammar of Assent.*
D. G. Rossetti: *Poems.*
Dickens died

ALPHABETICAL LIST OF WRITERS.

ADAMS, SARAH FLOWER	1805-1848
AINSWORTH, WILLIAM HARRISON	1805-1882
ALISON, SIR ARCHIBALD	1792-1867
ALLINGHAM, WILLIAM	1824-1889
ARNOLD, MATTHEW	1822-1888
ARNOLD, THOMAS	1795-1842
AUSTIN, JOHN	1790-1859
AYTOUN, WILLIAM EDMONDSTOUNE	1813-1865
BAILEY, PHILIP JAMES	1816-1902
BARHAM, RICHARD HARRIS	1788-1845
BARNES, WILLIAM	1801-1886
BATES, HENRY WALTER	1825-1892
BLACKIE, JOHN STUART	1809-1895
BLANCHARD, SAMUEL LAMAN	1804-1845
BORROW, GEORGE	1803-1881
BOSWORTH, JOSEPH	1789-1876
BRONTË, ANNE	1820-1849
BRONTË, CHARLOTTE	1816-1855
BRONTË, EMILY JANE	1818-1848
BROUGH, ROBERT BARNABAS	1828-1860
BROWN, DR. JOHN	1810-1882
BROWNING, ELIZABETH BARRETT	1806-1861
BROWNING, ROBERT	1812-1889
BUCKLE, HENRY THOMAS	1821-1862
BURTON, JOHN HILL	1809-1881
CAIRNES, JOHN ELLIOT	1823-1875
CALVERLEY, CHARLES STUART	1831-1884
CARLETON, WILLIAM	1794-1869
CARLYLE, THOMAS	1795-1881
CHAMBERS, ROBERT	1802-1871

CHAMIER, FREDERICK 1796-1870
CLARK, WILLIAM GEORGE 1821-1878
CLARKE, CHARLES COWDEN 1787-1877
CLARKE, MARY COWDEN 1809-1897
CLOUGH, ARTHUR HUGH 1819-1861
COLENSO, JOHN WILLIAM 1814-1883
COLERIDGE, HARTLEY 1796-1849
COLERIDGE, SARA 1802-1852
COLLIER, JOHN PAYNE 1789-1883
COLLINS, MORTIMER 1827-1876
COLLINS, WILLIAM WILKIE 1824-1889
CONINGTON, JOHN 1825-1869
CORY, WILLIAM 1823-1892
CRAIK, DINAH MARIA 1826-1887
CROKER, THOMAS CROFTON 1798-1854
DARWIN, CHARLES ROBERT 1809-1882
DE MORGAN, AUGUSTUS 1806-1871
DE TABLEY, J. B. LEICESTER WARREN,
   LORD 1835-1895
DE VERE, AUBREY 1814-1902
DICKENS, CHARLES 1812-1870
DISRAELI, BENJAMIN, EARL OF BEACONS-
   FIELD 1804-1881
DOBELL, SYDNEY THOMPSON 1824-1874
DOYLE, SIR FRANCIS HASTINGS . . . 1810-1888
DUFFERIN, HELEN SELINA SHERIDAN,
   LADY 1807-1867
DYCE, ALEXANDER 1798-1869
ELIOT, GEORGE 1819-1880
FERGUSON, SIR SAMUEL 1810-1886
FERRIER, JAMES FREDERICK 1808-1864
FINLAY, GEORGE 1799-1875
FITZGERALD, EDWARD 1809-1883
FORSTER, JOHN 1812-1876
FROUDE, RICHARD HURRELL 1803-1836
FROUDE, JAMES ANTHONY 1818-1894
GASKELL, ELIZABETH CLEGHORN . . . 1810-1865
GLADSTONE, WILLIAM EWART 1809-1898
GLASCOCK, WILLIAM NUGENT . . . . 1787?-1867

INDEX.

9731